QUEEN AND COUNTRY

QUEEN AND COUNTRY

The Life of
Elizabeth the Queen Mother

DAVID SINCLAIR

J M Dent & Sons Ltd

LONDON, MELBOURNE & TORONTO

First published 1979
© David Sinclair, 1979
All rights reserved. No part of this publication may be
reproduced, stored in a retrieval system, or transmitted,
in any form or by any means, electronic, mechanical, photocopying,
recording or otherwise, without the prior permission of
J. M. Dent & Sons Ltd
Phototypeset in 11 on 14 pt V.I.P. Palatino by
Western Printing Services Ltd, Bristol
Printed and bound in Great Britain
by William Clowes & Sons Limited
Beccles and London
for J. M. Dent & Sons Ltd
Aldine House, Welbeck Street, London

British Library Cataloguing in Publication Data

Sinclair, David
    Queen and country.
    1. Elizabeth, *Queen, consort of*
    George VI, King of Great Britain
    2. Great Britain – Queens – Biography
    I. Title
    941.084'092'4   DA585.A2

    ISBN 0–460–04436–2

Contents

Illustrations

The Yorks in Ontario, 1939 (*The Times*)
Family portrait, 1940 (Topix)
Bomb damage at Buckingham Palace, 1940 (*The Times*)
Visiting the East End, 1940 (Central Press)
Harvest-time at Sandringham, 1943 (*The Times*)

Between pages 144 and 145

Royal tour of South Africa, 1947 (*The Times*)
Wedding of Princess Elizabeth, 1947 (*The Times*)
Silver wedding, 1948 (Camera Press)
Royal Ascot, 1951 (*The Times*)
Mourning for George VI, 1952 (Keystone Press)
At the Castle of Mey, 1956 (John Adams, Wick)
Rhodesia, 1957 (Central Press)
Arriving on the *Ark Royal*, July 1958 (Syndication International Ltd)
With Prince Charles and Princess Anne, 1956 (Central Press)
With her grandchildren, 1960 (*The Times*)
Fishing in New Zealand, 1966 (Central Press)

Between pages 208 and 209

Arriving in Copenhagen, 1968 (Keystone Press)
Chelsea Flower Show, 1969 (London Express News Service)
Badminton horse trials, 1971 (Camera Press. Photograph by Serge
   Lemoine)
Best-loved grandmother (Camera Press. Photograph by Les Wilson)
In the North of Scotland, 1973 (Cowper & Co., Perth)
With Prince Charles and Prince Andrew, 1975 (Camera Press.
   Photograph by Norman Parkinson)
Wedding of Princess Anne, 1973 (London Express News Service)
At the Royal College of Music, 1973 (Press Association)
Visiting the new National Theatre (Camera Press. Photograph by
   Colin Davey)
Royal charade at Balmoral (*Stern* magazine)
Congratulating Sunnyboy at Ascot, 1976 (Central Press)
Birthday photograph, 1978 (Press Association)

Picture research by Michael Young

Introduction

Monday 4 August 1975 was greeted with a certain amount of quiet satisfaction at two offices in the City of London. The directors of a firm of medallists could congratulate themselves on a shrewd investment while at the headquarters of a leading insurance institution there was relief that an event which would have cost the company a large sum of money had not occurred. What did occur on that date was the seventy-fifth birthday of Her Majesty Queen Elizabeth the Queen Mother, and it was that anniversary which had been looked forward to in those City offices. The medallists had invested a great deal of money in producing a series of plaques in twenty-two carat gold to celebrate the Queen Mother's birthday and, to protect the investment, they had taken out an insurance policy against the risk of Her Majesty dying before 4 August.

Of course, the Queen Mother did not disappoint the hard-headed businessmen, and indeed a few days before her birthday it was pointed out by a number of newspapers that in her fifty-two years of royal life to date she could never be said to have disappointed anybody. 'An unbroken record of public service unmatched by any Briton' was one comment applied to her. It is a statement difficult to contradict. As Duchess of York,

9

and later when she unexpectedly became Queen Consort after the abdication of King Edward VIII, she displayed special qualities which assured her of a place in history, but since her husband King George VI died in 1952, the Queen Mother has made a contribution to the life of the nation which can only be described as unique, and as she has grown older there has been no sign of her settling down to the sedate retirement one might expect a queen dowager to enjoy.

If the Queen Mother had thought of retiring her seventy-fifth year would have been a good time to do it, with three-quarters of a particularly troubled and hectic century behind her. But a glance at her diary of official engagements for 1975 shows that a quiet life was no nearer by then than it had been ten years before. In March she opened a new headquarters for the London City Mission. On 6 April she took the salute at a review of the Greater London Territorial Army and Volunteer Reserve Association in Hyde Park and eight days later she flew to Iran for a five-day visit at the invitation of the Shah, after which she attended a service of thanksgiving at St George's Chapel, Windsor, to begin celebrations marking the five hundredth anniversary of the founding of the chapel. In May the Queen Mother opened a new civic centre in Enfield then travelled to Deeside and completed the month by touring the Channel Islands and the Isle of Wight in the Royal Yacht *Britannia*.

June was an especially busy month. On the 11th the Queen Mother was at Epsom to watch the Derby, two days afterwards she was attending the Aldeburgh Festival in Suffolk and on the 16th she was present at a luncheon party in Windsor Castle for the Knights of the Garter. On 24 June she visited Edinburgh for events connected with European Architectural Heritage Year and on the 30th she joined the Queen at a reception in Buckingham Palace for delegates attending the conference of the World Association of Girl Guides and Girl Scouts.

July began in Somerset, when the Queen Mother was guest of honour at a garden party at Montacute to mark the eightieth anniversary of the founding of the National Trust. On the sixth of the month the Queen Mother travelled to Edinburgh in preparation for a state visit by the King of Sweden, but before that there was a luncheon for Knights of the Thistle at Holyroodhouse. She attended a state banquet in honour of the Swedish King on 8 July and the following day was present at the colourful ceremony of Beating the Retreat in Holyrood Park. On the 10th it was back to London for a banquet given by the King of Sweden at Claridge's, and the Queen Mother rounded off the month by visiting Trinity College, Cambridge, and opening an extension to the Fitzwilliam Museum.

August was her birthday month, but there were no public celebrations, though the Queen Mother received hundreds of greetings telegrams and more than a thousand letters and cards. The day itself was marked by a dinner party for eighty members of the royal family and close friends in the Throne Room at Buckingham Palace. Later in the month the Queen Mother travelled to Scotland for her summer holiday and after that she returned to London to face an autumn and winter as full of engagements as the spring and summer had been.

From Scotland to the south-west of England, out into the Channel and even to the Middle East: the amount of travelling the Queen Mother did in her seventy-fifth year would alone have been enough to daunt most women of her age. But, like the shrewd men who insured themselves against her death, she knows that business is business and she believes that it is her business to be seen by as many people as possible and to take an interest in as many as possible of the things that people care about. This book is a record of how she has lived up to that belief for more than half a century.

Prologue: Crown in Crisis

The children singing carols in the streets of London during the weeks before Christmas 1936 had found new words to accompany a familiar tune:

> Hark the herald angels sing,
> Mrs Simpson's pinched our King . . .

For many people those lines summed up the situation. Edward the Eighth by the Grace of God of Great Britain, Ireland and the British Dominions beyond the Seas, King, Defender of the Faith, Emperor of India, had renounced his throne and fled his country for the sake of a twice-divorced American woman. The man who had once been regarded throughout the world as the great hope for the future of the British monarchy had led that ancient and awesome institution into a public scandal which threatened to destroy it. The fate of the Crown now depended upon a rather slight, diffident man and his pretty, pragmatic wife, who lived quietly with their two daughters in a comparatively modest royal residence at 145 Piccadilly: the Duke and Duchess of York had become, reluctantly and literally overnight, King George VI and Queen Elizabeth.

Never since the so-called Glorious Revolution of 1688 had the

13

English Crown been confronted by such a crisis, and at least on that earlier occasion there had appeared to be something to fight about, with a Roman Catholic King James II arousing the resentment and wrath of an overwhelmingly, one might say fanatically Protestant country. By contrast the Abdication of 1936 lacked any sense of grave national danger, but at the root of Britain's greatest constitutional upheaval of modern times lay a cause even more potent than religion – the cause of love. An infatuated Sovereign demanded the right to marry whom he chose, while a bewildered and disappointed people, who had placed this King at the very heart of their affections, tried to show him that if he were to reign over them he must respect their desires and emotions.

Inevitably the result was muddle, misunderstanding and tragedy. But in the strange way that fate sometimes has of repairing the damage it causes, the nation and the monarchy survived the debacle and even prospered as a result of it. That they did so owed much to the courage and wisdom of King George VI, and perhaps even more to the fortitude, high principles and simple devotion of his Queen, who, now as Queen Mother, is arguably the best-loved member of the Royal Family since Queen Victoria.

The Duke and Duchess of York had been married for thirteen years when they were suddenly called upon to fill the void left by the departing King Edward. Their marriage had been noteworthy: for the first time in two centuries the son of an English king had been allowed to marry a commoner (the previous occasion having been when another Duke of York, later King James II, was permitted to wed Lady Anne Hyde). On the day of the Yorks' wedding in 1923 the opinion was expressed that the bride, Lady Elizabeth Bowes-Lyon, 'is probably all the more welcome an addition to the Royal Family because the public knows nothing about her'.[1] She was in fact doubly welcome, not only to the public but also to the Royal Family, because there was at that time no sign of a prospective bride for the heir to the throne, the Prince of Wales, then approaching his thirtieth year.

Lady Elizabeth had hesitated for some time before accepting

the proposal of marriage from her royal suitor. As the daughter of a noble landowner she had grown up closer to simple country folk than to princes and courtiers, and she did not relish the prospect of life in the public domain. But Prince Albert, Duke of York, the second son of King George V and Queen Mary, was determined to make Elizabeth his wife, and finally she acquiesced – immediately demonstrating that she possessed at least the tact and grace of a royal personage when she expressed the hope that the people of her home county, Forfarshire, would not spend a large sum of money on a wedding present for her. Her father wrote to the county clerk:

> Lady Elizabeth wishes me to say that . . . she would dearly love to have some token on her marriage from friends and well-wishers in the county, but that she would infinitely prefer that no money should be spent on a wedding gift for her when unemployment and distress are so prevalent, and when almost everyone is feeling the pinch of bad times. . . .

The burghers of Forfarshire responded with admirable restraint, confining themselves to the presentation of an illuminated address to the new duchess, and honour was satisfied on both sides.

The public's lack of knowledge about the Duchess of York did not last long, as the newspapers published all the intimate details of her existence that it was possible or, in those more respectful times, deemed proper to print. She was well read and perfectly capable of writing herself the speeches she made at official functions. She was described as 'small, dark and piquante' and it was revealed that she was a good dancer, a keen tennis player, an accomplished hostess and an active Girl Guide (a district commissioner, no less). She was vigorous and high-principled. In sum, she was 'British to the core'. Whatever else was to be revealed about the royal new recruit the public learnt at first hand as the Duchess set about her duties with the enthusiasm and good humour that were to endear her to people the world over. She opened hospitals, visited horticultural shows, received the freedom of cities, toured schools and housing projects, became president of the Young Women's Christian

Association, inspected soldiers, accepted honorary degrees from universities and even broadcast on the emergent wireless with all the aplomb of one trained from the cradle to such a life.

But there was in her an extra, unexpected dimension which particularly appealed to those with whom she had official contacts: when she told the first residents of a new block of flats in poor, overcrowded Battersea that she wished them 'the very best of luck you could possibly have', they knew that she really meant it. Having been born a commoner (though that is a somewhat misleading description for the daughter of an earl descended from a Scottish king) and having mixed naturally with people far below her class, the Duchess of York displayed an everyday warmth and humanity which was not noticeable among the born royals of her generation, reared as they were in isolation, cut off from friendships and common experience lest they should be compromised in some way. It is no accident that the young princes and princess of today's Royal Family have grown up in an atmosphere as near to that of the 'real world' as is presently thought possible for the children of the Sovereign. When she joined the Royal Family, Elizabeth Bowes-Lyon brought with her a thorough understanding of the hopes, fears and needs of the British people, and that instinctive knowledge was to prove invaluable to the House of Windsor.

As the drama of the Abdication careered uncontrollably towards its final act, the Duke and Duchess of York remained unaware of or perhaps unwilling to recognize the responsibility that was about to fall upon them. The Duke was not consulted by the King, his elder brother, until the very last moment, when abdication was the only course left and the prophesy of their father, King George V, concerning his firstborn came true: 'After I'm dead the boy will ruin himself in twelve months.' In fact Edward VIII reigned for just three hundred and twenty-five days, and when he had gone there were not a few people who breathed heartfelt sighs of relief. His stubbornness, egotism and apparent lack of concern for others, and for the requirements of his great

Two-year-old Elizabeth
Bowes-Lyon with her
sister Rose at St Paul's
Walden Bury in the
summer of 1902.

St Paul's Walden Bury as
a visitor would have seen
it in 1923.

Elizabeth and David Bowes-Lyon with their dancing master, Mr Neill, at Glamis in 1909.

Elizabeth with her father during one of the cricket weeks which were a feature of summers at Glamis before the First World War. Lord Strathmore was a noted fast bowler.

Elizabeth Bowes-Lyon with her sister, Lady Rose Leveson-Gower, at Glamis during the First World War, shaking hands with a wounded soldier.

A 1923 portrait of the Duchess of York, painted by Philip A. de Laszlo. The picture was given by Lady Strathmore to David Bowes-Lyon as a wedding present.

The Duke of York with some of the Bowes-Lyons and their friends shortly after the announcement of Elizabeth's engagement to him in 1923.

Elizabeth leaving her parents' home at 17 Bruton Street for Westminster Abbey on her wedding day.

Honeymoon days: the
Duke and Duchess of
York at Polesden Lacey.

The Duchess of York with
Queen Mary at Balmoral
in September 1923.

The Earl and Countess of Strathmore escorting Bertie and Elizabeth at a Glamis garden party in 1923.

The christening of Princess Elizabeth in 1926. *Left to right*: Lady Patricia Ramsay, the Duke of Connaught, Queen Mary, King George V, the Duchess of York, the Duke of York, Lady Strathmore, the Earl of Strathmore, Princess Mary.

inheritance, had, as he had grown older, largely dispelled the image of the Prince Charming which he had enjoyed in his youth.

Had he been one of the younger sons of George V and Queen Mary, he might have been able to 'get away with it' (a favourite phrase of his). But Edward Albert Christian George Andrew Patrick David was born to be king, and in a century that has swept away so many royal houses, a constitutional monarch is not allowed to 'get away with' very much.

The birth of this controversial prince, in the rather gloomy surroundings of York Cottage, Sandringham, on 23 June 1894, seemed auspicious enough: it was the first time that a reigning English monarch had seen the birth of a great-grandson, and Queen Victoria pronounced herself very pleased. On the other hand, David – as the prince was always known to his family and friends – came into a world that was changing more rapidly than anyone cared to admit, as the massive edifice of nineteenth-century imperialism began to crumble; and he would be at the forefront of the generation called upon to rebuild the world after the demolition wrought by the Great War. Celebrating David's birth, *The Times* commented:

> The young Prince is heir to a noble inheritance, not only to a station of unequalled dignity, but more than all to the affection of a loyal people, which it will be his office to keep and to make his own. Our heartfelt prayer is that he may prove worthy of so great a trust.

Forty years later another editor of *The Times* would decide that the great trust was misplaced in the person of Edward VIII, and a humiliated Royal Family would wonder, in its darkest moments, whether it was going to survive. Queen Mary, stiff, over-formal and somewhat forbidding, though with her heart in the right place, wrote to her eldest son after the Abdication: 'I do not think you have ever realized the shock which the attitude you took caused your family and the whole Nation.'

David was accustomed to causing shocks. It was his way of rebelling against the strict discipline imposed in his youth by his father, a gruff old sailor who always viewed life as if from the quarter-deck and who charted the course to be followed by his heir with the words, 'the Navy will teach David all he needs to know'. As it turned out neither the Navy nor his parents taught David the requirements of modern kingship – they merely combined to ensure that, at least until he faced the reality of abdication, he never quite grew up.

He first caused flutters of alarm during the Great War when, as a popular Prince of Wales, he would dash in best *Boys' Own Paper* style to the front-line trenches in France. 'What does it matter if I am killed?' he asked gaily. 'I have four brothers.'[2] In the Roaring Twenties David began to acquire the kind of reputation as a ladies' man that had been earned by another Prince of Wales, his grandfather, in the Naughty Nineties. His liaisons with married women became the talk of the decadent café society, as did his clothes – loud check suits, tan suede shoes, and the dinner jacket he made popular as an alternative to white tie and tails. By the thirties his indiscretions had spread into politics as he sniped at British industry for being out of date, criticized the policies of the Government and the Foreign Office, and gave the German ambassador in London the impression that certain aspects of the Nazi cause appealed to him.

But while David's excesses drew complaints from his father, the King was shrewd enough to see that his son's gaiety, energy and zest for life could be employed to advantage in what were dangerous days for monarchs. The 1914–18 war had destroyed the Hohenzollerns in Germany, the Hapsburgs in Austria-Hungary and the Romanovs in Russia; and while the Windsors, having changed their name from Saxe-Coburg at the height of anti-German hysteria in 1917, had come out of it unscathed, there was a nagging fear that Queen Victoria's prophesy of the fall of the Royal House by 1930 might be fulfilled if the tide of republicanism swept towards the British Isles (indeed it was already at the flood in Ireland).

The handsome, dashing Prince of Wales was a definite asset in such circumstances, a man to whom people shocked by the effects of the 'war to end all wars' could look for leadership and regeneration, and the Prime Minister, David Lloyd George,[3] quickly put him to work. In 1919 the Prince was sent to show the flag round the bastions of the Empire – Canada, Australia and New Zealand. He was a sensation. In Canada he was greeted everywhere by vast, cheering crowds, and his parents became concerned at the amount of hand-shaking he was doing. While in Canada, the Prince was invited by President Woodrow Wilson to visit the United States, and the republican Americans took him to their hearts. After a brief rest at home he set off in the spring of 1920 for New Zealand and Australia, where he travelled 46,000 miles and delighted the rugged and determinedly unceremonious peoples with his good looks, physical prowess at sports and his lack of 'stuffiness'.

In the autumn of 1921 David went to India, where Mahatma Gandhi had recently launched his campaign of civil disobedience against the British Raj and threatened a boycott of official celebrations during the Prince's visit. Once again, however, David was a spectacular success and though there was some rioting this was not taken to be a protest against his tour. Marathas cheered him in Poona, thousands of Bombayites kissed the ground over which his car passed, and even in Allahabad, where official ceremonies were boycotted, multitudes turned out to watch the Prince play polo. His progress back to England – via Ceylon, Malaya, Hong Kong, the Philippines, North Borneo, Penang and Egypt – was triumphal, and a newspaper editorial greeting his return echoed the thoughts of many when it said: '*Habemus principens*: we have in him a Prince who lives up to the name, as a true leader of men, endowed with the prime requisites of leadership.'[4]

The Prince of Wales eclipsed all the other members of the Royal Family in popularity. There was profound respect and deep affection for the King and Queen Mary; there was much interest in the Duke and Duchess of York, and later on in their daughters; but it was the Prince of Wales who excited the imagination of the British people. David always gave the impression that to him the people mattered far more than the rituals of a Court still unable to move out of the long shadow cast by Queen Victoria, and there is no reason to doubt that he was sincere. As the grip of economic recession began to squeeze the industrialized world in the late 1920s, the Prince threw himself whole-heartedly into the task of relieving the suffering among rapidly growing numbers of unemployed workers and their families. In 1928 he became a patron of the National Council of Social Service and travelled extensively in the districts worst hit by the Depression. In a speech at the Albert Hall, London, in January 1932 he said: 'I am thinking now of each member of the unemployed population as a single, separate personality, beset by depression, labouring under a sense of frustration and futility.' In the silent Welsh mining valleys, the mean terraces of Tyneside, the grimy mill towns of Lancashire and the over-crowded tenements of industrial Scotland, the people knew he was speaking directly to them, and they loved him for it.

Such a man, with such a public following, might have been expected to go down in history as one of the world's great monarchs. With his capacity for hard work and his populist approach he could have dragged the throne out of the Victorian twilight into the glare of twentieth-century 'democracy'. It is ironic that his ultimate contribution to the modernization of the monarchy was to make way for a man who was much closer to the Victorian tradition than he himself was.

In his Abdication broadcast to the nation, Edward VIII made much of the fact that his brother, the new King, 'has one matchless blessing . . . not bestowed on me, a happy home with his wife and children', while he himself was unable to 'carry the heavy burden of responsibility and discharge my duties as King as I would wish to do, without the help and support of the woman I love'. That comparison, however, overlooked one vital detail: the Duke of York had chosen a bride who, though a commoner, could be accepted by the Royal Family and by the country as a whole; King Edward, on the other hand, was determined to marry a woman whom many people in a far less exalted station would have found difficult to accept as a daughter-in-law, let alone a queen.

'That woman', as King George V called her contemptuously, was born Bessie Wallis Warfield in Baltimore, Maryland, on 19

June 1896. Brought up in a shabby-genteel family, Wallis (she never liked the name Bessie) was married in her teens to an American air force officer but later divorced him and moved up the social scale by marrying Ernest Simpson, a shipping tycoon born in England but educated in the United States, who brought his bride-to-be to London and introduced her to fashionable society. The Simpsons had been married just two years when one of the most fateful meetings in royal history took place – they encountered the Prince of Wales at a weekend party at a country house near Melton Mowbray.

That was in 1930. In the spring of the following year the Prince met the Simpsons at a party given by Thelma, Viscountess Furness, who like Mrs Simpson was an expatriate American. The future lovers came together again when Mrs Simpson was presented at Court in June 1931 and the Prince gave her and Ernest a lift home in his car. In 1932 the Simpsons were invited to Fort Belvedere, David's beloved retreat near Windsor Castle, where during the next twelve months they were more or less permanent weekend guests. Evidence of a deepening relationship between the Prince and Mrs Simpson came in June 1933, when he threw a birthday party for her at Quaglino's restaurant in London, after which he became a frequent visitor to the Simpsons' flat in Bryanston Court. David had formed a series of attachments with married women, but Mrs Simpson was to be the last of the line.

The turning point was reached early in 1934 when the Prince's current companion, Lady Furness, found herself obliged to go to New York and entrusted her friend Wallis with the task of making sure that 'the little man', as they called David, was not lonely during her absence. Mrs Simpson was only too successful and Lady Furness returned to England to discover that she had been supplanted in the affections of 'the little man'. That summer Mrs Simpson – accompanied this time not by her husband but by her elderly Aunt Bessie – joined the Prince's holiday party in Biarritz and later on a cruise in the yacht *Rosaura*, owned by Lord Moyne, one of the leaders of the Conservative Party. After the cruise David gave Wallis a diamond and emerald charm to wear on her bracelet. To her it was the symbol of a dream world made all the more wonderful by the fact that she, a *petite bourgeoise* from Baltimore, was right at the centre of it: 'Wallis in Wonderland' was her description. She knew that no one would ever describe her as 'beautiful' or even 'pretty' – her jaw was too large and her nose too long – yet here she was at the side of a handsome prince who could have been the hero of any girl's wildest fantasies. It is hardly surprising that at this time she cared little for the consequences of such a liaison, if indeed she ever considered them.[5]

The first consequence seems to have been of not much import-ance to her. She came back from a winter holiday with David and his friends in 1934 to a marriage which had sunk into sullen silence, a development she appears not to have expected and for which she later blamed her husband (though his reaction to his wife's close friendship with another man would seem to have been quite natural and perfectly predictable). It made no difference, however, as her relationship with the Prince became more and more intimate. She had been introduced to his parents in the autumn of 1934, a meeting which did not please the King and Queen, who resolved that they would never receive her again. At the same time David, captivated by this bright and ambitious woman, was resolving to marry her if and when she was free. A powder keg was being placed under the throne, and it would be only a matter of time before it exploded.

The fuse was lit in 1936, a year filled with tragedy and menace. On 7 March Adolf Hitler sent his Nazi troops to reoccupy the Rhineland which, for the sake of French peace of mind, had been declared a demilitarized zone after the Great War. On 8 May Benito Mussolini proclaimed a new Roman Empire after completing his invasion of Abyssinia. On 16 July the Spanish Civil War began. In Britain the year opened on a mournful note with the death of King George V on 20 January. A few months earlier the nation had surprised the King by its show of love and loyalty on the silver jubilee of his accession; now it grieved with equal fervour – though there was also a tremendous sense of excitement as people looked forward to the reign of their glamorous new King, a man they thought they knew much better than the austere and remote George V. If the people had known what was going on behind the scenes, if they had known that when their fine new monarch watched his accession being proclaimed at St James's Palace Mrs Simpson was standing beside him, their welcome for Edward VIII might have been muted. But the King's subjects were ignorant of the pressure building up behind the palace doors, and thanks to an astonishing conspiracy of silence by the noble proprietors of the national newspapers they remained in ignorance until the hallowed portals were blown wide open.

The Duke and Duchess of York, like the rest of the Royal Family, were almost as much in the dark as the new King's subjects. Of course, they knew of David's relationship with Wallis Simpson and were worried about it, but they took the view that the heavy responsibilities of kingship would end the affair. The Yorks had become a popular royal couple, the more so since the birth of their two daughters, Princess Elizabeth and Princess Margaret Rose, and now the Duke was heir presumptive to the throne because Edward VIII had no heir. Throughout 1936 they continued their round of official engagements blissfully unaware of what the Duke's new status would mean.

In February 1936 the Conservative Prime Minister, Stanley Baldwin,[6] heard indirectly that the King intended to marry Mrs Simpson, but he dismissed the idea as pure speculation. He could not know that Wallis had told David that she was going to divorce her husband and that the King had sent her to see his solicitor, who had found her a divorce lawyer. In any case, Baldwin was far more concerned at what he saw as the King's thoughtless and haphazard approach to his duties and his lack of interest in affairs of state. David had reduced the staffs of the royal homes at Sandringham and Balmoral without a care for the loyal service many of those dismissed had given to his father. He was unpunctual and inconsiderate with his servants and he shocked members of his Household by sending furniture and plate from Buckingham Palace to Mrs Simpson. He did not like the social obligations of his position and he could not grasp the finer points of the British constitution, which in any case he found boring.

Baldwin could not understand how the popular and hard-working Prince of Wales had become a king to whom he could not send certain state papers for fear that they would be left lying about during one of the many private parties at Fort Belvedere, to which David escaped at every opportunity. But the King's Private Secretary, Major Alexander Hardinge,[7] thought he knew the reason for his master's behaviour: he had come to the conclusion that the King's thoughts were entirely taken up with Wallis Simpson, that she alone could influence him and that he consulted her before taking any decision, no matter how minor.

The British have a highly developed talent for ignoring problems in the hope that they will go away, but in the summer of 1936 it became obvious that something would have to be done about the problem of the King's dependence upon Wallis Simpson. The Duke and Duchess of York, with the two Princesses, were at Birkhall, their holiday home near Balmoral. Stanley Baldwin, nearing the age of seventy and in uncertain health, had been ordered by his doctor to take a three-month vacation. Meanwhile the King was cruising on the yacht *Nahlin* in the Adriatic – with Mrs Simpson and a party of friends. As a result of that cruise, the fate of the King and of the Yorks was sealed. The voyage of the *Nahlin* turned David's romance into an international scandal. It was, as the American humourist H. L. Mencken put it, 'the greatest story since the Crucifixion', and the Press in Europe and the United States made the most of it during the 'silly season', the newspaperman's name for the summer, when news is hard to come by. Every day Americans were treated to lip-smacking accounts of the royal progress with 'Wally', the all-American girl who had landed a king, while the French papers waxed lyrical and scandalous over *l'amour du Roi*.

Only in Britain was the Press silent about the *Nahlin* cruise, respecting the usual request from Buckingham Palace that the monarch should be allowed to enjoy privacy while on holiday abroad. But if the British public was denied the juicy story, the Foreign Office, the Prime Minister's office and the Royal Family were only too painfully aware of the details as reports censored from foreign publications available in Britain were relayed to them. Unfortunately, no one felt able to raise the matter with the King, not even members of his family. When in September David returned home from his holiday and dined at Marlborough House with his mother, the only comment Queen Mary saw fit to pass was, 'Didn't you find it terribly warm in the Adriatic?' The Duchess of York made her dislike of Mrs Simpson quite plain when she arrived at Balmoral to find Wallis playing hostess, but still no attempt was made to explain to the King the outrage he was provoking and the damage he was likely to do to the Crown.

When Baldwin returned in mid-October from his long rest he was immediately plunged into the bubbling cauldron of 'The King's Matter'. His staff showed him letters which had arrived from shocked and bewildered British people living abroad who had read the richly embroidered stories of their King's carryings-on. Baldwin called in the Foreign Secretary, Anthony Eden,[8] and learnt that he too had been receiving such letters. To make matters worse, Mrs Simpson's name had appeared in the published list of impending divorce actions: she was the petitioner in an undefended suit to be heard at the Suffolk Assizes in Ipswich on 27 October. (Wallis later claimed that there was no room for the action in the schedule of the London courts that year, but divorces were often heard at provincial assizes to avoid unwelcome publicity.) It seemed certain that the King's romance would now be thrown into the public arena at home as well as abroad. Alexander Hardinge wrote to Baldwin asking the Prime Minister to intercede with the King and if possible to have the divorce proceedings stopped. At ten o'clock on the morning of Tuesday 20 October the King and his Prime Minister met in the octagonal drawing-room at Fort Belvedere.

Baldwin was understandably nervous. He poured himself a whisky (upon offering one to the King he received the cold reply that His Majesty never touched alcohol before seven o'clock in the evening) and lit his pipe. Finally he steeled himself to begin the crucial conversation, emphasizing that he was speaking as a friend as well as the King's constitutional adviser. He spoke of the role of the Crown as the vital link between Britain and her overseas Dominions, of the importance of public opinion both in Britain and abroad, and then of the foreign Press reports that were so damaging to the Crown. At length he came to the point, or as near to it as he dared come, saying that he could foresee a nation divided after a divorce decree had been granted to the 'woman in the case'. Then he asked whether the petition really had to go ahead. The King replied quickly that it would be wrong for him to interfere in the woman's affairs simply because she happened to be a friend of his, and the interview ended with neither man having stated his position clearly. Baldwin, relieved that the distasteful meeting was over, went away feeling that he had done his duty, while the King was comforted by his Prime Minister's expressions of friendship and understanding. In fact, both men had been less than frank, each relying upon the ancient English arts of understatement and insinuation, which on this occasion proved to be tragically unreliable. Baldwin did not know that the King definitely intended to marry Mrs Simpson after her divorce, and the King could not gauge the true strength of the opposition he would have to face.

The simple fact was that, as King, David was titular head of the Church of England, Defender of the Faith. The laws of the Church of England, insisting that a marriage made before God cannot be dissolved at the whim of man, forbid the remarriage in church of a divorced person and refuse to recognize any subsequent civil marriage of a divorced person. There was therefore no possibility of the Church of England consenting to the marriage of the King and Mrs Simpson. Apart from that, Mrs Simpson was non-royal and American, and it was unlikely that the people of Britain would accept her as their queen. A moment's thought should have told David that he was reaching for the moon. But the King was a man in love.

Even before his meeting with Baldwin, David had been alert to the dangers of widespread publicity for the Simpson divorce case, so he had called in Lord Beaverbrook, the owner of the *Daily Express*, and asked him to do what he could to protect Mrs

Simpson. Beaverbrook, with the aid of Esmond Harmsworth (son of Lord Rothermere, proprietor of the *Daily Mail*), had persuaded all the Fleet Street papers to be discreet, and on 28 October all that was reported was that someone called Wallis Simpson had obtained a decree nisi at Ipswich. But there was one Fleet Street man who was determined not to let 'The King's Matter' rest: Geoffrey Dawson, the editor of *The Times*, felt that it was the duty of his newspaper to uphold the standards of Church and State, and became one of the King's leading opponents.

The day before Mrs Simpson's petition was due to be heard, Dawson suggested the possibility of the King's abdication when he called on Alexander Hardinge and Baldwin and left them each a copy of a letter which said, in part,

> I cannot refrain from saying that nothing would please me more than to hear that Edward VIII had abdicated his rights in favour of the Heir Presumptive, who I am confident would be prepared to carry on in the sterling tradition established by his father. In my view it would be well to have such a change take place while it is still a matter of individuals, and before the disquiet has progressed to the point of calling in question the institution of monarchy itself.

The letter was signed 'Britannicus in Partibus Infidelium' and is thought to have come from a man in East Orange, New Jersey, who described himself only as 'a Briton who has been resident in the United States for several years'. (Beaverbrook later claimed that the letter had been written in the offices of *The Times*, and certainly it bore a striking resemblance to Dawson's own views: perhaps the truth of the matter is that the letter was genuine but not entirely unsolicited.) 'Britannicus' dealt at length with the American Press reports of the King's love affair and drew attention to the harm they were doing to Britain's image in the eyes of the American public. His most important paragraphs were the last two, where he predicted the rise of republicanism in Britain if the King carried on as he had been doing, and put forward his drastic remedy. In the prevailing atmosphere *The Times* could not publish the letter, but Dawson knew how to use it.

On the day that Dawson handed copies of the 'Britannicus' letter to Hardinge and Baldwin, the seriousness of the situation was revealed by a report in the *New York Journal*, a report made all the more significant because it was the paper's first mention of the affair. The story said:

> Within a few days Mrs Ernest Simpson of Baltimore will obtain her divorce decree in England and some eight months thereafter she will be married to Edward VIII, King of England. King Edward's most intimate friends state with the utmost positiveness that he is very deeply and sincerely enamoured of Mrs Simpson, that his love is a righteous affection, and that immediately after the Coronation he will take her as his consort . . . he ardently loves her and he does not see why a King should be denied the privilege of marrying the lady he loves.

The owner of the *Journal*, William Randolph Hearst, had been staying in Britain and it was assumed that, as a fellow-countryman of Mrs Simpson, he had obtained his information from her American friends in London.

On 27 October Mrs Simpson returned to London from Suffolk to be told by the King of his meeting with Baldwin. She began to feel frightened of what might lie ahead, but David reassured her that he could fix things. There was plenty of time. Her divorce did not become absolute until April and the Coronation was not until 12 May. When the couple discovered the following morning that the newspapers had treated Wallis's divorce with commendable discretion, it seemed that perhaps things would work out after all.

Geoffrey Dawson, Alexander Hardinge and Stanley Baldwin, however, thought differently. Hardinge had already called on the Duke of York at his home in Piccadilly and suggested that King Edward's abdication could not be ruled out if he really intended to marry Mrs Simpson. Dawson told Baldwin that he was preparing an editorial on the matter since he felt *The Times* could not remain silent indefinitely. Baldwin was consulting representatives of the Canadian and Australian Governments, upon whose attitude much would depend. At one point the Prime Minister was heard to say that he understood why people had been locked up in the Tower of London in the old days and he wished he could put Mrs Simpson there.

There now occurred something of a lull. On 3 November the King opened his first (and last) Parliament, on the following Sunday he attended the Armistice Day service at the Cenotaph in Whitehall, and the next three days he spent visiting the Home Fleet at Portsmouth. When he returned to London on Friday the 13th, however, he received a severe blow in the form of a letter from his anxious Private Secretary. Hardinge had been unable to contain himself any longer and, after consulting Dawson, he had written to the King warning him that the British Press would not maintain its reticence about Mrs Simpson and that there was a possibility the Government would resign, causing a general election in which the King's private life would be the main issue. To avert such a crisis, Hardinge implored the King to consider sending Mrs Simpson abroad.

The King was furious, not only at the contents of the letter but also at its formal and unfriendly tone; he assumed that it was some sort of ultimatum and that Hardinge was being disloyal to him. When Wallis read the letter she was stunned and told David that perhaps his Private Secretary was right, perhaps she should go abroad for a while. But David's pride had been hurt, and he would not hear of Wallis leaving the country. If his opponents wanted a fight, they could have it. Was he not one of the most popular figures in the world? The people would stand by him even if the politicians, and his own staff, would not. That was his fatal misjudgment.

The King's first move was to appoint an intermediary with the Government, by-passing Hardinge whom he felt he could no longer trust (though in fact the Private Secretary seems to have acted with his master's best interests at heart – his fault was in the way he expressed his concern). The man chosen to carry on the delicate negotiations was Walter Monckton, KC,[9] a friend of David's from university days who had held the office of Attorney-General to the Prince of Wales. The King told Monckton that he was going to send for Baldwin and inform him that if the Government opposed the planned marriage he was ready 'to go'. He seems to have thought that his threat would make the Government back down, in view of his personal popularity, but what it actually meant was that he was manoeuvring himself into a position for which the other side, prompted by 'Britannicus' and Dawson, was already prepared.

Baldwin was received by the King at Buckingham Palace at 6.30 on the evening of Monday 16 November. The King said he understood there were fears of a constitutional crisis arising from his friendship with Mrs Simpson. The Prime Minister pointed out that if His Majesty were to marry Mrs Simpson she would automatically become queen; the people must have a say in the choice of queen, and it was unlikely that they would approve of Mrs Simpson. The King replied that he wanted the Prime Minister to be the first to know that he had made up his mind to marry Mrs Simpson, that nothing would shake his resolve and that he would abdicate if necessary. Baldwin went away in great distress but not nearly as upset as Queen Mary was later that evening when her eldest son dined at Marlborough House and told her of his decision. He asked her if she would receive Mrs Simpson. She refused. The following day David told his brothers that he would abdicate in the face of continued opposition from the Government: the Duke of York was so shaken that he could make no reply, and a few days later he was writing of his fear that the whole fabric of the monarchy would collapse under the strain. No one knew quite what to do.

On 18 November the King left London for a two-day tour of the most depressed districts of South Wales. On 29 November the Yorks left London for Scotland, the Duke to be installed as that country's Grandmaster Mason and the Duchess to receive the Freedom of Edinburgh. The Duke said he felt like a lamb being led to the slaughter – and he was not referring to the Freemasons' ceremony. When the Yorks returned to the capital on Thursday 3 December they were met by newspaper placards proclaiming 'The King's Marriage': the gaffe had been well and truly blown.

It had come about because a provincial bishop, who said he had never even heard of Mrs Simpson, had taken it upon himself to remind the King of his obligations as Defender of the Faith, and the Press, assuming that he was talking about the Simpson affair, had removed its self-administered gag. The Duke of York dashed off to see Queen Mary, and then his brother, who said he was preparing to broadcast to the nation so that the people might decide his fate. Later the King told Queen Mary, in the presence of the Duke of York, that he could not live alone and must marry Wallis Simpson, then he asked his brother to visit him at Fort Belvedere the next morning. The Duke telephoned the Fort on the Friday but was told his brother could not see him until Saturday. Then he was put off until Sunday, then Monday. At 6.50 on the evening of Monday 7 December, David telephoned his brother and asked him to call at the Fort after dinner, but the Duke replied that he would come immediately, and when he arrived the King announced that he had definitely decided to abdicate.

The next three days were hectic, with the Duke rushing from his London home to Fort Belvedere and back. The Duchess, meanwhile, at the hour of the greatest crisis in her life, had been forced to retire to bed with influenza, faced with the frightening prospect of being Queen in a few days' time. The frantic activity ended on the morning of Thursday 10 December when Edward VIII, with all his brothers at his side, signed his Instrument of Abdication. At 3.43 that same afternoon, Stanley Baldwin walked to the Bar of the House of Commons and said to the Speaker: 'A message from the King, sir, signed by His Majesty's own hand.' He passed the document to the Speaker then went back to his seat, wiping tears from his eyes, as the announcement of the abdication was read out. Afterwards he told the Commons the story of his 'repugnant task' in making the King aware of the position into which he was putting himself and of the King's 'unwavering intentions'.

While all this was going on an angry and humiliated Queen Mary was at 145 Piccadilly, sitting by the sickbed of the Duchess of York, the Scottish peer's daughter who had married a prince and had now become Queen Consort.

1

The Girl Who Would Be Queen

The woman who received the Queen's Ring from the Archbishop of Canterbury during the Coronation Service in Westminster Abbey on 12 May 1937 may truly be described as a
daughter of the twentieth century, having been born during its
infancy, on 4 August 1900. Her parents, Lord and Lady Glamis,
were liberal-minded Victorians and the spirit of the times was
what we now think of as Edwardian (though the King who gave
his name to that pleasure-loving decade did not accede to the
throne until 1901). But Elizabeth Angela Marguerite Bowes-
Lyon, as the baby was baptized on 23 September 1900, was born
at just the right moment to take advantage of all that was worth
retaining from the nineteenth century and yet to adapt to the
exigencies of an epoch beset by changes both more radical and
more rapid than in any preceding age.

The ninth child of a happy, secure and close-knit family,
Elizabeth was what is often referred to as 'an afterthought': her
mother, who was thirty-eight years old at the time of the future
Queen's birth, had last produced a child seven years previously,
so the new baby was doted upon by five big brothers and two
sisters (the firstborn, Violet Hyacinth, having died of diphtheria
at the age of eleven).[1] But the childbearing years of Lady Glamis

did not end with Elizabeth. In 1902 she gave birth to a sixth son, David, and she nicknamed him and Elizabeth 'the Benjamins', because they were so much younger than her other offspring. Elizabeth and David became inseparable companions, almost like twins, and were the delight of family and friends.

The background against which 'the Benjamins' grew up could hardly have been more stable. Lord and Lady Glamis celebrated their twentieth wedding anniversary the year after Elizabeth was born, and they seem to have been a perfectly matched couple. Lord Glamis, born Claude George Bowes-Lyon in 1855, the heir to the thirteenth Earl of Strathmore and Kinghorne, was a quiet, dignified man with an unshakable sense of duty but lacking the rigidity of so many Victorian fathers. Tall, ramrod-straight and heavily mustachioed, he had endured rather than enjoyed service as a Guards officer before being granted by his father the tenancy and income of a large and beautiful estate in Hertfordshire, St Paul's Walden Bury. His wife, the former Nina Cecilia Cavendish-Bentinck, a cousin of the Duke of Portland, was a charming, gifted woman with seemingly inexhaustible reserves of understanding and sympathy. It was said that she never spoke harshly to her children but maintained maternal authority by the sheer force of her personality. Her joy in mother-hood, her flair for creative gardening, her accomplishment in music and the decorative arts and her skill as a housekeeper and hostess made her the ideal wife for a country landowner. Lord Glamis rejoiced in the responsibilities of his land and properties – becoming an expert in forestry and a noted authority on all country matters, and taking a keen interest in the welfare of all the tenants and staff who depended upon him for their survival – while Lady Glamis, eschewing the doctrine of parental remoteness favoured by the gentry of the day, took an active role in the upbringing of her children, directed operations in her extensive gardens, and in her own admirably casual way gener-ally organized a settled, peaceful, rural existence. Were there such a thing as a genius for family life, it has been said, then Lady Glamis would have been the epitome of it.

Apart from all the love and security Elizabeth found in her

birthplace, St Paul's Walden Bury provided an environment not far short of a children's paradise. The house, a rambling Queen Anne mansion of red brick hung with honeysuckle and magnolia, and its outbuildings were an endless source of pleasure to 'the Benjamins' – particularly a place they called the Flea House, once used for brewing but by then deserted, where Elizabeth and David would hide to escape morning lessons and enjoy a hidden store of fruit, chocolate, biscuits and even illicit cigarettes. What Elizabeth loved best, however, were the gardens, and most of all a star-shaped wood laid out so as to give the impression of a great forest far from civilization, whereas in fact every part of it was well within earshot of the road leading up to the house. Here Elizabeth would wander through the groves of oak, beech, fir and silver birch with her brother David and her Shetland pony Bobs in tow. Sometimes they would find a dead bird, which they would bury, with suitable piety, in a little box lined with rose leaves. One bird, a pet bullfinch called Bobby, received what almost amounted to a state funeral, with a coffin fashioned from a pencil box by David and what seemed like interminable obsequies devised by Elizabeth.

There were plenty of other animals at St Paul's upon which Elizabeth could lavish affection – horses, dogs, tortoises, Persian cats, chickens, goats, rabbits, two black Berkshire pigs called Lucifer and Emma, and two ring-doves poetically named Caroline-Curly-Love and Rhoda-Wriggly-Worm which shared a wickerwork dovecote in an enormous old oak at the bottom of the garden. One of the pigs gave rise to a tragedy almost as profound as the premature death of Bobby the bullfinch when the children discovered one day that Lucifer had been given away as a prize in a local charity raffle. Horror-stricken, Elizabeth and David scraped together as much money as they could (they received ninepence a week in pocket money) and rushed to where the raffle was being held. They had enough money to buy almost half the tickets on sale, and having done this they waited anxiously as the draw was made – only to dissolve into tears when the number chosen proved to be on one of the tickets they had not managed to buy, and Lucifer was lost forever.

St Paul's Walden Bury really was an enchanted garden for the two youngest Bowes-Lyons, but before long they were introduced to a completely different kind of magic. When Elizabeth was four years old her father inherited the ancient Scottish earldom of Strathmore and Kinghorne, and with it a castle at Streatlam in County Durham and Glamis Castle in Forfarshire, not far from Dundee. Streatlam was for occasional visits only, but Glamis became the home of the new Earl and his family in the late summer and autumn each year. It was as different from St Paul's Walden Bury as could be imagined, but greatly superior to the Hertfordshire manor in its ability to weave spells in young minds.

The history of Glamis stretches back to the eleventh century, when it was a hunting lodge much favoured by early Scottish kings. In the fourteenth century it was given by King Robert II (grandson of Robert the Bruce) to his daughter Jean and her husband Sir John Lyon, from whom the Bowes-Lyons are directly descended. Three hundred years later, the third Earl of Strathmore opened the doors of Glamis to the Old Chevalier, James Stewart – son of the deposed King James II of England and father of Bonnie Prince Charlie – and later died fighting for the Jacobite cause at the bloody battle of Sheriffmuir. But what really gives Glamis its magic, of course, is Shakespeare's use of it as the setting for *Macbeth*. In the first act of the play, the ill-fated King Duncan arrives at the castle for the first time as the guest of Macbeth, the Thane of Glamis:

DUNCAN: This castle hath a pleasant seat; the air
Nimbly and sweetly recommends itself
Unto our gentle senses.

BANQUO: This guest of summer,
The temple-haunting martlet, does approve
By his lov'd mansionry that the heaven's breath
Smells wooingly here: no jutty, frieze,
Buttress, nor coign of vantage, but this bird
Hath made his pendent bed and procreant cradle;
Where they most breed and haunt, I have observ'd,
The air is delicate.

There is a story that Shakespeare visited Glamis shortly before writing the play in about 1605 and that the murder of Duncan is set in the old guardroom of the castle, which to this day is known as 'Duncan's Hall'.

The Glamis Elizabeth Bowes-Lyon knew as a child was five hundred years old in parts, but most of it had been built of sandstone in the seventeenth century in the style known as Scottish Baronial, with turretted embellishments copied from the classic French châteaux of the Loire. The family lived mainly in one wing which had been refurbished in the nineteenth century, but the children loved to play in the central, older part of the castle, with its mementoes of Bonnie Prince Charlie, its tales of ghosts and past bloodshed, and the all-pervading smell of history. Elizabeth claimed to have seen a female ghost in sixteenth-century dress on the stairs, but more tangible were the phantoms 'the Benjamins' fashioned out of materials from their dressing-up box and left in 'King Malcolm's Room' or 'Hangman's Room' to frighten visitors.

Outdoors there was the tree-dotted splendour of Angle Park, nestling in the fertile valley between the Sidlaw Hills to the south and the lowering bulk of the Grampians to the north. Through the castle grounds meandered Glamis Burn and Dean Water, and later on there was a magnificent formal garden – with terrace, fountain and surrounding yew hedge – designed by Lady Strathmore.

As the daughter of an earl, Elizabeth was accorded the courtesy title of 'Lady', but it was not long before she became known to the family, in an unconscious act of prophesy, as 'Princess'. From her earliest years she was precocious in the best sense of the word, walking and talking early and displaying a rare strength of character. Astrologers say that the conjunction of the Sun, Mercury and Venus under Elizabeth's birth sign of Leo bestowed on her beauty, grace, charm and gentle good humour to blend with a confident, outgoing approach to life, an innate warmth and friendliness, and a desire to lead and to be admired by others. Such indeed were the qualities she showed as a child, and hence her prophetic nickname. She had the quiet dignity of her father and to complement it the lively intelligence and *joie de vivre* of her mother. Small for her age, she was pretty and appealing, with cascading curls, large grey-blue eyes and a bright, responsive manner. What impressed people most, however, was the fact that she could always make conversation and had an unerring instinct for the right thing to say. At the age of three she drew an important guest away from the drawing room and into another room for a 'talk' that lasted forty-five minutes. Whenever the Strathmores were entertaining and there was a lull in the conversation, the message went out, 'Find Elizabeth'. She had an intuitive knack of putting people at their ease, and that ability is the thing most noticed by people who meet the Queen Mother today.

Such were the virtues of Elizabeth Bowes-Lyon as a child. Her vices appear to have been few. Once, at the age of six, she took a pair of scissors and cut to ribbons some new sheets, but her confession of the deed was sufficient to make amends in her mother's eyes. Lady Strathmore, asked how it was possible to rebuke such a clever and attractive child, replied that all she had to do was say *'Elizabeth!'* in a sad voice and that would make her sorry for whatever it was she had done wrong. Otherwise, apart from a passion for chocolate cake and cream biscuits, she seems to have been something of a paragon, though perhaps she was a little given to showing-off, a fault for which she was once upbraided at her London day school when, at the age of nine, she began an essay with a Greek quotation.

Elizabeth was educated mainly at home, though contemporary fashion dictated that girls as well as boys should be sent away to school. Lady Strathmore taught her 'Benjamins' to read and write and instructed them in the arts of music, dancing and drawing. Also, since both their parents were deeply religious, the children had, by the age of six or seven, acquired a sound knowledge of Bible stories and a simple, direct faith which was to be the mainstay of Elizabeth's testing life. Following their mother's teaching was a succession of governesses, of whom, Elizabeth wrote at the time, some were nice and some were not. A fluent reader by the age of six, Elizabeth spoke French well at

ten and later learnt German. In London, where her father leased
a house in St James's Square, she spent two terms in 1909 at a
day school in Marylebone High Street under a young, Froebel-
trained headmistress named Constance Goff. Miss Goff was
able to testify to her nine-year-old pupil's panache after being
invited to St James's Square for tea: Lady Strathmore had been
delayed and was not at home to receive the guest, but when she
did arrive she found that Elizabeth had taken Miss Goff into the
drawing room, rung for tea, poured it and was deeply engaged
in polite conversation.

The music and dancing lessons begun by Lady Strathmore
also continued in London, under the direction of professional
tutors. Like her mother, Elizabeth showed a talent for playing
the piano and after only six months' tuition was 'top of the bill' at
a concert arranged by her piano school. The principal of the
school, Mme Matilde Verne, recalled a tense moment during a
practice session in preparation for the concert:

> One day, in what we called the Paderewski Room, I heard some-
> one being taught an exercise that all pupils, old and young, detest.
> It seemed to me that the struggle was going on too long, so I went
> into the torture chamber and found that little Elizabeth was the
> victim. 'We have only just begun,' said the teacher firmly. I looked
> at the child. Though reverent in face, there was a warning gleam in
> her eyes as she said to the teacher, 'Thank you very much. That
> was wonderful', and promptly slid off the music-stool, holding
> out her tiny hand in polite farewell.

Having made her point, Elizabeth allowed herself to be cajoled
back onto the piano-stool and the session ended successfully.
The piano lessons went on until shortly before Elizabeth's
engagement to the Duke of York was announced in 1923, and
after her marriage she invited Mme Verne to tea, greeting her
with the words: 'You must give the Duke of York some piano
lessons. I have already begun to teach him his notes, and he
knows three.'

As well as learning the piano, Elizabeth was taught by her
mother to play the small organ in the chapel at Glamis. On one
memorable occasion she caused a good deal of embarrassment

during a service by playing variations in the style of Handel on the theme of a popular song.

Music teachers, governesses, butlers, footmen and drawing room teas were commonplaces of the comfortable, secure and privileged world in which the little 'Princess' grew up. While she played with her pony in the wood at St Paul's Walden Bury, a ten-year-old working-class child might be slaving for twelve or thirteen hours a day as a grocer's messenger for four shillings and sixpence a week. While the traditional piper played stirring airs in the dining room at Glamis, the family of a Glasgow shipyard worker would most probably be sitting down to an evening meal of bread and jam washed down with tea. Such contrasts were one of the chief features of society in Edwardian Britain. Profits in industry and commerce were soaring (the value of income tax assessments on profits and interest rose by 55 per cent between 1896 and 1913), but the wages of the workers were steadily losing their purchasing power – a decline of 10 per cent between 1896 and 1913. Britain, still the workshop of the world, was booming, but all the benefits were going to the rich. As the American trade union organization Industrial Workers of the World put it: 'The working class and the employing class have nothing in common. There can be no peace so long as hunger and want are found among millions of working people and the few, who make up the employing class, have all the good things of life . . .' In eastern Scotland, where Glamis Castle is situated, 24 per cent of the working population were unemployed in the early years of the century: between 1900 and 1910 a quarter of a million Scots left their native land in search of a better life. Of course, none of this intruded upon the idyllic childhood of Elizabeth Bowes-Lyon, but it was not too long before she was confronted by the kind of suffering that afflicts both rich and poor, and she learnt something of the workings of 'ordinary' people's minds.

Her formal schooling virtually ended and her real education may be said to have begun on her fourteenth birthday. On the evening of 4 August 1914 she was taken to see a variety show at the London Coliseum where, at the end of the programme, it was announced that as from 11 pm Britain was at war with Kaiser Wilhelm's Germany. The audience burst into an ecstasy of patriotic fervour, watched from a box by the incredulous Elizabeth. To her the Kaiser's War was to bring a broader outlook on life which would serve her well when she was called upon to take her place at the head of the new, uncertain and unstable society that emerged from the conflict.

Elizabeth's cosy world was changed almost overnight by the declaration of war. Her brothers Patrick, John, Fergus and Michael rushed off to join their regiments and preparations were immediately made to turn Glamis into a military hospital. Hardly a week had gone by before Elizabeth was at the castle among, as she later said, 'the bustle of hurried visits to chemists for outfits of every sort of medicine and to the gunsmith's to buy all the things that people thought they wanted for a war and then found they didn't'. She also helped with the task of providing comforts for the men of the local Black Watch battalion – her job was to crinkle tissue paper until it became soft enough to use as lining for sleeping bags. At that stage the war was an adventure, almost fun, and its remoteness was emphasized for the Bowes-Lyon family in September 1914 when, on the 17th, Fergus married Lady Christian Dawson-Damer and on the 29th John married the Hon. Fenella Hepburn-Stuart-Forbes-Trefusis. But all too soon the realities of the conflict were to strike home.

The first shots had been fired at the Battle of Mons on 22 August, leaving sixteen hundred men dead or wounded, and on 26 August the British IInd Corps had suffered three thousand casualties at Le Cateau. The day before Fergus Bowes-Lyon's wedding, the British commander-in-chief, Sir John French, issued orders leading to a new kind of combat which depended upon the construction of an elaborate system of trenches, and within a month the carnage was beginning in earnest. The British army effectively smashed itself to pieces at the month-long battle of Ypres, which started on 12 October. By the time it was over more than half of the young Britons who had landed in France to oppose 'The Hun' had been killed or wounded. The people who had so wildly cheered the royal proclamation of 4 August now realized that the struggle might be long and costly. There had been talk of winning the war by Christmas, but many grim Christmases were to follow before the killing stopped.

Glamis received its first wounded soldiers from France in December 1914. Lady Strathmore met the men at the main door of the castle and settled them in sixteen beds arranged round the panelled walls of the vast dining room. For the next five years those beds would never be empty. The medical care of the troops was supervised by Elizabeth's elder sister, Rose, then aged twenty-four, who had been trained as a nurse at a hospital in London. Elizabeth herself was considered too young to join the nursing staff at Glamis, but there was plenty for her to do in the scullery and on the ward. She made sure that the soldiers were supplied with cigarettes and tobacco, helped them to write their letters to loved ones, served meals and tea to those who were bedridden and could not eat with the others in the castle crypt. But her main task was to put the men at their ease in their strange and somewhat daunting surroundings, and to keep them entertained. She sang for them, played whist with them and, through her friendly good humour, generally took their minds off their wounds and the horrors they had experienced in the trenches. One day in 1915 she dressed up her brother David in skirt, cloak, furs, hat and veil and presented him to the patients as a rather grand female cousin. David toured the ward asking all the right questions and behaving exactly like a distinguished visitor. It was not until the following day that the joke was revealed to the soldiers, and what they said about it is not recorded.

Corporal Ernest Pearne, who found himself at Glamis in August 1915 after being severely wounded in the shoulder, wrote down his impressions of life at the castle, and recalled another practical joke played by the aristocratic mischief-maker. Shortly after his arrival at the castle, the corporal was exploring the dim recesses of the crypt, with its menacing suits of armour and its rats, when he was confronted by a huge brown bear, standing on its hind legs and with its mouth wide open. 'Of course,' he wrote, 'I got a rare fright, and I must have shown it because, on looking across the room, I saw a smiling face at a little window . . .' The bear was a stuffed memento of a former Earl of Strathmore and the smiling face belonged, as the corporal discovered to his embarrassment the same evening, to Lady Elizabeth Bowes-Lyon.

Elizabeth and the corporal became firm friends, and he remembered her thus:

> She had the loveliest pair of blue eyes I've ever seen – very expressive, eloquent eyes that could speak for themselves. She had a very taking habit of knitting her forehead just a little now and then when she was speaking, and her smile was a refreshment. I noticed in particular a sort of fringe at the front of her shapely head. Her teeth were even and very white and well set, and when speaking, she struck me as being a most charming little lady and a most delightful companion.

She was not always so charming, however. Corporal Pearne recalled the day when Elizabeth really lost her temper with him:

> One red-hot day I climbed to the top of the castle tower. Lady Elizabeth was there and we got talking about plays and so on. The Union Jack was lying at the foot of the flagstaff. I said it would look better at the top, so we decided to haul it up. We did so, and just as it reached the top the wind entangled it over the top of the staff, and try as we might it wouldn't right itself.

The corporal said he would climb the flagpole and free the flag, but Elizabeth said that he must not do it for fear of damaging his shoulder (his arm was still in a sling). The corporal begged her pardon and said he was going to try it anyway.

> At that she stamped her little foot, and called me 'stubborn', 'pig-headed', 'foolhardy', anything to stop me. Then she ran away to get someone else to prevent me. It was a difficult job, but I managed to scramble up and slide down slowly dragging the flag with me. When I descended to the crypt I met Lady Elizabeth coming back, and told her it was done. She stared at me amazed. 'Well, Ernest,' she said, 'I didn't think you could have done it. You *are* stubborn!'[2]

Soldiers like Pearne would stay at Glamis for six months or

more, and parting from them was a real wrench for Elizabeth and her family. But the war was to lay a much heavier hand on the Bowes-Lyons. In September 1915 news came that Fergus, a captain in The Black Watch, had been killed on the first day of the idiotic Battle of Loos. He was just twenty-six years old. Three days before the battle, he had been at Glamis on leave to see his first child, a daughter, born in July 1915. Lady Strathmore was heartbroken, and the men in the ward who had escaped from the hell of the trenches with their lives, felt deeply for her. They agreed among themselves that during the days of mourning they would not go upstairs to the billiard room, which had been opened for their recreation; they would not play games on the lawns; they would keep down the noise of the gramophone and the piano; and above all they would not use the main door of the castle, so as not to intrude upon the family. But when the soldiers sent a letter of sympathy to Lady Strathmore, she expressed her thanks and told the men they must carry on just as they had done before the terrible news, since they were guests at the castle.

The shock of Fergus's death and the onset of ill-health meant that Lady Strathmore was forced to take a rather less active part in the running of Glamis, both as a hospital and as a home, and Elizabeth gradually assumed greater responsibility, particularly after May 1916, when Rose left home to marry. If the war turned boys into old men, it certainly turned a teenage girl into a woman, burdened as she was not only with the anxieties of a family which had lost one of its sons and risked losing another three but also with the cares of looking after a group of men who, as well as suffering the pain of their wounds, relived the nightmares of the Western Front. It is hardly surprising that in later life, and during another cataclysmic war, Elizabeth was able to display such courage, calmness and devotion to duty. She learnt the hard way.

Her courage was dramatically tested in December 1916 when fire broke out in the ninety-foot-high keep at Glamis. Elizabeth was the first person to notice the smoke and flames and she immediately telephoned the fire brigade. The hoses of the

Glamis firemen, however, were not long enough to draw water from the Dean, a few hundred yards from the castle, and neither were those of the Forfar brigade. It was feared that the entire building might be destroyed, but Elizabeth had shown great presence of mind by telephoning the Dundee fire service as well, and after what seemed an eternity they arrived to quell the blaze. In the meantime Elizabeth had not been standing idly by: a huge lead water tank under the roof of the keep had burst and sent hundreds of gallons of water cascading down the spiral staircase of the building, threatening the drawing room and other apartments, with their furniture, pictures and other valuables. Elizabeth and David quickly organized a team of servants, tenants and villagers to brush the torrent aside into less vulnerable halls and corridors. Then, as the flames still crackled and black smoke billowed from the keep, the contents of the apartments were passed from hand to hand along a human chain to safety. Glamis and its historic treasures were saved, though it was to be many years before the damage could be completely repaired.

The Great War ended abruptly on 11 November 1918 when Germany followed Turkey and Austria-Hungary into surrender. No one knew quite what to do. In the trenches the troops sat stunned as the guns fell silent. In London, virtually all work ceased and crowds thronged the streets, singing, dancing and drinking. Total strangers made love in doorways as an act of celebration. A bonfire lit at the base of Nelson's Column in Trafalgar Square left smoke stains on the plinth which are still visible today. At Glamis, however, life went on much as it had done since the end of 1914: the flow of wounded continued unabated, and as well as caring for them the Bowes-Lyons had to entertain officers from Australia and New Zealand while they awaited passages back to their own countries. It was not until 1919 that the last soldier took his leave of the castle and the last member of the family to return from the war – Michael, who had been wounded and taken prisoner in 1917 – came home to it.

For Elizabeth there was now a lot of catching-up to do. The society into which she might have been expected to 'come out', as the saying goes, had been suspended for five years and instead of going to finishing school or looking forward to the thrill of wearing her first long dress to a ball, she had performed duties no upper-class teenage girl of the day could have imagined in peacetime, and she had come to understand and respect people from backgrounds about which she would have known nothing had it not been for the war. She had lost, or at least postponed part of her youth, and in a way that was an advantage. Youth is said to be wasted on the young, and though Elizabeth was still only eighteen years old when the war ended, her experiences had given her a maturity well beyond her years. When in 1919 the time came to attend balls and parties and otherwise to enjoy the social life of her class, she was wise enough to appreciate it fully, and to realize that pleasure was merely a fleeting stimulant, not a way of life, as had been the case during the giddy, carefree, long summer afternoon that the nobility had enjoyed in Edwardian Britain.

There was no 'coming out' ball to herald Lady Elizabeth Bowes-Lyon's official entry into upper-class womanhood, but as the worries of war gave way first to the relief and later to the uncertainties of peace, the great social merry-go-round of London began to revolve at full speed again and the twenty-year-old 'Princess' was soon caught up in the whirl of parties, dinners, formal dances, country house weekends and theatre-going. She was noticed at Ascot in a white lace frock; she was frequently among guests at Number One Carlton House Terrace, the home of the fabulous Curzons; and she rapidly acquired a reputation as 'the best dancer in London'. But there were two aspects of the social round that did not appeal to Elizabeth: its formality and its traditional function as an aristocratic marriage market. Her reaction to the first of these is best expressed in the story of a rather stuffy and boring luncheon she was obliged to attend, when she arranged beforehand with a friend that the two of them should burst into uproarious laughter every time Elizabeth gave the signal by raising her left eyebrow. As for the marriage stakes, she had no intention of offering herself to the field, and though a

45

number of suitors soon appeared they were all firmly rejected.

Perhaps one reason for Elizabeth's lack of interest in marriage prospects was the fact that she was in no hurry to leave home. The family was still the centre of her life and she was never happier than when she spent tranquil weekends among the greenery of St Paul's Walden Bury or passed golden Augusts at Glamis, entertaining friends and playing tennis. In her two homes, she said later, she found perfection. Apart from that, she felt she was very much part of the communities which were so closely linked with her family. At St Paul's Walden, for example, one of the villagers remembered how for many years Elizabeth called at his cottage at Christmas time with a present for his daughter, who had once been frightened by a dog belonging to the Strathmores. At Glamis, Elizabeth was an enthusiastic Girl Guide and in 1920 became district commissioner, adored by the girls because of her sense of fun.

It was the Girl Guides that provided Elizabeth with her introduction to royal circles through a friendship with Princess Mary, George V's daughter,[3] whom Elizabeth met when the Princess inspected the Glamis Guides. The friendship blossomed quickly and Elizabeth, three years younger than the Princess, was soon a regular visitor to Buckingham Palace. Princess Mary, however, was not the only member of the Royal Family to take an interest in the Scottish earl's daughter – there was also the King's second son, Prince Albert, Duke of York. Bertie, as the Duke was always known, had first met the girl with whom he was to fall in love at a children's party (the story goes that Elizabeth gave him three glacé cherries from the top of her cake at tea), but he did not recall this meeting when he was introduced to Elizabeth at a ball in London during the summer of 1920. The shy, twenty-four-year-old Bertie was immediately attracted to Elizabeth and on their second meeting a few months later, when he and Princess Mary were guests of the Strathmores at Glamis, it began to dawn on him that he was in love with her.

Elizabeth, however, was not in love – or if she was she did not know it. Marriage, even to a prince, was very far from her thoughts. She was still catching up with the years of her youth lost during the war, while at the same time she had formulated a set of high standards for the man, whoever he might be, whom she would eventually choose to share her life: he had to be kind and brave; he had to be unswervingly loyal and honest; he had to possess unimpeachable morals and he had to be firmly committed to his religious faith. These were the ideals Elizabeth set for herself, and she was not about to marry anyone until she was convinced that he shared her principles. It was going to take all Bertie's courage, patience and perseverance to win her.

In any case, Elizabeth was much too busy in 1920 to take a courtship seriously. Early that year the Strathmores had been obliged to give up their London house in St James's Square and a good deal of their time was spent in searching for a new Town residence. Finally, in October, they settled on 17 Bruton Street, a few steps to the east of Berkeley Square, and there was all the excitement of having the house altered to suit their needs and decorated to their taste. While the house-hunting was going on there was a busy summer of entertaining at Glamis, culminating in not only the arrival of the Duke of York and Princess Mary but also the grand and important Forfar Ball and a large party given to mark the visit of Elizabeth's elder sister Rose, home for a few months from Malta where her husband, the Hon. William Leveson-Gower,[4] was stationed with the Royal Navy. Then at Christmas there was a big family party at St Paul's Walden Bury, when Aunt Elizabeth was much in demand by the younger members of the growing Bowes-Lyon clan. Elizabeth enjoyed it all immensely. When the children were about she would join in their play; when friends came to stay she would entertain the company by singing popular songs with the words adapted by her to suit the personalities and idiosyncracies of the guests – and her talent for mimicry was such that it was once said she could have been a star of the music-hall. She also loved dressing up for the glamorous occasion. At the party given for Rose she turned many a head with her pink brocade gown and pearls shining in her dark hair.

The following year was equally busy, and its requirements of Elizabeth were rather more testing. In May 1921 Lady Strathmore became ill and despite predictions that the summer break at Glamis would improve her health, her condition worsened and she was bedridden for several months, undergoing two operations before she began to recover. As well as worrying about her mother, Elizabeth had to shoulder the responsibilities and anxieties of housekeeper and hostess at Glamis, with its continuous parade of summer guests. That she succeeded admirably in both departments is not to be doubted. Friends from those days have recalled Elizabeth's efficiency, calmness and indefatigable cheerfulness. It is remembered, too, that she had the knack of making people want to please her – an effect she still markedly produces today.

Among the visitors to the castle during that summer of 1921 was, predictably, the Duke of York, who went for the start of the grouse shooting season on 12 August and also to further his cause with regard to Elizabeth. It was at this time that Bertie first revealed his feelings for the Strathmores' youngest daughter to his mother, who was staying with Princess Mary at Cortachy Castle, the home of Lady Airlie, a few miles from Glamis. Intrigued, Queen Mary decided to visit Glamis herself and motored over for tea. The newspapers of the day were probably right in speculating that the Queen's trip constituted an inspection of a possible royal bride, but they were quite wrong in hinting at the identity of the prospective bridegroom. They assumed that the Queen was considering a partner for her eldest son David, the Prince of Wales, then twenty-seven years old and causing some concern in official circles by his apparent lack of interest in marriage. It was to be some time before the true story came out, and when it did the Press and the public were taken completely by surprise.

Elizabeth had not been exactly encouraging to her royal suitor, but in 1921 he plucked up the courage to propose marriage to her. It was her strength as much as her charm and good looks that moved him. She was kind, gentle and good-humoured, but underneath her mild exterior was a forceful personality ever willing to express opinions, steadfast in beliefs and powerful in argument. Bertie needed a lot of love and understanding, but he also needed support and a certain amount of firmness. He knew it, his mother knew it, and so did Lady Strathmore, who said of him that he would be made or marred by the woman he married. Elizabeth seemed the perfect choice. But she turned him down, and it is not difficult to see why.

Bertie was of a serious, sometimes even morbid turn of mind, introspective and occasionally prey to a feeling of self-pity. He was painfully shy, agonizingly modest and he suffered from a severe stammer that made his diffidence all the more acute. He had a wild temper, inherited both from his father and the fierce old Duke of Teck, his maternal grandfather. He was courageous, high-principled and endowed with deep warmth and sympathy towards his fellow man, but his personality had been warped by an upbringing that was, to say the least, depressing.

From the day of his birth in 1895 it seemed that the fates were against him, for that event occurred on 14 December, the day held in mournful reverence by the aging Queen Victoria as the anniversary of the death of her beloved Prince Albert. The boy's family were extremely nervous about the old Queen's reaction to the news of his birth on that of all days and his grandfather, the Prince of Wales (later Edward VII), found it necessary to reassure Bertie's parents, then Duke and Duchess of York, that Grandmama was not annoyed with them, though she regretted their unfortunate timing. As a palliative, the Prince of Wales suggested, the Yorks should propose to the Queen that they call the boy Albert. The Duke followed his father's advice and Victoria was duly mollified. She wrote: 'I am all impatient to see the new one, born on such a sad day, but rather the more dear to me, especially as he will be called by that dear name which is the byword for all that is great and good.' The boy was baptized Albert Frederick Arthur George.

But having survived the embarrassment of his birth-date, Bertie had other problems to face. He was left-handed and knock-kneed; he lived in the shadow of an elder brother who would not only inherit the throne but was also blessed with

49

immense charm; and in early childhood he was systematically neglected by a mentally unstable nurse who fed him so badly that he would suffer from digestive troubles for the rest of his life. And then, of course, there were his parents – a father of both stern and idiosyncratic disposition and a mother who placed duty above everything (she once said she could not forget that the father of her children was also their King). His father's requirements of Bertie were straightforward enough: on his fifth birthday the King said to him, 'I hope you will always be obedient and do what you are told.' Doing what he was told involved being obliged to write with his right hand and to wear splints on his legs which caused so much pain that he could neither concentrate on his lessons by day nor sleep properly at night. By the time he was seven years old Bertie had acquired his stammer and was subject to nervous tension and uncontrollable outbursts of temper.

Bertie was naturally expected to go into the Navy, as his father and elder brother had done, and accordingly he went to the Royal Naval College at Osborne on 15 January 1909. He had not proved to be an outstanding scholar when taught at home by the royal tutor, Henry Peter Hansell – who, though he inspired a deep devotion in the young Princes under his care, would have been the first to admit that he was not the best teacher they could have had – and Osborne did nothing to improve his academic standing. To the dismay of his father, Bertie was found to be indifferent to his college work and to the rebukes he earned through his consistently low placing in his class. At one point it was doubted whether he would do well enough to gain entry to the senior naval college at Dartmouth, but though in his final examinations at Osborne Bertie was placed sixty-eighth out of sixty-eight students, he was able to go to Dartmouth in January 1911.

If the naval colleges did nothing to improve Bertie scholastically they certainly did their bit towards forming the more positive sides of his nature. For the first time in his life he was able to mix freely with boys of his own age and he formed friendships which he would sustain for many years. He was popular with both his officers and his fellow cadets for his generosity, sense of fun, good manners and consideration for others, whether they were his naval superiors or college servants. He was, it is true, still volatile of temperament, but much better able to control himself than formerly. He learnt to ride well, to sail, to play creditable tennis (left-handed) and to devote some concentration at least to his lessons. By the end of his two years at Dartmouth he had risen a few places above the bottom of the class and his officers were full of praise for his determination and the general quality of his character. And after all the doubts, the resounding admonitions from his father, he could fulfil 'the dearest wish of Papa and Mama' and join the Royal Navy.

In January 1913 Bertie sailed from Devonport in the cruiser *Cumberland* on a six-month training voyage that developed into something of an endurance test for him. First, he fell victim to seasickness, which was to cause him trouble throughout his naval career. Then, as the ship made its way to Canada via Tenerife and the Caribbean islands, he found himself besieged at every stage by wildly enthusiastic crowds clamouring to see and even to touch the King's son, and he was followed by hordes of newspapermen anxious to interview him. The Prince had a horror of appearing in public and when, in Jamaica, he was asked to open an extension to the yacht club in Kingston, his carefully rehearsed speech was ruined by his stammer. Thereafter he saved himself some embarrassment by persuading one friend to appear for him at lesser functions and another to impersonate him during a Press conference. However, the cruise had both its pleasures – horse-racing in Barbados, salmon fishing in Newfoundland – and its benefits. Bertie returned home more mature and a little more confident in himself than he had been. His father was greatly pleased.

The Prince now began his naval career in earnest, joining the battleship *Collingwood* as a midshipman, under the alias of 'Mr Johnson', and it was there that he was to be found manning gun turret 'A' on 4 August 1914. Much to his chagrin, however, his war service was interrupted by repeated attacks of stomach trouble which necessitated long periods of shore leave. Indeed, he was in the sick bay aboard the *Collingwood* when, as part of the Home Fleet's First Battle Squadron, she joined the Battle of Jutland on 31 May 1916. Exhilarated by the prospect of at last seeing some action, Mr Johnson, newly promoted to sub-lieutenant, leapt from his bunk and raced to his station in 'A' turret. The battle proper lasted no more than five minutes and was inconclusive in terms of naval supremacy, but it had a profound psychological effect on the Prince. The ear-splitting roar of the twelve-inch guns, the sight of great ships exploding and disappearing beneath the waves, the huge shells whistling overhead so close that one could see what colour they were, made Bertie feel that he had proved himself as a man and 'done his bit' for his country. His only regret was that the *Collingwood* bore no battle scars.

Jutland was the last action the Prince saw. Most of the next eighteen months he spent in command of a desk and at the end of November 1917 his seafaring days were cut short when he underwent an operation to remove a duodenal ulcer. But if he could not continue in the senior service there was a place for him in a very junior one – the Royal Naval Air Service, shortly to be amalgamated with the Royal Flying Corps to form the Royal Air Force. With the rank of flight-lieutenant, Bertie went to the embryonic flying training school at Cranwell in Lincolnshire and soon became the first member of the Royal Family to qualify as a pilot.

With the war over, King George V decided that it was time his second son played a greater part in public affairs, but before he could do so he had to master the mysteries of the British con-stitution and learn about the delicately balanced relationship binding together the Crown, the government and the people. In October 1919, therefore, Bertie went up to Trinity College, Cam-bridge, where he spent a year studying history, civics and economics. At the end of his time at the university, the King conferred upon Bertie the titles Baron Killarney, Earl of Inver-ness and Duke of York. These were the titles George V had held for the best part of a decade and their bestowal on his second son constituted a recognition by the King that he had imbued Bertie with the high moral and personal standards he himself held so dear. What he apparently failed to realize was the damage he had wrought in trying to mould a member of the new generation in the image of the old.

The negative sides of Bertie's upbringing were only too obvious to Elizabeth Bowes-Lyon when the Duke proposed to her in 1921. He had matured late and in trying too hard to rise to the strict and unbending standards laid down by his father he had placed a strain upon himself which showed in his petulance – though it was directed mainly against what he considered to be his own shortcomings, his temper also hurt other people – and in his bouts of depression. If she were ever to marry him, he needed to show her that his virtues were capable of final victory over his faults. There were other factors, too, which influenced her decision. For one thing, Bertie had little experience of the sort of family life which was so dear to her, and what knowledge he did have had been gained at second hand through living with his old naval friend Dr Louis Greig and his wife while at Cranwell. Also, the Duke was a public figure robbed of privacy wherever he went by reporters, photographers and gawping crowds. The Bowes-Lyons, though always conscious of their public responsibilities as members of the landed aristocracy, were accustomed to guarding their privacy and their freedom to do as they pleased; these rights were special to Elizabeth, and she would not easily give them up. Lady Strathmore, not one to be dazzled by the prospect of a royal connexion, fully understood her daughter's decision, though at the same time she liked Bertie, sympathized with his cause and made it clear that he would always be welcome at St Paul's Walden Bury and Glamis.

Bertie, depressed but by no means defeated after his rejection by Elizabeth, made the most of the Strathmores' open door. Ostensibly it was his passion for shooting which took him during the autumn to St Paul's Walden (where he endeared himself to the locals when, during days out with the guns, he lunched at the village pub, the Strathmore Arms), but there were many places where he could have peppered the partridge and the pheasant, and it is obvious that Elizabeth was the real attraction. For the time being, however, Elizabeth was keeping him at arm's length. When, for example, he visited Glamis she would keep him waiting before she appeared to greet him; when he contrived to have himself invited to parties or on outings where she was among the guests, she would refuse to let him hold her hand.

Elizabeth did have a wedding on her mind but it was certainly not her own. Her friend Princess Mary had become engaged to Viscount Lascelles,[5] and they were married at Westminster Abbey on 28 February 1922. Elizabeth was one of the eight bridesmaids, in a beautiful cloth-of-silver gown and wearing a big silver rose at her waist. At the wedding breakfast she sat next to the Duke of York, little dreaming that in barely more than a year the attention of the entire nation would be upon her as she walked up the aisle at the Abbey.

Shortly before the wedding of Princess Mary, Elizabeth asked the servants at St Paul's Walden Bury and the wives of the tenants on the estate to a party at the manor house so that they could see her in her bridesmaid's dress. It was an action which, in the 'democratic' climate of today, might seem condescending and even rather insulting, but in fact it was no more than the perfectly natural response of someone brought up to accept the benevolent leadership and generous paternalism of the ruling class – and there is nothing to suggest that it was viewed by those for whom it was intended as anything but an act of kindness and thoughtfulness. Indeed, it would be hardly worth recalling, except as an example of how the English class system in those days was supported by people on both sides of the great divide, were it not an early indication of what Elizabeth's contribution to the monarchy was to be. When she became Queen Consort her attitude towards the people of Britain was precisely the same as her attitude towards her father's tenants and staff had been: without lowering the stature of the throne, she treated its subjects as people towards whom she had a responsibility and with whom she shared a mutual interest and interdependence.

Of course monarchs have always realized that 'the people' are an important factor in their survival or otherwise, but the problem has always been to strike a balance in the relationship between Crown and country. Many rulers have suffered death or banishment because they remained too aloof from their subjects, while others have contributed to the erosion of their own powers, rights and privileges in seeking popularity by descending nearer to the level of the common people. As Queen, Elizabeth would enjoy the advantage of having been brought up close enough to ordinary life to understand it yet far enough away not to have lost the natural aloofness which may be accepted in one born to a superior social position. Part of the reason why the British Crown has not been trampled underfoot in what has been called 'the long march of Everyman' is that at a time when the tide might easily have turned in favour of republicanism there was a Queen who was able to win the confidence and affection of the nation as a woman without sacrificing any of the dignity of the throne.

In the spring of 1922, though, there was not the faintest hint of a suspicion that Elizabeth Bowes-Lyon would become Queen, and indeed she was a long way from any royal status other than by nickname. Lady Strathmore's health was by now improving and it seemed that her daughter could look forward to a year less fraught than the previous one had been. Elizabeth's first thought, though, was for a dear friend of hers, Diamond Hardinge, daughter of the British Ambassador in Paris,[6] who was seriously ill. To Paris Elizabeth went in June 1922 to nurse her friend through convalescence after a major operation – a purpose very different to her visit the year before, when she had moved a guest at an embassy ball to liken her to 'an English rose, sweet and fresh as if with the dew still on it'.[7] On her return from Paris there was a Glamis summer waiting and afterwards a winter of parties and dances and the London theatre, followed by the traditional family Christmas at St Paul's Walden Bury.

It was a year, too, during which five eligible young men proposed marriage to Elizabeth, but as 1922 drew towards its

55

close the talk within a restricted circle of courtiers and Strathmore relatives and friends was all of Elizabeth and Bertie. It was obvious that the Duke was going to propose to her again, but this time Elizabeth was not so sure about what her answer would be. On the one hand she was anxious to please Bertie but on the other she dreaded the responsibilities involved in sharing her life with a member of the Royal Family. She had satisfied herself that Bertie possessed the qualities she expected of a man, but she still had doubts about becoming part of his role as a prince.

On 13 January 1923 the Duke of York arrived at St Paul's Walden Bury as a weekend guest of the Strathmores. There is a charming legend that on the following day, Sunday, Elizabeth and Bertie excused themselves from church and took a walk in the wood Elizabeth had so loved as a child, and that there he proposed to her. However, the official biographer of King George VI, Sir John Wheeler-Bennett, who had the advantage of being able to inspect the Royal Archives at Windsor, has recorded that on the 13th itself the Duke dispatched a telegram from St Paul's Walden to his parents at Sandringham with the message 'All right – Bertie', the prearranged code that told the King and Queen he had been accepted.

If the acceptance surprised Bertie (and his father, who had told him he would be a lucky chap if she said 'yes') it was no less of a surprise to Elizabeth, who a few days afterwards described herself as happy but quite dazed. It has been suggested by some people that she found she just could not do without Bertie and by others that she felt it was her duty to marry him and did not fall in love with him until later. The truth of it seems to be that she let her heart rule her head, making her decision entirely on impulse. While logically the prospect of becoming a royal duchess may have dismayed her, emotionally it appealed to her. She was much surer of Bertie than she had been in 1921 and she knew a great deal more about his royal responsibilities; having grown up as a 'star' of the Bowes-Lyon family she enjoyed being the centre of attention and knew that she could cope with being constantly in the public eye; and she liked to be busy, to do something useful and worthwhile, for which there would be plenty of opportunity in royal life. Not for nothing had her family nicknamed her 'Princess'. The loss of much personal freedom and the relinquishing of most of her life to the public domain was a sacrifice, but not all that much of a sacrifice in view of what royal status offered in return. And so Elizabeth Bowes-Lyon agreed to marry the Duke of York.

A few years later the *Manchester Guardian* summed it up in easily understandable terms: 'It was known to be a love match . . .'

2

'A Princely Marriage'

A royal wedding was just the kind of tonic Britain needed in 1923. The Great War had cemented over the cracks which had appeared in the fabric of British society during the early years of the century, but when the euphoria of victory passed the war-time spirit of national unity went with it. The traditional ruling class, feeling that it had given up much of its privilege and descended nearer to the level of its social inferiors for the sake of the war effort, sought to regain its old unquestioned supremacy. The middle classes, who in the previous century had come to regard themselves as the backbone of the Empire, struggled to retain their position in the face of aspirations from below. The war-weary workers and demobilized soldiers waited impatiently and with growing frustration for the realization of that vision of a better life which had inspired them through the sacrifices and the slaughter.

On 12 November 1918, the day after the signing of the Armistice, the *Daily Mirror*, the workers' penny paper, looked into the future:

> We shall then not disgrace our peace with thoughts and things unworthy of the sacrifice made for us. We shall be glad, but we shall be grave in our gladness. A new chapter in the world's

history is beginning. It is for us to write it and we can write only the thoughts we have within us, draw only the figure and image of ourselves. That form can be noble or base . . . By our thoughts and actions we shall be responsible, during the next few months, for the future of the world for centuries – a tremendous duty. Our dead have placed their achievement in our hands, for us to use or misuse . . .

But upheavals on the scale of the Great War can never be controlled by mere mortals and it was not long before the British Government which had held the nation together throughout the war found the peace slipping from its grasp, in spite of the fact that it continued to use its wartime powers for almost three years after the conflict ended. (Some practices introduced between 1914 and 1918 remain to this day – strict control of licensing hours, the imposition of British Summer Time, and the playing of the National Anthem at the end of theatre and cinema performances.)

At first it did indeed look as if the new Promised Land was going to be created, but after an economic boom in 1919 and 1920 there followed what was described by *The Economist* as 'one of the worst years of depression since the industrial revolution'. There was widespread industrial unrest, unemployment was rising – by 1923 one man in six was out of work – and there was a desperate shortage of housing owing to building restrictions in force during the war. Ireland was in turmoil, while India, the jewel of the Empire, was pressing for independence, alienated from Raj rule by the Amritsar massacre of demonstrators in 1919. Fired by the example of the Bolsheviks in Russia, communism was gaining a foothold in Europe – the Communist Party of Great Britain was founded in 1920.

Political difficulties were accompanied by changes which tended to upset what had been a pretty rigid social structure. Formality, largely discarded under the stress of war, was now relegated to the wardrobe for use on special occasions: the gentleman's garb of top hat and frock coat gave way to the classless lounge suit except at Court, at the races and among diehard politicians or other public men. Cigarette-smoking, previously the preserve of the smart trend-setters (while the wealthy smoked cigars and the poor puffed pipes), became universal. At a more fundamental level, better hygiene and medical services meant that working people tended to live longer and more of their children survived to adulthood, so the working class grew in proportion to the population as a whole, which meant, of course, that its voice became louder and its aspirations more important. At the same time a decline in the birthrate among the upper and middle classes, brought about by the fact that contraception was becoming readily available to them, further upset the accepted social balance.

Such were the beginnings of the polarization which has dogged Britain for the past half-century, and when in 1922 Lloyd George resigned as Prime Minister after his Liberal Party had been abandoned by its coalition partners, the Conservatives, the old Establishment saw its chance to seize the advantage. The new Prime Minister, Andrew Bonar Law[1] – the former Unionist Party leader brought out of retirement to lead the Tories – included in his Cabinet six peers of the realm, of whom three were from great landowning families and a further two carried inherited titles rather than created ones. The battle lines were drawn for a class struggle which, in the minds of many people, is still being fought today.

In the unsettled climate of the early twenties, the position of the monarchy remained certain. A king may be a force for change, but more often than not he is a symbol of the status quo, and so it was with George V, who, if he had possessed the power, would have made the nineteenth century go on forever. Yet if he was the emblem of the established order, the King was also held to be the epitome of all that was best in Great Britain – with the emphasis on the 'Great' – and no matter how loud was the clamour for change the vast majority of the nation, regardless of class, could be counted on to stand firm behind him. And a royal event such as the engagement and marriage of the Duke of York added an extra dimension to the unifying force of the monarchy. Bearing this in mind, Bertie's choice of Elizabeth Bowes-Lyon could be regarded by the Establishment as politi-

60

cally sound. Not only did she come from outside the remote ranks of royalty, making it easier for ordinary people to identify with her, but she also came from a Scottish family, and Scotland was one of the places where the growing socialist movement had its deepest roots.

The engagement was announced in the Court Circular of 16 January 1923:

> It is with the greatest pleasure that the King and Queen announce the betrothal of their beloved son the Duke of York to the Lady Elizabeth Bowes-Lyon, daughter of the Earl and Countess of Strathmore, to which union the King has gladly given his consent.

Letters, cards and telegrams of congratulation began to arrive by the sackful at the Strathmores' London home in Bruton Street, while reporters hovered round the door. In her innocent enjoyment of all this interest and her lack of experience in public life, Elizabeth talked very frankly to the Press – revealing among other things that she had not yet received her engagement ring but had set her heart on a half-hoop of a sapphire and two diamonds. The King soon put a stop to such indiscretion with an order that she must give no more interviews.

Exactly a week after accepting Bertie's proposal, Elizabeth went with her parents to Sandringham to discuss the wedding arrangements with the King and Queen, who were genuinely delighted at their son's choice. They found Elizabeth pretty, charming and refreshingly natural. 'Bertie is supremely happy,' Queen Mary noted. The King, who had no taste for what he regarded as the strident and anarchic modern woman, was pleased to discover on closer acquaintance with Elizabeth that she embodied the old-fashioned feminine virtues he admired and this greatly increased his affection for her: she would get away with things no one else could in his presence.

The practical aspects of the Strathmores' visit were soon settled. The King and Queen were due to visit Italy in May and since there appeared to be no reason for delay it was decided that the wedding should take place before the Italian trip – Thursday 26 April was the date chosen. All that remained was to fulfil the formal requirements of the Royal Marriages Act of 1772, which specifies that members of the Royal Family may not contract lawful marriages without the consent of the Sovereign unless they are over the age of twenty-five and have given twelve months' notice of their intention to marry to the Privy Council. This was the Act that would snare Princess Margaret a quarter of a century later, but in the case of her parents no obstacle was seen and accordingly on 12 February 1923, at a meeting of the Privy Council, the King signed a document formally signifying his consent to the marriage of the Duke of York.

The decision to have the wedding ceremony at Westminster Abbey indicated its political importance as a public morale-booster. Not since the thirteenth century had a king's son been married at the Abbey. Royal weddings were customarily held in a private chapel at one of the royal palaces: Queen Victoria's wedding had taken place at the Chapel Royal, St James's, as had that of George V when he had been Duke of York; Edward VII, as Prince of Wales, had married Princess Alexandra of Denmark at St George's Chapel, Windsor. The idea of making royal weddings a public spectacle was born of the spirit of national celebration following the victory of 1918 – Princess Patricia of Connaught[2] had set the trend in 1919 by marrying at the Abbey and her example had been followed by Princess Mary. By the time it came to the turn of Bertie and Elizabeth the need for some sort of national rejoicing was again keenly felt.

Even before her wedding Elizabeth began to take part in royal life. Her first mention in the Court Circular (other than the announcement of the engagement) came on 4 April 1923 when she accompanied the King and Queen, the Prince of Wales and, of course, her fiancé, to a performance of *Elijah* at Eton College, from where she had collected her brother David for many an afternoon outing while he had been a scholar. And the celebrations for the marriage began three days before the event. On 23 April the King and Queen had six hundred guests at Buckingham Palace for a party; the following day the staffs of the Royal Household and the Strathmores were entertained at the Palace, and on the 25th there was an afternoon reception for still more people.

Meanwhile wedding presents were flooding in from relatives, royalty, organizations, societies and individuals all over the world. (More than £250,000 worth of gifts had to be returned because they did not conform to the rule that the donors had to be known or in some official way connected with royalty.) Among the 'official' gifts were china from the city of Worcester; antique silver given by the City of London; a remarkable clock, sent by the citizens of Glasgow, which played march tunes; cutlery and a grand piano from Windsor; a thousand gold-eyed needles presented by the Needlemakers' Company. Perhaps the most unusual gift, though, was from another of the Guilds of the City of London, the Patternmakers. It was an oak chest containing wellington boots, rubber shoes and goloshes. When the chest was presented to Elizabeth at Buckingham Palace she made her first 'royal' speech: she looked forward to testing the contents of the chest, she said, straight-faced.

The personal gifts were, of course, splendid. Elizabeth received from Bertie a diamond and pearl necklace with matching pendant, and she gave him a platinum and pearl watch chain. From the King, Elizabeth received a suite of turquoise and diamond jewellery and from the Queen a sapphire and diamond necklet with matching ring, brooches and pendant, as well as a fan of lace on a mother-of-pearl frame and handle. Queen Alexandra gave to Elizabeth a pearl and amethyst necklace with an amethyst pendant, and to Bertie an antique silver box. The Strathmores were not to be outdone by their royal relatives-to-be: to Elizabeth they gave a platinum and diamond tiara, a pearl and diamond necklace, and a second necklace of pearls and diamonds with a matching bracelet; to Bertie, Lady Strathmore gave a diamond-framed miniature portrait of Elizabeth. A less glamorous but more practical gift came from Princess Mary and her husband – a set of the finest linen. The American Ambassador gave Elizabeth a sketch of the Duke of York, while Prince Paul of Serbia presented Bertie with a framed sketch of his bride. From the members of Bonar Law's aristocratic Cabinet came a writing set comprising inkwells, stamp boxes and four candle-sticks, all in silver.

The newspapers were avid for details of the wedding presents, as they were for information about Elizabeth's bridal gown. At last the design was made public: it was a dress on simple medieval lines in ivory coloured chiffon and with sleeves and a train made from Nottingham lace. The Press was not slow to see the significance of the lace. The industry in Nottingham was in the deepest depression, caused by cheap foreign imports, and commentators felt that it would receive great benefits by contributing to the royal occasion. The lace made for Elizabeth's dress was displayed at an exhibition organized by the Duchess of Portland to revive interest in the Nottingham lacemakers. The gown itself was embroidered with silver thread and decorated with pearls. With it Elizabeth would wear a train of old lace (over the Nottingham train) and a tulle veil, both lent by Queen Mary. For her trousseau, the women's magazines cooed, Elizabeth had chosen simple dresses in light, summery materials and two furs – a full-length sable coat and an evening wrap of white lapin.

The success of all the publicity may be judged by the effect the marriage had on the nation. On the wedding night the Savoy Hotel arranged dancing in four ballrooms; the big London stores, like Harrods and Selfridge's, brought in military bands, searchlights and a dazzling array of flowers. Though it rained all night on the wedding eve, and it was still raining as spectators began to claim their vantage points in the early morning, more than a million people thronged the streets between Bruton Street, the Palace and the Abbey. Walter Bagehot, that brilliant interpreter of the English constitution, was being proved right: 'A Royal Family,' he had written, 'sweetens politics by the seasonable addition of nice and pretty events . . . It brings down the pride of sovereignty to the level of petty life . . . a princely marriage is the brilliant edition of a universal fact, and as such it rivets mankind . . .'[3]

At 9.30 on the morning of the wedding, the rain stopped and by ten o'clock three thousand guests were assembled in the Abbey – except for Winston Churchill,[4] who was late. In the manner of such events, the timetable was arranged to the last minute, so it was at precisely 11.12 that Elizabeth emerged from 17 Bruton Street and climbed into a state landau escorted by four mounted policemen; one minute later the Duke of York with the Prince of Wales, his chief supporter (the royal equivalent of the best man), and Prince Henry of Gloucester, left Buckingham Palace. The King and Queen had set off five minutes before him.

Bertie wore the uniform of a Royal Air Force group captain, with the Riband and Star of the Order of the Garter and the Star of the Order of the Thistle (newly awarded to him by the King as a tribute to his Scottish bride). At his right shoulder were the golden aiguillettes of a Personal Aide-de-Camp to the Sovereign and on his left breast was a single row of medals. He made a handsome, manly figure, yet even on this day he was almost eclipsed by the dashing, gifted Prince of Wales, resplendent in the uniform of the Grenadier Guards.

At exactly 11.30 the landau carrying the bride drew up outside the Abbey. Elizabeth stepped out and was joined by her two eleven-year-old trainbearers, her nieces the Hon. Elizabeth Elphinstone and the Hon. Cecilia Bowes-Lyon, and her six bridesmaids – Lady Mary Cambridge, Lady May Cambridge, Lady Mary Thynne, Miss Betty Cator (who later married Michael Bowes-Lyon), Lady Katherine Hamilton and Miss Diamond Hardinge. The attendants all wore dresses of ivory coloured georgette trimmed with Nottingham lace. They had sashes of green tulle held by a silver thistle and a white rose, and sported crystal brooches carved into roses surrounding the initials E and A formed of diamonds – these had been presented to them by the Duke of York. Elizabeth took the arm of her father, who was dressed in the scarlet uniform of a county lord lieutenant, but before they could proceed into the Abbey someone had to retrieve the bride's small white handbag, which she had left in the landau. There was a further pause when one of the clergymen attending Elizabeth fell down in a faint. During the delay Elizabeth left her father's side and placed her bouquet of white York roses and white heather on the Tomb of the Unknown Warrior.

The service was read by the Archbishop of Canterbury, Randall Davidson, and the address was given by the Archbishop of York, Cosmo Gordon Lang, who told the couple:

> You have received from Him at this altar a new life wherein your separate lives are now, till death, made one. With all our hearts we wish that it may be a happy one. But you cannot resolve that it shall be happy. You can and will resolve that it shall be noble. The warm and generous heart of this people takes you today into itself. Will you not, in response, take that heart, with all its joys and sorrows, into your own?

The Archbishop had a special word for Elizabeth, who, he said, in your Scottish home have grown up from childhood among country folk and friendship with them has been your native air', thus she was well equipped for her new and important role in the life of the British people. He concluded: 'On behalf of a nation happy in your joy, we bid you Godspeed.' As the bride and bridegroom led royalty and relatives into Edward the Confessor's Chapel for the signing of the registers, the choir sang the anthem 'Beloved, Let Us Love', which Elizabeth had last heard at Princess Mary's wedding, for which it had been specially written. Then it was Mendelssohn's Wedding March and the couple's exit from the Abbey to the cheers of the crowds now standing in brilliant sunshine.

So that as many people as possible should see them, Bertie and Elizabeth drove to Buckingham Palace by way of Marlborough Gate, St James's Street, Piccadilly, Hyde Park Corner and Constitution Hill. The simple landau of Elizabeth's journey to the Abbey had given way to a royal coach magnificent in gold and scarlet; the four mounted policemen had been replaced by an escort of the Household Cavalry. With a wedding ring of Welsh gold on her finger, Her Royal Highness the Duchess of York was now the fourth lady in the land, next in precedence to her friend and sister-in-law Princess Mary.

At the Palace, as the multitude jostled in front of the railings, Bertie and Elizabeth appeared on the balcony. They were joined for a short time by the King and Queen and were then left to receive the cheers by themselves. But if one ordeal, the Abbey ceremony, was over, another lay before the newly-weds – the wedding breakfast. One hundred and twenty-three guests had gathered in the State Dining Room and the Ball Supper Room, at tables adorned with white lilac and pink tulips, and containing elaborate menu cards in gold and crimson. The repast created by the royal chef, Gabriel Tschumi, was as regal as the surroundings: consommé à la Windsor; suprême de saumon Reine Mary; côtelettes d'agneau Prince Albert; chapons à la Strathmore (boiled and jointed chicken covered in white chicken sauce and garnished with truffles and tips of tongue); jambon et langues découpés à l'aspic, salade royale; asperges, sauce crême mousseuse; fraises Duchesse Elizabeth. There was also fruit, and there were pastries in baskets fashioned from sugar, which the guests could take away with them. One and a half hours elapsed between the serving of the first course and the toast, proposed by the King: 'I ask you to drink to the health, long life and happiness of the bride and bridegroom.'

There was some interest among the guests in the matter of how Elizabeth would manage to cut the cake, its four tiers stretching upwards for nine feet and weighing a total of eight hundred pounds. (To emphasize the Scottish connexion, it had been made by the Edinburgh firm of McVitie and Price.) But nothing is left to chance on royal occasions, and the diminutive Duchess was not expected to perform her task unaided: a large slice of the cake had been cut previously, leaving only the icing to be divided before the slice could be freed by a gentle tug on a satin ribbon.

When the cake had been distributed and the toast had been drunk, Bertie and Elizabeth could at long last escape. In a landau drawn by four grey horses they left the Palace through a hail of confetti and rose petals and were driven to Waterloo Station, where they boarded a special train that took them to Great Bookham, in the spring-fresh Surrey countryside. The first few days of their married life were spent at Polesden Lacey,[5] a charming, two-storey Regency mansion near Bookham which had been lent to them by the Hon. Mrs Ronald Greville, a longstanding friend of the Royal Family. Bertie had been a frequent visitor to the house and now he took pleasure in showing his bride round its thousand-acre estate, walking with her beneath the rustic pergolas of the walled rose garden, strolling along the quarter-mile-long terrace with its fine southerly views across the rolling Ranmore Common, and playing golf.

On 7 May the couple left the peace of Polesden Lacey behind them and returned to London. They called on the Strathmores at Bruton Street and later the Prince of Wales – who was to describe Elizabeth as a breath of fresh air in royal circles – accompanied them to Euston Station where they took a train to Glamis. The weather in the neighbourhood of Elizabeth's Scottish home showed just why the Strathmores tended to leave their visits until much later in the year: there were gales, there was rain, and there was even snow. To make matters worse, Elizabeth developed whooping cough and most of the couple's stay at Glamis was spent in the specially prepared first-floor suite that they would continue to use whenever they visited the castle. It must have been with a certain amount of relief that they travelled south again on 19 May to stay at Frogmore House, the residence in Windsor Little Park so rich in associations with Queen Victoria and *her* beloved Prince Albert, from whose influence the Royal Family had as yet made no effort to free itself.

And then the honeymoon was over. The little girl who had been nicknamed 'Princess' by her family had grown up to become Her Royal Highness in fact. She was about to discover just what that meant.

Elizabeth's first royal task was to organize and learn how to run her new home. At the instigation of Queen Mary, the King had granted to the Yorks the rambling, isolated 'grace and favour' residence of White Lodge in Richmond Park. The Queen had a special affection for the Lodge because it had been given to her parents, the Duke and Duchess of Teck, in 1869. Bearing in mind Queen Mary's passionate attachment to anything that had connexions with her family's past, the granting of the Lodge to Bertie and Elizabeth showed how completely the young commoner had been accepted at the Palace.

The much renamed White Lodge started life as a hunting lodge for George I and was later used as a home by Caroline of Anspach, wife of George II. Queen Caroline's daughter, Princess Amelia, was the next occupant and she caused two wings to be added to the building, as well as giving it the name White Lodge. In 1802 King George III awarded the house to Henry Addington, perhaps better known by his later title of Lord Sidmouth, whose main claim to fame is that he was the Tory Prime Minister who filled the gap between the two administrations of William Pitt. Next the Lodge was the home of the Duchess of Gloucester, widowed daughter-in-law of George III, and some time afterwards it was occupied by the Prince of Wales who was to become Edward VII. By the time it came to be considered as a home for the Yorks, White Lodge was in need of some refurbishment, so while Bertie and Elizabeth were on their honeymoon Queen Mary supervised a programme of modernization, applied her impeccable taste to the arrangement of the furnishings, and made sure that the gardens were in a state that would have met with the approval of the old Duke of Teck, who had been mainly responsible for laying them out.

The Yorks moved into White Lodge on 7 June 1923. Elizabeth was delighted with her new home and her new way of life. She liked to show off her splendid jewellery to friends who visited the Lodge, and another thrill for her was to walk out to the garage, which had been created from the old stable block, and look at the beautiful cars there, each with its white rose insignia. It was like the happy ending of a fairytale, but Elizabeth was not the sort of young woman who would let herself be carried away on a tide of romance. It was exciting – even deliciously nerve-wracking – to entertain the King and Queen to lunch (as the Yorks did shortly after settling in at White Lodge, though Elizabeth thought it prudent to warn Their Majesties that her cook was not up to providing anything but the plainest fare), but the new Duchess found just as much pleasure in entertaining girls from Dr Barnado's Homes at her royal residence. Her entry into the social stratosphere made it all the more important to her that she should maintain contacts with everyday life, and at the same time she felt that she had to work for the privileges which had come with her royal marriage. Perhaps, too, she knew instinctively the lesson of the royal blood spilled in Russia and Serbia and the lost thrones in Bulgaria, China, Persia and Greece: that in the twentieth century a royal house had to be seen to be taking a genuine interest in the welfare of its subjects and had to adapt to their changing requirements. The Duke of York was certainly aware of this. His involvement in efforts to improve the conditions of the working classes, and in industrial life generally, was so marked that his elder brother David had dubbed him 'The Foreman'.[6]

The *Morning Post* noted:

> At once the Duchess of York bore her rank as if it had been hers by right of birth. She took her place simply and naturally in the ever-expanding public life of her husband. He was especially interested in the social welfare of boys and men; she did similar work among women and girls. While he went over factories and workshops and shipyards, she was unwearied in visiting maternity centres, girls' clubs and housing colonies. They were together all over the United Kingdom and Ulster, crowding their days with beneficent duties, obviously happy in their strenuous work and in each other, and whether she was happier gracing State ceremonies in London, Edinburgh and Belfast, or equipped with a handkerchief drawn over her hair, to go down a Durham coal-mine, there was no means of determining. That special faculty for absorption in the occasion never deserted her.

A French visitor put that last point more simply after watching the Duchess lay a foundation stone: 'I suppose Her Royal Highness has laid many foundation stones, yet she seems this afternoon to be discovering a new and delightful occupation.' This responsiveness, this joy in pleasing other people – even when, as sometimes happened, she was doing it at eight official engagements in a single day – was the secret of Elizabeth's great success as Duchess of York and it is the basis of the affection shown to her wherever she goes today, as Queen Mother.

But the instant public success of her early royal years is only part of the story. There was another, more private and, to Elizabeth, more satisfying reward. She was able to provide a stable, loving home for Bertie, to build round this shy, over-modest and under-confident prince a cocoon of affection, reliability and warmth such as had been provided for her and had allowed her natural gifts to grow to maturity. Denied parental support except on the rigid terms of the King and Queen, eclipsed at almost every turn by his dynamic and forceful elder brother, Bertie had developed something of an inferiority complex, and though his native courage kept him going, the strain was great. Now with Elizabeth beside him at every possible opportunity – and writing to him daily when royal duties separated them – he could feel that someone loved and respected him for himself, believed in him, thought him important. He never would have the strength of the autocrats and martinets who preceded him as King – indeed when he came to the throne one person close to him expressed the opinion that it was the Queen who ruled the roost – but in Elizabeth he had a wife and later a consort who complemented him so exactly, making up for what he lacked in pride and confidence, that his stature was immeasurably increased. He was a brave, resolute, steadfast man, a fine war leader, and he deserves to be remembered as a good king; but there is no doubt that it was his marriage to Elizabeth which allowed him to realize his potential to the full and overcome his limitations.

In the early days of his life with Elizabeth, it was a great comfort to Bertie, when the pressure of public life was at its greatest, to be able to escape to the homely peace of White Lodge, with supper on a tray in front of the fire, someone to share the strain, and cosy privacy. There was, however, one area of some friction between the newlyweds: time. Like his father and his grandfather, Bertie was a stickler for punctuality – he had grown up with it, for Palace life under George V was regulated like that on a ship of the line. Elizabeth, in contrast, had been brought up in a large and cheerfully irregular family, and it soon began to look as if her husband might encounter, to a lesser degree, the sort of difficulties experienced by Edward VII with Queen Alexandra, who was even late for the Coronation. (At Sandringham, Edward ordered the clocks to be kept half an hour fast so that the Queen would be encouraged to get a move on.) But Bertie's position was undermined somewhat when Elizabeth's unpunctuality did not produce the expected result in a certain quarter: when the Yorks arrived late for dinner with the King and Queen, Elizabeth's apology was airily brushed aside by her father-in-law, who said dinner must have been called too early. Later the King said that if Elizabeth were not late sometimes she would be perfect, and that would be horrible.

Her capture of George V's heart was complete. She was even able to do what no one else could in mediating between him and the Prince of Wales during their frequent disagreements over David's conduct. But her special position in the eyes of the King would never have been achieved if she had not felt for him the same affection and respect that he held for her. When George V died Elizabeth confessed how much she would miss him, recalling that in twelve years he had never spoken unkindly to her and that she had known him as a warm, sympathetic man with hidden depths of humour.

Queen Mary was equally captivated by her first daughter-in-law, and full of admiration for Elizabeth's ability to speak in public and her ease of manner. The Duchess was as much of an asset when the King and Queen were entertaining as she had been when the Strathmores had received guests, and for the same reason. When Elizabeth was among the company the ice of formality was quickly broken; she always had something to say and as a result other people who were perhaps feeling nervous or overawed found it easier to talk. On occasion she astonished and delighted her parents-in-law by sitting down at a convenient piano and leading dignified guests in Glamis-style singing. In another person such 'informal' behaviour might easily have caused offence, but Elizabeth did it so naturally, with such panache and obvious sincerity, that people could not help but join in.

All this went on behind the scenes, of course, unknown to the public, who were keen to see how the Duchess would perform as a royal personage. Elizabeth's first big public engagement took place before some eighty thousand people when she accompanied the King and Queen, with Bertie, to the Royal Air Force Pageant at Hendon in June 1923. The following month she was in Scotland with her parents-in-law for the rededication of Holyroodhouse in Edinburgh as a royal palace. Then in October came her first royal visit abroad, for the christening of the Crown Prince of Yugoslavia and immediately afterwards the wedding of Prince Paul, cousin of King Alexander, and Princess Olga of Greece.[7]

Bertie had not intended to accept the invitation from the ill-starred royal house of the new Balkan state. He was enjoying an autumn holiday with Elizabeth at Holwick Hall, one of the properties the Strathmores owned in County Durham thanks to their connexion with the local Bowes family, when on 23 September the King sent a telegram from Balmoral explaining that for political reasons the Foreign Secretary, Lord Curzon, thought it advisable for the Duke and Duchess to agree to be the godparents of the infant Prince Peter and to represent George V at Prince Paul's wedding. Bertie was annoyed at the interruption of the holiday and at the haste with which he and Elizabeth were obliged to make arrangements for the trip. He complained that the Foreign Office should have allowed for the fact that it is more difficult for a married man than for a bachelor to make last-minute changes of plan.

But duty had to be done, and on 18 October Bertie and Elizabeth set off for Belgrade. Their quarters at the royal palace in the Yugoslavian capital, which was crowded with European royalty, were none too comfortable, and they bemoaned a lack of hot water. On top of that the long and complicated christening ceremony – in which Bertie, as godfather, played the major role – was marred by the fact that the baby was dropped in the font by the elderly Patriarch who was conducting the service and, having been rescued by Bertie, rendered the rest of the proceedings almost inaudible by his screaming. The wedding, however, passed off without any untoward incident, and the Duke was pleased to note that Elizabeth was a great favourite among the assembled royals.

Back home there were plenty of events, social, royal and

public, to keep the Yorks occupied. In November there were two royal weddings – those of Lady Louise Mountbatten and of Princess Maud – and, with Christmas approaching, there was work to be done on behalf of the disabled and also for poor children, two groups in which Elizabeth took a special interest. But there was time for relaxation, too. Bertie had leased The Old House at Guilsborough, in Northamptonshire, so that he could enjoy hunting with the Pytchley and the Whaddon Chase. Elizabeth did not hunt, but attended meets and followed the progress of the riders by car. There was a lot of travelling to and from London for official engagements while the Duke and Duchess stayed in Northamptonshire, but while this made life rather hectic it was better than living at White Lodge, which was shrouded in autumn fogs and where modernization work was still going on. Indeed the disadvantages of White Lodge as a home had quickly become apparent, and for some time much of the energies of Bertie and Elizabeth were devoted to avoiding the place. The house took a heavy toll on staff because of its seemingly endless corridors and its size made it extremely expensive to run – White Elephant might have been a better name for it. In the spring of 1924, therefore, the Yorks gratefully accepted an offer from Princess Mary – who was living serenely in Yorkshire and expecting her second child – that they should have the use of her London home, Chesterfield House, at the junction of Curzon Street and South Audley Street, just behind Park Lane.

It was as well that the Yorks had acquired a London base, for the year 1924 turned out to be a particularly busy one. The previous twelve months, as Elizabeth was to learn, had been no more than a practice run for the never-ending round of state occasions, public appearances and private entertaining that was the lot of a much sought-after royal couple. The year had hardly begun before Elizabeth was called upon to attend her first Court since joining the Royal Family: she stood behind the King and Queen on the dais as they received curtseys from the women who were being presented to them. This was followed on 15 May by a state ball in honour of the King and Queen of Romania, and on 26 May by the state visit of the King and Queen of Italy. In July it was the turn of the Crown Prince of Ethiopia, Ras Taffari, who later became the Emperor Haile Selassie.[8]

More fun than all this ceremonial were two visits Bertie and Elizabeth made to the British Empire Exhibition at Wembley, which was opened by the King on 23 April. The opening day was full of excitement because for the first time the voices of members of the Royal Family – the King and the Prince of Wales – were to be broadcast by the British Broadcasting Company, forerunner of the BBC. The Prince of Wales was unlucky: his short speech inviting his father to perform the opening was lost in the airwaves and heard by none of the three million or so people listening to the wireless (so much more romantic than the name 'radio'). Fittingly it was left to King George V to make history when, in what were described as 'clear, rich tones', he said: 'I declare this exhibition open.' The Yorks' second visit to the exhibition was less formal. This time their destination was the huge amusement park, where Elizabeth sat next to the Prince of Wales in the front seat of one of the cars on the giant switchback.

On 19 July the Duke and Duchess began a busy, week-long visit to Northern Ireland, which had been granted its own parliament and executive government in 1920. The Six Counties were passionately royalist – indeed their Protestant majority still is in these tragic and violent times – and George V had been impressed by the enthusiasm of the welcome for him in 1921, when he had opened the inaugural session of the Belfast Parliament. The Duke and Duchess of York were received with no less fervour. Bertie confessed himself astounded at the size of the crowds, the sound of the cheering and the obvious sincerity of the demonstrations of loyalty to the Crown – and, he told his father, the Ulster people simply loved Elizabeth.

Enjoyable though the visit to Northern Ireland was, it was eclipsed in the autumn of 1924 by the Yorks' first great adventure together – a tour, part holiday and part official, to East Africa and the Sudan. For Elizabeth it was the first encounter with a continent she would grow to love, and her first sight of the great Empire which would grow to love her.

Leaving London on 1 December, Bertie and Elizabeth went first to Paris and thence to Marseilles, where they boarded the P. & O. liner *Mulbera*, which sailed for Port Said on 5 December. The five-day Mediterranean crossing was made in rough and cold weather, and no one was sorry when it was over. From Port Said the royal party travelled through the Suez Canal into the Red Sea, south to Aden, where Bertie and Elizabeth went sightseeing, round the Horn of Africa and down the coast to Mombasa, principal port of the Crown Colony of Kenya, where the *Mulbera* docked on 22 December. Waiting to meet the royal visitors were the popular Governor of the colony, Sir Robert Coryndon (who was to die only a little more than a month later, after a surgical operation), and five thousand Africans from every tribe in the area, who presented a vast and colourful dance festival to the sound of horns and the intoxicating rhythm of the tomtom. It was an unforgettable experience, but it was followed by an even greater thrill for Bertie and Elizabeth, a three-hundred-mile journey in the Governor's train across the wild interior of Kenya to Nairobi, the capital. Some of the time the couple sat on a special platform erected in front of the engine so they could get a better view of the zebra, ostrich, hartebeeste, wildebeeste and other animals that roamed the huge game reserve through which the train passed.

They came even closer to the game during the next six weeks, when they went on safari. The Duke, who was an excellent shot, was put off at first by conditions very different to the damp and windswept grouse moors of Scotland, but he soon got his eye in and bagged big game with as much success as he brought down birds at home. Elizabeth, in khaki shirt and slacks and a floppy hat, also proved herself no mean marksman, having been taught to shoot by the head keeper at Glamis. With a Rigby rifle she collected a rhino, a hartebeeste, a buffalo, a gazelle, an oryx and several more beasts. At that time there was no vociferous conservation lobby to protest about the carnage, and game was so plentiful in Africa that there were no real fears for endangered species, but even so the weekly reports from the Press corps following the Yorks did give rise to criticism at home, along the lines that killing God's wild creatures was not a pursuit which should quicken royal blood, or indeed female blood. But what concerned most people, including the King and Queen, was that the Duke and Duchess might be taking unacceptable risks facing all those fierce animals. Bertie and Elizabeth, though, were enjoying the element of danger and the pleasure of living rough, eating in the open air off a folding table, riding about the bush on mules and sleeping under canvas. They were young and fit, they were away for a time from the official openings, the stone-layings, the speeches, and they were happy.

The Kenyan safari came to an abrupt end, however, on 10 February with the news of the sudden death of Sir Robert Coryndon. Bertie and two aides returned to Nairobi to attend the military funeral of the Governor, and Elizabeth, who was staying with one of the leading figures in Kenya's European community, joined her husband later. Shortly afterwards the Duke received another shock when a message from London told him that his father, who was then in his sixtieth year, had been taken ill with acute bronchitis. Almost thirty years later Bertie's daughter, Princess Elizabeth, would be on holiday in Kenya when news came of her father's death and her accession to the throne. In 1925, however, the tidings of the King's health were not grave and, reassured that his father was recovering, Bertie decided he and Elizabeth could continue their holiday, though he felt that out of respect for Coryndon they should seek their pleasures elsewhere. They moved on to Uganda, sailing in the steamer *Clement Hill* across Lake Victoria, stopping at the Rippon Falls, which are said to be the source of the White Nile, and landing finally at Entebbe.

During their eighteen-day stay in Uganda, the Yorks visited the cathedral in Kampala, the capital, received a pair of handsome elephant tusks from the Kabaka of Buganda (whom the Duke had invested as a Knight Commander of the Order of St Michael and St George), and went hunting their own elephant on a week-long safari. Bertie shot two elephants and a white rhino with a tusk thirty-three inches long. Elizabeth, meanwhile, sat on the deck of the riverboat *Samuel Baker* and fished in the waters of the White Nile.

The final stage of the African adventure began at Nimule, in the far south of the Anglo-Egyptian Sudan, where Bertie and Elizabeth left their steamer and travelled an arduous ninety miles by car to Rejaf. They embarked on another steamer and set off down the Nile to Khartoum, a thousand miles away, breaking their journey to watch twelve thousand Nubian warriors display their prowess in the martial arts, and, in complete contrast, to view the march of modern technology in the construction of the Makwar Dam. At Khartoum, etched for ever on the British consciousness by General Gordon, the Duke and Duchess stayed in the grand building erected on the site of Gordon's last stand and were guests of honour at a splendid reception given by the Governor of Sudan, Sir Geoffrey Archer. On 9 April they boarded a P. & O. liner, the *Maloja*, for the ten-day voyage home, where they were met by Princess Mary and her husband and themselves greeted the King and Queen a few days later when Their Majesties returned from a holiday rather more sedate than the Yorks' – a Mediterranean cruise.

For Elizabeth, who had never before travelled farther than Italy, where her maternal grandmother lived, the African tour had been an experience to challenge her both mentally and physically. Now it was back to the narrower horizons and different challenges of the hospital visit, the foundation stone, and the state occasion.

The Britain to which Bertie and Elizabeth returned after an absence of almost five months had entered a period of revival and reconciliation after the tensions and worries of the immediate postwar years. Bonar Law had died of throat cancer on 30 October 1923 and his successor as Prime Minister, Stanley Baldwin, had been forced into a general election in December of that year. Left without an overall majority, mainly through sweeping electoral gains by the emergent Labour Party, Baldwin's Government had been defeated in Parliament in January

1924 and the King, somewhat apprehensively, had invited Ramsay MacDonald to form the first ever Labour administration – causing panic among the middle classes, who foresaw the imposition of socialism on the Soviet pattern. MacDonald's reign had been short, however: just nine months and one day. At the end of September 1924 Labour's minority Government had lost a censure motion put down by the Conservatives over what they described as political interference in the Campbell case, the prosecution (dropped at MacDonald's prompting) of J. R. Campbell, a known communist, on charges of incitement to mutiny. In the subsequent general election there was a Tory landslide, thanks mainly to the decline of the Liberal Party and partly to the middle-class fears of what Labour might do if it were allowed to continue in office.

Baldwin, a pipe-smoking fifty-seven-year-old ironmaster from Worcestershire, found himself presiding over 419 members of Parliament out of a total of 615, and with his Government's position thus rendered unassailable he sought a peaceful life for his country and himself. Winston Churchill, as Chancellor of the Exchequer, put Britain back on the Gold Standard, from which it had withdrawn in 1919; Baldwin fathered the Locarno Pact to guarantee peace in Europe; MacDonald and the Prime Minister were complementary personalities and thinkers, so party conflict was reduced; a steadily rising standard of living and an embryonic welfare state mitigated class strife. In short it was a Britain restored, at least for the time being, to something like the tranquillity that many people fondly remembered from the days before the First World War (though that very peace itself had been largely illusory). A new mood of calm and confidence was abroad in the land, and the Royal Family – more particularly the Duke and Duchess of York – were called upon to symbolize and consolidate the feeling of unity and goodwill.

As soon as he returned from Africa Bertie took over from the Prince of Wales as President of the British Empire Exhibition, then entering its second year. On 21 April 1925, the Duke issued a personal message:

The British Empire Exhibition aims to complete in 1925 the educational work for Empire unity and Empire trade so well begun in 1924. The task of showing fresh aspects of our great heritage has been taken up with vigour and enthusiasm, and the new picture of the Empire will be even more vivid than the old. I ask for it the fullest measure of public support.

Bertie was in need of some support himself, for on the day of the second opening of the exhibition, 10 May, he had to make a speech in public, in front of his critical father, and into a microphone for broadcasting throughout the land. To a man with a stammer that sometimes afflicted him even in private – and especially when he was talking to his father – the speech was a daunting, indeed terrifying prospect and in the short time available to him before the dreaded day Bertie rehearsed endlessly, both at home and at the Wembley exhibition centre. When the moment came the tension was felt by more people than the Duke. Afterwards Bertie expressed the opinion that the speech had gone better than he had expected and the King was relieved that it had not been a complete disaster, but the hearts of many people listening to the wireless went out to the Duke as he struggled to enunciate the words. 'It was an agonizing experience to hear him,' according to one woman, now in her seventies, who remembers the broadcast.

Other duties that year were less of an ordeal. At the end of June the Duke and Duchess were in York where, at the Minster, Elizabeth unveiled the restored Five Sisters, a series of beautiful lancet windows dating from the thirteenth century which had been removed during the war in case they should be damaged, and were now returned to their position in the north transept as a result of contributions from women all over Britain in memory of those of their sex who had died during 1914–18. The Duchess 'captivated us all,' said a local newspaper, 'and there is no one who is not proud to think that she bears the name of our historic and wonderful city'. The couple remained in the North-East for the celebrations, at the beginning of July, marking the centenary of the Stockton and Darlington Railway, that cradle of the transport revolution in the nineteenth century. They opened a huge

80

New Zealand, 1927: the trout was caught by the Duchess of York.

Gown show: the Duchess visiting Lady Margaret Hall, Oxford, in 1928.

Family group: the Yorks with Princess Elizabeth (*right*) and Princess Margaret at the circus in January 1935. The lady in the background is the childrens' nurse.

Coronation day, 1937: the Princesses to the fore on the balcony at
Buckingham Palace.

Above left. Unconventional royal dress for Queen Elizabeth aboard the liner *Empress of Australia* at the start of the royal tour of Canada and the United States in 1939.

Above right. Queens are tourists, too. Elizabeth filming the arrival in Canada.

Below. Even more unconventional crowns for the King and Queen at a nickel mine in Ontario.

A family portrait issued on the fourteenth birthday of Princess Elizabeth.

'I'm glad we've been bombed.' The King and Queen inspecting the damage at Buckingham Palace after the bombing of September 1940.

Looking the East End in the face during the London Blitz.

Dig for victory: a royal inspection of the harvest at Sandringham in 1943.

railway exhibition at Faverdale Wagon Works in Darlington then went on to watch a procession of fifty-three locomotives ranging from George Stephenson's Locomotion No. 1, which had inaugurated the Stockton and Darlington service, to the London and North Eastern Railway's most modern 'Flying Scotsman' train. After unveiling a commemorative plaque at Stockton-on-Tees, Bertie and Elizabeth received as mementoes silver models of Locomotion No. 1 and the 1825 passenger coach 'Experiment'.

During the summer the Yorks divided their time between the Strathmores at Glamis and the King and Queen at Balmoral, and when they returned to London in October they moved into Curzon House, Curzon Street, since they still had no permanent home in London. Then, on 19 November, while Bertie was away hunting in Leicestershire, came news that Queen Alexandra, a few weeks short of her eighty-first birthday, had suffered a heart attack at Sandringham. Next day Bertie and the Prince of Wales set off by train for Norfolk, but they arrived too late to take their leave of their beloved grandmother: she died at 5.25 on that gloomy Friday afternoon, 20 October. The nation was stunned. Queen Alexandra had inspired in the people the same spontaneous love and devotion that the Queen Mother enjoys today, and her passing signified for many the close of a chapter in history when God had been in His Heaven somewhere over England and all had been well. The mourning was not only for a remarkable woman but also for an age.

For the Royal Family, though, there was good news to lighten their grief. In the very month that Queen Alexandra died it was confirmed, though it was not made public, that the Duchess of York was expecting a baby.

3

Home and Family

On a wet Wednesday morning in April 1926 a small crowd stood on the glistening pavements of Bruton Street gazing up at the windows of Number 17. There was a buzz of excitement when the Duke of York was seen behind the lace curtains on the first floor, then the event everyone was waiting for was confirmed when the smiling face of a nurse appeared at a window: there had been a royal birth.

The Home Secretary, Sir William Joynson-Hicks, who by custom had been present at the birth,[1] caused a statement to be issued saying that, 'Her Royal Highness the Duchess of York was safely delivered of a Princess at 2.40 am today, Wednesday, April 21st.' A medical bulletin added that 'a certain line of treatment was successfully adopted' – meaning in plain English that the birth had been difficult and the baby had been delivered by Caesarean section – and a further bulletin said that the Duchess 'has had some rest since the arrival of her daughter. Her Royal Highness and the infant Princess are making satisfactory progress.' It was still raining and there was still a crowd in the afternoon when the King and Queen arrived from Windsor, where, having left strict instructions before going nervously to bed the previous night, they had been woken with the news shortly after three o'clock in the morning.

Bertie, who had done his fair share of floor-pacing throughout the night, was ecstatic. Here was the beginning of the happy family life he had long yearned for. As he waited for his parents to arrive, however, he reflected on what the King's reaction might be to the fact that the first grandchild of the male line was not a boy, and it sounded a little like an excuse when he told his father that Elizabeth had wanted a girl. He need not have given a thought to the matter. Their Majesties were delighted with their grand-daughter, and the little Princess was to prove the greatest blessing of the King's last years.

The Press welcomed the arrival of the Princess warmly but without a great deal of fuss. The baby was, of course, third in line to the throne, but it was probable that the Yorks would have more children of which one would possibly be a boy, and it was naturally assumed that in any case it would not be too long before the Prince of Wales, then almost thirty-two, would follow the usual procedure for an heir to the throne and marry a foreign princess who would contribute to the line of succession. Apart from those considerations, the newspapers had on their minds events which were at the time of far greater moment than the birth of the Yorks' first child. At the end of March 1923 the Samuel Commission on the coal mines had infuriated the miners' union by supporting demands from the coal owners for reductions in wages. On 30 April, just nine days after the birth of the Princess, a government subsidy which had maintained miners' wages came to an end and lock-outs began at the pits. The next day, May Day, the Trades Union Congress announced that a general strike in support of the miners would begin at midnight on the following Monday, 3 May.

Weekend attempts to avert the General Strike came to grief when machine operators at the *Daily Mail* refused to print the paper because it contained a rabidly anti-strike leader written by the editor, Thomas Marlowe. This 'gross interference with the freedom of the Press' infuriated Stanley Baldwin, who summoned the leaders of the Trades Union Congress to Downing Street and handed them a letter which more or less told them to strike and be damned. For the next nine days normal life was suspended. Thousands of clerks, lawyers, doctors, businessmen and housewives abandoned their usual activities and volunteered to drive lorries, trains, buses and trams; to man power stations; and to unload food cargoes from ships which, because the dockers were on strike, put in at seaside resorts. Eleven thousand special constables were mobilized and more were sworn in. Troops guarded food convoys and there were riots at strike meetings in the North of England and the Midlands. Hyde Park became a miniature town with services provided for the volunteer workers.

Through it all the Duchess of York remained quietly at home enjoying her new baby. Bertie, however, had less time for fatherhood: his knowledge of and abiding interest in industrial affairs made him the royal expert on the strike, though the constitutional position of the monarchy made it impossible for him or indeed the King, who was greatly worried by the strike, to intervene. (The King did use his remaining power to warn Baldwin against promulgating an Order in Council to stop the banks paying out money to 'any person acting in opposition to the national interest' – an attempt to freeze union strike funds. 'Anything done to touch the pockets of those who are now only existing on strike pay might cause exasperation and serious reprisals,' the King wisely told his Prime Minister.) Bertie was in the House of Commons every day throughout the strike, listening to the debates and seeing at first hand how difficult it is to retreat from an extreme position once it has been adopted. A decade later he was to find the experience invaluable when, as king, he became the one constant force in the alternating currents of politics.

The General Strike ended without achieving very much – indeed in the case of the miners it achieved absolutely nothing, since they were forced to accept lower wages and longer hours – and the Duke of York was able to turn his attention once more to domestic affairs. The most pressing matter was naming the little Princess and arranging her christening. Queen Victoria had decreed that children born close to the throne should bear either her own name or that of her beloved Albert, but Elizabeth and

Bertie felt that they need not observe the old Queen's directive and proposed to name their daughter Elizabeth Alexandra Mary. 'Elizabeth of York' sounded nice, they thought, assuring the King that no confusion would arise from having a second Elizabeth in the family. The King agreed that it was a pretty name, and there could be no objection to Alexandra and Mary: it was just that there was no Victoria – but after all the new Princess was not really likely ever to come to the throne, so perhaps the solemn injunction could be ignored. The King consented to the names the parents had selected.

The christening of Her Royal Highness the Princess Elizabeth Alexandra Mary took place in the chapel at Buckingham Palace on 29 May. The choral service was conducted by the Archbishop of York and the baby was baptized, in the silver gilt font made for Queen Victoria's eldest daughter in 1840, with water from the River Jordan. The godparents were the King and Queen, Princess Mary, the old Duke of Connaught, Lord Strathmore and Lady Elphinstone, the eldest sister of the Duchess of York. Almost as soon as she was brought into the chapel the little Princess began to cry, in spite of the attentions of her mother and her royal grandmother, and the wailing continued until the service was over and she was given back into the care of her nurse.

Now that they had a child it was imperative that the Yorks should have a home of their own, and their heavy programme of royal duties determined that the house should be in London. They had hoped to find somewhere in Carlton House Terrace, at the back of The Mall, but there was no property available in that location. What did present itself was a house nobody seemed to want – a rather dull, four-storey mansion owned by the Crown Estate at 145 Piccadilly, about ten minutes' walk from Buckingham Palace across Green Park. The house had been unoccupied since 1921 and the Crown Estate Commissioners despaired of finding a tenant (in fact at one stage the commissioners considered converting the mansion, with its twenty-five bedrooms, into a block of flats). Then the Yorks became interested in the property and after some hard bargaining it was agreed that they should rent the house and that the Crown Estates Office should carry out necessary repairs.[2] There was all the fun of choosing the décor – Elizabeth selected mainly the newly fashionable pastel colours which are now regarded as being so typical of twenties taste – and furnishing the multiplicity of rooms. But events on the other side of the world ensured that it would be a long time before Bertie, Elizabeth and their daughter were able to move into their first family home. Indeed not only was this pleasure to be delayed, but the Yorks were to suffer a long separation from Princess Elizabeth within a few months of her birth.

The Commonwealth of Australia had just built itself a new capital at Canberra (previously the seat of government had been Melbourne) and the first meeting of the Dominion Parliament in its new home was due to take place on 9 May 1927. In June of the previous year the Australian Prime Minister, Stanley Bruce, contacted George V to ask if the King would send one of his sons to open this inaugural Parliament. When he heard the reply Bruce may well have wished that he had not asked, for the King decided to send the Duke of York.

The reasons for the choice were sound enough: the obvious candidate, the Prince of Wales, had already visited Australia (in 1920) and the King felt it was time his second son should be given a task of prime importance in the royal scheme of things. But there was the problem of Bertie's stammer. Stanley Bruce had heard the Duke of York speak in public and knew how bad it could be: for example, the consonant 'k' or hard 'c' sound frequently brought Bertie to a halt, which meant that he could never refer to 'the King' but had to say 'my father' or 'His Majesty'. The prospect of the Duke making a major speech at the State Opening of Parliament filled the Australian Prime Minister with forebodings.

Since his marriage, Bertie's speech had improved slightly, with Elizabeth helping him, giving him confidence and suggesting words which he could substitute for the ones he found difficult to articulate. But even Elizabeth felt that the ceremony in Canberra might prove too much for her husband. Nevertheless, the King had made up his mind, had shown his own confidence in Bertie, and it was up to the Yorks to prove that such confidence was justified. Bertie had undergone speech therapy with little effect, but when in the autumn of 1926 the name of a new therapist was suggested to him, Elizabeth begged that he should have just one more try.

Appropriately enough the new therapist was an Australian. His name was Lionel Logue and, though he had no medical qualifications, he had acquired such a reputation in Australia for his speech improvement techniques that in 1924 he had felt justified in moving to London and setting up a practice in Harley Street. To Logue's consulting rooms the Duke of York went on 19 October 1926. The initial interview lasted for two hours and at the end of it Bertie already had one foot on the road to victory over his impediment. Logue understood the psychological background to certain speech defects and the mainspring of his treatment was convincing stammerers that their complaint was curable and instilling into them the confidence to overcome the affliction.

That was only the beginning, of course. Logue believed that the physical cause of Bertie's stammering was a lack of co-ordination between the brain and the diaphragm and he devised a series of exercises designed to correct and control the Duke's breathing. He made no secret of the fact that, while the Duke could be cured if he had the will, it would take a long time and a lot of hard work. As always, Elizabeth was at hand to aid and encourage. She visited Logue several times herself so that she could fully understand her husband's problem and the recommended treatment. Within a month there had been a noticeable improvement in Bertie's speech and, most important, his dread of speaking in public was beginning to recede (he never did grow to enjoy the experience, but at least it became bearable). By the time the Yorks were ready to leave in January for Australia, on what had grown into a world tour, the Duke was able to express himself full of confidence to face the ordeal that lay ahead.

Little Princess Elizabeth was to be shared by her grandparents during the absence of her father and mother. She spent Christmas with her parents and the King and Queen at Sandringham, then was taken to her mother's childhood home at St Paul's Walden Bury. Finally, at the house where she had been born in Bruton Street, she watched her parents leave for their long journey. Her mother burst into tears at the moment of parting, and it was some little time before the smile which by then had become famous could be seen at the window of the car taking her and Bertie to Victoria Station. It was just the kind of situation Elizabeth had feared when Bertie had proposed marriage. Private life, private happiness even, had to take second place: the country and the Empire took priority. But Elizabeth had made her choice and she was not the sort of woman to indulge in self-pity or regret. She had a job to do and, whatever the personal cost, she would do it to the best of her ability.

The emotions of the Duchess of York at leaving her eight-month-old daughter were not visible to the crowd assembled at Portsmouth on 6 January 1927 to watch the departure of the battle cruiser *Renown* and its royal passengers. As the huge ship glided out of the harbour to the music of the Royal Marines band, Elizabeth stood on the deck smiling and waving a handkerchief to the cheering throng. She was less radiant a couple of days later when an Atlantic gale buffetted the *Renown*, but she proved to be a better sailor than her husband – indeed one of her great advantages as a royal figure is that she is a very good traveller – and she still managed to take a turn on deck.

After four days the ship docked in the Canary Islands, where the Yorks met British émigrés, then it was on to Jamaica for a three-day visit. On 25 January the *Renown* reached the Panama Canal, pausing at Panama City for a ball, shopping and sightseeing, and three days later she sailed into the Pacific, where her first port of call was Nuku-Hiva, the largest of the Marquesas Islands, which are part of what were then rather poetically called the 'French Settlements in Oceania' (later French Polynesia). The French Governor came aboard and the Marines gave a band concert for the Marquesans, who responded with a dancing display. Next it was Fiji – where Bertie was obliged to drink the foul-tasting local liquor called *kava*[3] but gallantly protected Elizabeth from the ordeal – and finally the royal party arrived in New Zealand on 22 February.

The New Zealanders had requested the visit when it became known that the Duke and Duchess were going to Australia and it had been decided that New Zealand should receive them first. The Australians were somewhat chagrined at thus being upstaged, but from the Yorks' point of view the schedule was well planned, for their rapturous welcome in Auckland filled them with confidence for the heavy task in front of them. Everywhere they went crowds pressed in on them, anxious to talk, shake hands, touch Elizabeth's clothes and feel the warmth of her smile. The New Zealand Prime Minister, Joseph Coates, reported to Sir Charles Fergusson, the Governor-General, that one of the country's best-known communists had been so captivated by Elizabeth that he had renounced his marxist faith – royals were human after all, the reformed Red had cried incredulously.

The official duties also went better than had been expected. Lionel Logue's therapy was doing wonders for Bertie: within a few hours of landing in Auckland the Duke had made three public speeches and was well pleased with his performance. Even so, Bertie believed that it was not to hear him speak that the people flocked – it was to see his wife, to bask in the sunshine of her interest as she mixed with ex-servicemen who had recovered from war wounds at Glamis, or asked experienced questions of Girl Guides formed up to greet her, or chatted with some of the thousands of cheering children who seemed to appear everywhere she went. 'She smiled her way straight into the hearts of the people', the newspapers said. Bertie himself paid her an unusual tribute when he leapt prematurely from their train as it pulled into a station and, unnoticed, ran with the waving, cheering crowd by the carriage window where she stood smiling.

With intervals for fishing trips in the Bay of Islands (Elizabeth' had been a keen angler since girlhood), the Yorks travelled to

Rotorua, where they were greeted by two thousand Maoris singing and dancing, then to Napier and Wellington, completing their tour of the North Island. It was when they reached the town of Nelson, near Christchurch, South Island, on 11 March that the strain of the visit caught up with Elizabeth and she succumbed to a severe attack of tonsillitis. Bertie was all for calling off the rest of the New Zealand programme, but Elizabeth would not hear of it, so while she remained in her sickbed at the Commercial Hotel in Nelson the Duke went on to receive a rapturous welcome which even he, in his shyness and modesty, could not pretend was for his wife rather than himself. For the first time he realized that he was popular in his own right.

At the hotel Elizabeth was inundated by gifts of fruit and flowers and throughout her illness received daily visits from the mayor of Nelson. Bulletins on her condition were issued and motorists passing the hotel were met by notices instructing them to drive quietly. Bertie telephoned every evening to see how Elizabeth was progressing and to tell her of all the things he had been doing. After a week or so Elizabeth was fit enough to return to Wellington and recover her strength at Government House, then she joined the *Renown* which sailed south to Invercargill to collect Bertie and make the twelve-hundred-mile voyage across the Tasman Sea to Australia.

Sydney was reached on 26 March. The *Renown* sailed in to an eerie silence because the myriad boats in the magnificent harbour had been asked not to blare out their greetings until the cruiser had been secured at her moorings. Once this operation had been carried out the National Anthem was played – and all hell broke loose in the form of hooters, bells, the firing of guns and the full-throated roars of the expectant citizens of Sydney. Australians are not a people to stand much on ceremony, so the keynote of the visit was informality. One rather daunting development for the royal couple was the 'public reception' (of which the Prince of Wales had been the innovator): the Duke and Duchess had to stand on a platform being stared at by queues of people passing them in line abreast, a sort of march-past in reverse of which the purpose was not for the dignitaries to review the parade but for the members of the parade to inspect the guests of honour. It was rather like being a rare exhibit in a zoo, but at least it meant that as many people as possible saw their royal visitors at fairly close quarters – and it was much less tiring for the Yorks than rounds of hand-shaking.

One of the most emotional moments of the tour came on Anzac Day, 25 April, when Bertie and Elizabeth were in Melbourne for a service and march-past in memory of the Australian and New Zealand dead in the 1914–18 war. Elizabeth, dressed entirely in black, stood next to her husband as he took the salute at the parade of twenty-five thousand ex-servicemen, including seven hundred permanently disabled by war wounds and forty holders of the Victoria Cross. The Duke made a moving speech and spoke personally to many of the veterans of the Gallipoli landing, the Palestine campaign and the battlefields of France and Belgium.

The Yorks saw an Aborigine carnival in Queensland, attended a state ball in Victoria, danced at a party in a woolshed, visited a cattle station, gazed at the Blue Mountains, drove under an arch of apples in Tasmania and reviewed Boy Scouts and Girl Guides in Adelaide (where Elizabeth wore the uniform which had been so much part of her life at Glamis). But extensive and popular as their tour was, the day everyone was waiting for was 9 May and its ceremony in Canberra. Fifty thousand people gathered in the new capital to watch the royal procession and the Duke's opening of the Parliament building with a golden key. It said much for Bertie's newly acquired confidence that he insisted, against opposition from officials, on making an extra speech on the steps of the building for the benefit of the spectators and the radio listeners throughout Australia. The address was word-perfect, as was his speech in the crowded Senate House, when he read a message from the King. Immediately afterwards a telegram was sent to Lionel Logue informing him how spectacularly good his treatment was proving to be. At the same time, however, Bertie had been nervous to a high degree the night before the ceremony and was glad to have Elizabeth by his side to support and encourage him.

So the visit came to its glorious end. Elizabeth and Bertie returned to Melbourne and boarded the *Renown*, which – with various stops on the way – sailed for Fremantle to begin the voyage home on 23 May. The cruiser may well have been lying a little lower in the water than on the outward journey, for the Yorks were taking back with them three tons of gifts, many of them toys for Princess Elizabeth. They also took with them the hearts of the Australians: Sir Tom Bridges, Governor-General of South Australia, told George V that the people had been profoundly touched by Bertie's unaffected manner, and, he added, the entire continent had fallen in love with Elizabeth.

Three days out into the Indian Ocean, in fine sunny weather, the captain of the *Renown*, Captain N. A. Sulivan, ordered the crew to stand by to abandon ship. Leaking oil in the boiler room had caused a serious fire. Four sailors were in the sickbay after being burned and gassed. The fire was still raging and at any time might spread to the main oil tanks and blow up the ship. Throughout the afternoon Bertie watched firefighting parties battling to contain the flames and finally extinguish them. Meanwhile the rest of the crew went about their normal duties so as not to alarm Elizabeth, but the air of studied calm was somewhat overdone. 'Every hour someone came and told me that it was nothing to worry about, so I knew there was real trouble,' the Duchess told Captain Sulivan wryly a few days later. At last, about ten o'clock in the evening, the blaze was put out and repairs were made. The remainder of the journey, by way of Mauritius, Malta and Gibraltar, passed without incident, and on Monday 27 June the *Renown* docked at Portsmouth.

The Yorks were greeted at the dockside by Bertie's three brothers, then went on to Victoria Station in London for the official welcome by the King and Queen (Bertie had been told by his father to take his hat off when he kissed his mother and not to embrace the King in front of so many people). But the meeting they most anxiously awaited was still to come – reunion with the daughter they had not seen for six months.

Princess Elizabeth, blonde haired and blue eyed, was by then fourteen months old, accomplished in the art of crawling and just beginning to stand. Bulletins and photographs of her progress had reached Bertie and Elizabeth almost every day during their absence. Now they were anxious to see for themselves, and nervous about the toddler's reaction to the mother from whom she had been parted so early. The reunion was meant to take place in the new home at 145 Piccadilly, into which Princess Elizabeth had lately moved with her nurse, but Queen Mary knew that the delay would be unbearable for her daughter-in-law, so when the royal party arrived at Buckingham Palace from the station, the Princess, in the arms of her nurse, was waiting to greet them. The little girl already had a small vocabulary, of which the most important word was 'Mummy'. The Queen took her grand-daughter from the nurse and carried her towards the Duchess. 'Look,' she said, 'there's Mummy.' For a few seconds nothing happened, then the child smiled, held out her arms and was swept into the embrace of the delighted Elizabeth. The homecoming was complete.

When the black double-doors of 145 Piccadilly closed behind them for the first time in June 1927 it seemed that the Duke and Duchess of York would settle down to a life as quiet and homely as was possible for the King's second son and his wife. There were constant calls on their time, of course, for their success in Australia and perhaps even more their status as the parents of the child closest to the throne, whose every gurgle by now excited the entire populations of Britain and the Empire (or so the newspapers seemed to believe), meant that the Yorks were regarded as the most suitable royals available to be patrons, presidents, official openers and guests of honour. The Prince of Wales still outshone them in popular appeal, but on the one hand he was heir to the throne and could not be expected to give of his valuable time in order to attend functions which did not match his exalted position, and on the other hand he had no one to take care of the distaff side of royal responsibilities. The Yorks' great advantage as public figures was that they were a family –

and as Walter Bagehot said, a royal family 'brings down the pride of sovereignty to the level of petty life'. But there was still plenty of time left for Bertie and Elizabeth to enjoy their home, and that was where they were happiest.

The hub of the Piccadilly house was the morning room, at the far end of the pillared hall. It had started out as Bertie's study, but its generous proportions and its French window leading to Hamilton Gardens appealed to Elizabeth, and she persuaded the Duke to move into a smaller room. Elizabeth had a large desk in the morning room where – in the morning, naturally enough – she dealt with her correspondence. The other furnishings included a gramophone, a wireless, a big cabinet finished in scarlet lacquer, small tables on which stood framed family photographs, bookshelves and a fish tank. Princess Elizabeth's toys could usually be seen lying about, for though the top-floor nurseries were her domain she often played in the morning room. Sometimes guests were entertained to dinner there because the dining room on the first floor was a rather forbidding chamber and in any case could seat no more than about a dozen people.

It may seem surprising that a family of three needed a house with twenty-five bedrooms, and even more odd that the Duke should have thought it necessary to have a twenty-sixth added, but when the number of living-in staff is taken into account it may be seen that 145 Piccadilly was not over-large. The Yorks employed a butler, an under-butler, two footmen, a housekeeper, a cook, three housemaids and three kitchenmaids, a nurse and her assistant, a dresser for the Duchess and a valet for the Duke, an odd-job man, a boy who worked in the steward's room, an orderly from the Royal Air Force, a night watchman and a telephone operator – a total of more than twenty people, of whom all but two lived in the house.

Elizabeth, however, was not the kind of woman to leave the running of the household entirely to her staff. She had a great interest in the activities of the kitchen, frequently passing on recipes handed down through generations of Bowes-Lyon wives, and she and Bertie took personal charge of their daughter's upbringing, spending as much time with her as royal duties permitted. The little Princess saw her parents first thing in the morning, when she tripped into their bedroom, and last thing at night when they took part in the fun and games of bathtime. As she grew older, Princess Elizabeth was included in the Yorks' entertaining, both personal and official, in much the same way as her mother had taken part in the social life of her parents. Royal status did impose some limitations, however. Just across the road from 145 Piccadilly was Green Park, which to Elizabeth's nurse, Clara Knight, seemed the perfect place for outings in the pram. Unfortunately it was also very public, and after several times finding herself besieged by well-intentioned but worrying crowds Mrs Knight was forced to abandon these perambulations, and Princess Elizabeth took the air first in the gardens at Buckingham Palace and later by way of carriage rides through Hyde Park.

In the meantime the other, public, life of the Duke and Duchess continued unabated. In the summer of 1927 Elizabeth received the Freedom of the City of Glasgow, and her voice was heard on the wireless for the first time when she made her acceptance speech. Later in the year she became Colonel-in-Chief of the King's Own Yorkshire Light Infantry, which involved her in many regimental duties – receiving newly appointed colonels, entertaining officers and their wives, presenting colours, visiting barracks and several times taking part in the annual distribution of roses in commemoration of the Battle of Minden on 1 August 1759. As Christmas approached she was again busy on behalf of poor children, and on 2 December she attended a festival organized by the Sunshine Guild, where she joined in with nearly nine hundred children for a sing-song.

The first function of the New Year, 1928, was a particularly colourful and exciting affair – the Costermongers' Carnival held in Finsbury Town Hall in January. Elizabeth and Bertie danced the lancers with some of the pearly kings and queens elected by street traders in the various London boroughs, and the Duchess was crowned with a paper hat. Later the couple danced a foxtrot together and presented prizes for a fancy dress competition.

Reporting on the occasion, *The Times* bemoaned the fact that the costermongers' costumes, covered in thousands of pearl buttons, were becoming so rare on London streets. The tradition was honoured, however, with the presentation of a 'pearly' doll for Princess Elizabeth.

The remainder of the year passed conventionally enough for Elizabeth: she visited the Ideal Home Exhibition at Olympia (where she bought two inlaid brass cigarette boxes, two Chinese lacquer standard lamps and, for the little Princess, a toy caravan and two carved wooden birds); she became Commandant-in-Chief of the St John Ambulance Brigade Nursing Division; she presented prizes at a community music festival in the East End of London; she visited a hospital for disabled children in Surrey, and she revisited Great Bookham, where she had spent the first days of her honeymoon.

The year ended sombrely, however. In November the King caught a feverish cold, which rapidly developed into bronchitis (associated with the fact that, like his father, George V was a heavy smoker) and septicaemia located at the base of the right lung. The Prince of Wales, who was in East Africa, set off for home having been told that there was 'cause for anxiety'. The Duke of York returned to London from hunting in Northamptonshire. On 1 December the King's doctor, Lord Dawson of Penn, felt that the situation was grave enough to issue a bulletin saying that the strain of the illness was beginning to affect the King's heart. Three days later a group of Privy Councillors, including Bertie, gathered outside the King's sickroom and watched him sign, with great difficulty, an Order appointing a Council of State to fulfil the official functions of the Sovereign. The Councillors were the Queen, the Prince of Wales, the Duke of York, the Archbishop of Canterbury, the Lord Chancellor and the Prime Minister.

On 11 December, the day the Prince of Wales reached London, Lord Dawson decided that he must perform an operation to save the life of the King: a rib was removed and the infected lung was drained. But the crisis was far from over. Churches remained open throughout the night so that prayers might be said for the King's deliverance, and in bitter weather anxious crowds waited by the railings at Buckingham Palace for news of their Sovereign's fight for survival. By the end of December it became clear that he was going to recover – it has been said that it was only his willpower that pulled him through. The nation heaved a sigh of relief, and so did the Yorks, for this intimation of mortality had brought it home to them that if the King did die and the unmarried Prince of Wales took his place, a great weight would fall upon Bertie as heir presumptive. How great the burden would eventually be was something no one could foresee, except perhaps George V, who once expressed the wish that the Prince of Wales would never marry and that in due time his second son and then his beloved grand-daughter would sit on the throne.

But the King did not die, though he never fully recovered his strength. In February 1929 an ambulance took him to convalesce at Bognor Regis, where early the following month he was joined by Princess Elizabeth, by then almost three years old and the only person who could really keep up the King's spirits in the face of the physical weakness and mental depression that followed his illness. He called her 'Lillibet', after the first stumbling attempts she made to pronounce her name (and it was immediately taken up by the rest of the family); she called him 'Grandpapa England' and thoroughly enjoyed being indulged by the man whose own children had been terrified of him. The Yorks, while repeating patient and good humoured admonitions that Lillibet should not be spoiled – as parents always do to fond grandparents – looked on with wonder at their child's taming of the old martinet and with pleasure at the joy she was able to bring to the King in the hour of his greatest need.

While Lillibet took her grandfather for walks along the seafront at Bognor and enlisted his aid in building sandcastles on the beach, Bertie and Elizabeth were off on their travels again, though this time they went no farther than northern Europe. Elizabeth herself had been ill with influenza at the beginning of 1929 and reports of her condition had been appearing in the newspapers next to those about the health of the King. She was fit enough, though, to accompany Bertie to Norway in March for the marriage of Crown Prince Olav, a nephew of George V, and Princess Marta of Sweden.

On their way to Oslo the Yorks passed through Germany, still reeling from the effects of disastrous inflation during the early twenties which had at one point sent the exchange rate of the German mark to a staggering nineteen million to the pound. There was nothing official about the visit of the Yorks, but the fact that they were the first members of the British Royal Family to set foot in Germany since the end of the Great War indicated a change in European relations. Irritated by the military, political and colonial ambitions of France, the British people and their politicians (displaying the old national characteristic of sympathy for the underdog) had put aside the residual bitterness of the war and begun to feel a certain warmth towards a nation which not so long before had been reviled as the horrible Hun. It was this renewed feeling of Anglo-Saxon kinship – after all, Britain had supported a German monarchy, or at least one with a German name, until 1917 – that led the British into the traps which were to be set by Adolf Hitler.

When the Duke and Duchess returned from Norway Bertie had a particularly historic duty to perform which involved a visit to Elizabeth's beloved Scotland. On 28 March it had been announced that the Duke was to be Lord High Commissioner to the General Assembly of the Church of Scotland, the ancient office of the Sovereign's representative at the deliberations of the Church's ruling body. In 1929 the appointment of the Duke was especially noteworthy, because not only was it the first time for more than two centuries that a member of the royal house had held the office but it was also the year in which opposing wings of the Church were reunited after a rift lasting almost ninety years.[4]

On 20 May the Duke and Duchess arrived in Edinburgh and were installed at Holyroodhouse, the official residence of the Lord High Commissioner, and the following day Bertie opened the General Assembly. The royal engagements in Edinburgh, however, were not all concerned with the Church of Scotland, for the Assembly happened to coincide with the six-hundredth anniversary of the granting of the city's charter by Robert the Bruce, and the citizens were proud and pleased to have a royal 'Scots lassie' in their midst to join the celebrations. *The Scotsman* commented:

> The association of the King's son and the little Duchess who had become the darling of the people transformed the routine welcome into rapture . . . Her Royal Highness waved freely to the crowds, took special notice of the children, of whom there were many, and did not forget to bestow frequent acknowledgement to spectators in high windows . . .

For her part Elizabeth noted that the Scots were disappointed because Princess Elizabeth was not in Edinburgh, and she confessed to Queen Mary that she found the public adulation of her daughter almost frightening, owing to the adverse effect it might have on the child's personality.

A month later the Scots honoured Elizabeth with a Doctor of Laws degree at St Andrews University, but the following year they had real cause to celebrate when 'their' Duchess was delivered of her second child at Glamis, the first royal birth in Scotland since 1602. The Yorks had been hoping for a boy, but at 9.22 on the stormy evening of Thursday 21 August 1930 a new princess was born. Next day a beacon was lit on Hunter's Hill, some two miles from the castle, and the Glamis pipe band played for hundreds of wildly excited dancers. In London a forty-one gun salute was fired at the Tower and the bells of St Paul's broadcast the good news.

Confident that the child would be a boy, Elizabeth and Bertie had given little thought to girls' names, but within a week they had decided that their daughter should be called Ann Margaret. Unfortunately the King did not like the name Ann and would not even countenance a transposition to Margaret Ann. Elizabeth was disappointed, for Ann had been her own choice while Margaret – to which the King had no objection – had been suggested by relatives. Bertie, who would never cross his father, counselled that the King should have his way, and on 6 September Elizabeth wrote politely but firmly to Queen Mary telling

her that she and Bertie had *decided* to name their baby Margaret
Rose (the second name in honour of the Duchess's sister, Lady
Rose Leveson-Gower) and she hoped Their Majesties would
like it. Thus was the Princess baptized by the Archbishop of
Canterbury at Buckingham Palace on 30 October – though as far
as Lillibet was concerned, her name was 'Bud', on the ground
that she was not yet a full-grown Rose.

Princess Margaret was a lively, intelligent child and everyone
who saw her was struck by her good looks. Her mother used to
say that Margaret took after her father, and she certainly inherited his temper. Also like the Duke of York, she felt the disadvantages and frustrations of being the second-born, difficulties
which may arise in any family but are so much more likely in a
royal one, since the rules of seniority are more obvious and more
rigid. The Duke was very much aware of his younger daughter's
position and tried to make up for the problems by giving her
extra attention (indeed some people say she was his favourite
and that he spoiled her). Later events, however, seem to show
that Princess Margaret – known cryptically as 'P.2' to courtiers
and staff in her younger days – is temperamentally as near to her
uncle, King Edward VIII, as to her father.

The Home Secretary who certified that Princess Margaret Rose
was the true child of the Duchess of York was a man very
different to his predecessor, the patrician Sir William Joynson-
Hicks who had been present at the birth of Princess Elizabeth.
His name was Joseph Robert Clynes and he was a former mill-
worker from Oldham who had risen to eminence by way of the
Lancashire Gasworkers' Union. It almost goes without saying
that when he had stood for Parliament in 1910 it had been in the
Labour interest. Britain, having given its first Labour Government a resounding vote of no-confidence in 1924 and flocked
towards Stanley Baldwin's Conservatives, had five years later
divided more or less equally between left and right, leaving the
Liberal Party out in the cold, from which it has never re-
emerged. The general election of May 1929 resulted, because of
constituency boundaries, in a parliamentary advantage of

twenty-eight seats to Labour and Stanley Baldwin resigned, making way for a Government whose lack of an overall majority placed serious restraints upon its effectiveness.[5] The formation of Ramsay MacDonald's second administration and the political shambles that followed it were to have a direct influence on the lives of the Duke and Duchess of York.

First, early in 1931, the Labour Secretary of State for the Dominions, James Henry Thomas, vetoed a proposal to send the Duke of York to Canada as Governor-General. The appointment of a royal Governor, Thomas said, would make Canadians feel less democratic than their American neighbours. This was patent rubbish, but though it infuriated the King his constitutional position made it impossible for him to ignore the advice of his minister, so Bertie and Elizabeth remained at 145 Piccadilly, and there is no reason to suppose they felt any sense of loss at that. (Curiously enough, the Canadians themselves were to suggest a quarter of a century later that the then widowed Queen Elizabeth should become their Governor-General, an idea which in 1958 led a newspaper diarist to speculate on the possibility of the Queen Mother becoming Governor-General of each of the Dominions in turn for one year, since 'it will seem a pity to many that she should not be given an opportunity to use her energy and knowledge in more directions'.)[6]

The second incursion of politics into the otherwise peaceful life of Bertie and Elizabeth came not from the Labour Government itself but from the so-called National Government which MacDonald formed in the wake of his Cabinet's inability to withstand the first shockwaves of the Depression that swept through Europe in the summer of 1931. An emergency Budget passed in September that year raised the rate of income tax to 25 per cent and cut the pay of all state employees, including Members of Parliament and the judiciary, by between 5 and 15 per cent. (The police were at the lower end of the scale of reductions, teachers at the higher, which says something about the Government's priorities; on 15 September revisions were made to the cuts in service pay after a 'mutiny' among the men of the Atlantic Fleet based in Scotland.) Once again the Gold Standard was suspended and on the foreign exchange markets the value of the pound fell from almost five dollars to an average of three dollars and forty cents.

Since everyone else in the pay of the state was losing income, the Royal Family felt that it had to share the burden and the King informed MacDonald that he would accept a reduction of £50,000 in the annuity paid to him in the Civil List. The Prince of Wales gave a similar sum to the nation, and the Duke of York was required to make a cut in his allowance, which was £25,000 a year. Bertie decided that he must give up hunting and sell his string of six horses. The sale took place at Leicester on 7 November 1931 and the Duke watched his horses go for a total of 965 guineas – not a vast sum of money to save, yet a sacrifice which, in those panicky times, was appreciated.

But while two and a half million men did their best to keep their families on dole payments, the Depression had little real effect on the Yorks' life. There was Royal Ascot to be enjoyed, there was a visit to Paris during which Bertie and Elizabeth opened a British Week, and there was the usual run of engagements, which during 1931 included a banquet with three thousand guests given by the Freemasons at Olympia, and a trip to Oxford, where Elizabeth opened a new maternity department at the Radcliffe Infirmary and received an honorary Doctor of Civil Laws degree from the University. Indeed, that grim September opened up new horizons for Bertie and Elizabeth when the King gave them a country house – The Royal Lodge, Windsor, with its memories of the Duke of Cumberland, the 'Butcher' of Culloden, and the Prince Regent.

The house had been severely knocked about by successive occupants and was in rather a shabby state when the Yorks took it over. They spent more than a year renovating it, adding to it and, most pleasurable of all as far as they were concerned, putting in order the overgrown garden. In the Royal Family's photograph album there is a picture taken by Queen Mary of Bertie, Elizabeth, Lillibet and Margaret, all grubby-faced and dressed in old clothes, during one of their gardening weekends at The Royal Lodge. Towards the end of 1932 a very unusual building appeared in the fifteen-acre garden: *Y Bwthyn Bach* (The Little House) was a model Welsh cottage, some fifteen feet high and containing six rooms under its thatched roof, presented by the people of Wales to Princess Elizabeth on her sixth birthday.

In 1932 there was every reason to suppose that the Duke and Duchess of York had settled in to a way of life that would occupy them for the rest of their days. They had two homes which they loved; though they had no son they seemed perfectly happy with their two daughters; and they enjoyed a secure position in the Royal Family and in the affections of the nation. They clearly enjoyed the public duties they carried out and they certainly made the most of their private hours.

The children took up a good deal of their time at home. Following the example of her mother, Elizabeth read Bible stories to her daughters and joined enthusiastically in their games. In the morning room at 145 Piccadilly were two little dustpans and brushes with which the Princesses could do make-believe chores, and Princess Elizabeth made the most of her little house in the grounds of The Royal Lodge to develop housewifely skills (though of course there was little chance that she would ever need them other than in a theoretical sense). The Duchess of York believed that the basis of a good and useful life was a happy childhood, and it was towards love and happiness that the girls' upbringing tended. But it was not forgotten that Elizabeth and Margaret were princesses, and much attention was paid to forming character and imparting a sense of self-discipline. The Duchess passed on her own simple, straightforward religious faith and she trained the girls for their royal life to come by acting out charades in which she pretended to be the Queen (soon to become fact) or the Prime Minister or some other dignitary with whom the Princesses had to deal. Lillibet and Margaret found it all great fun and at the same time they learnt how to conduct themselves with dignity and to treat other people with respect.

Elizabeth was keen to build on her own training by sending Lillibet to school when she reached the age of seven, but the King put his foot down: the Princess was third in line to the throne and, though her accession did not seem very likely at the time, heirs to the throne were always educated at home. (It would be left to Princess Elizabeth herself to change all that when she did become Queen.) So Lillibet's governess, Marion Crawford, evolved a schedule of lessons covering six days a week and giving over the mornings to academic studies while afternoons were left free for such pursuits as music, dancing and drawing.

It was Princess Elizabeth, incidentally, who founded the corgi tradition in the Royal Family, and made the little Welsh dogs the second most popular breed in England. The first royal corgi, known as Dookie, arrived at 145 Piccadilly in the autumn of 1933 and was followed by a second one called Jane. The Yorks had many other dogs – among them labradors and a Tibetan lion dog – but it was the corgis which caught the imagination of the public, in spite of the fact (or possibly because of it) that corgis are notorious for their uncertain temper and are wont to go for the heels of anything that moves.

The happy family life of the home-loving Yorks did much to establish their position in the hearts of loyal subjects throughout the world – a fact that was put into words when in 1932 Elizabeth opened the new headquarters of the British College of Obstetricians and Gynaecologists in Queen Anne Street, London. The president of the college, Sir W. Blair-Bell, summed it up:

> We believe that the sanctity of the family means a great deal to the spiritual and physical welfare of our race. Your Royal Highness has given to us all a vision of the happiness of married life, and in a very beautiful way, through the little Princesses, the people have been permitted to share your joys and show their devotion to the Crown.

As if to underline this symbolic role, Newfoundland chose Elizabeth's head to appear on its seven cents stamp in 1932.

But the Duchess was more than a symbol of the ideal family. She was also more immediately human than most people expected royal personages to be. One small example of her responsiveness came in 1934, when she visited Sheffield and was taken to see the Deep Pit allotments, formerly derelict land which through the efforts of twelve hundred working men had been turned into a vast vegetable garden. Bertie was suffering from a poisoned hand at the time and was unable to go with his wife, which caused some disappointment among the allotment holders who had been hoping that he would dig up some 'Duke of York' potatoes. Feeling this sense of anticlimax, Elizabeth told the men, 'I'll try to take his place', and – wearing high-heeled shoes and white kid gloves – she picked up a garden fork and dug out the potatoes. A couple of years later she earned the respect of miners in County Durham when, with Bertie this time, she went down the Glamis pit at Kibblesworth and hewed her very own piece of coal at the face with a small pickaxe provided for her. It was the same wherever she made public appearances. Her warmth and natural friendliness captured the hearts of all who saw her.

A Bishop of London once said: 'What the Duchess's smile has done for the British Empire we shall find out in years to come.' He could not have foreseen it at the time, but Britain and its Empire was to demand a great deal more than a smile from the Duchess of York.

The Three Kings

The year 1935 marked the silver jubilee of King George V and accordingly the Duke and Duchess of York were involved in even more public appearances than usual. In July Elizabeth became the first royal visitor to Manchester since 1888, and among other places she visited that year were Barrow-in-Furness, Wimbledon, Wigan, Putney, the Isle of Dogs and Edinburgh. She also made her first journey by air when she and Bertie went to Brussels to attend a British Week. But early in 1935 there were signs that the year would end sadly. In February the King suffered a serious attack of bronchitis and spent the following month in convalescence at Eastbourne. Somehow he found the strength to go through the jubilee celebrations in May and to review the Fleet at Spithead in July. But a prayer written by the Poet Laureate, John Masefield, that the King should enjoy many more years of his reign, was not to be answered. In December Anthony Eden, who had become Foreign Secretary in a new National Government, this time headed by Stanley Baldwin, travelled to Sandringham to see the King and found him coughing painfully, though he remained in good spirits.

The Yorks did not go to Sandringham that Christmas, for Elizabeth was suffering from influenzal pneumonia and was advised to remain at The Royal Lodge. Princesses Elizabeth and Margaret, however, did go to stay with their grandparents for the festive season: though they did not realize it, it would be the last time they would see their dear Grandpapa. On 16 January he was so ill that he had to take to his bed. Four days later he presided at his last Council of State, when he barely had the strength to sign his name. The anxious Queen had summoned her children to Sandringham, and on the evening of the 20th they all saw that he was dying and took their farewells. That evening a medical bulletin was issued: 'The King's life is moving peacefully to its close.' He died at five minutes to midnight. His last words are said to have been, 'How is the Empire?'

On 22 January the Duchess of York, still weak from her illness, travelled to Sandringham, returning to London the same day with the Queen and Princess Mary in a closed railway carriage immediately behind the one that carried the King's coffin. The body of George V lay in state for five days at Westminster Hall, and on the last night before his funeral his four sons stood watch at each corner of the catafalque. On 28 January, a cold, gloomy day, the coffin was borne on a gun carriage to Paddington Station then taken by train to Windsor, where the funeral took place in St George's Chapel. After the service, the new King remained a little apart from the rest of his family. It was assumed that he was thinking of the responsibilities which had fallen upon him, and of the great hopes the nation had for him. No one knew then that one of the matters uppermost in his mind was what he was going to do about Mrs Wallis Simpson.

At first, though, Edward VIII was determined to be a thoroughly modern monarch, sweeping away the last vestiges of what he had seen as his father's private war against the twentieth century. During the six months of full mourning for George V he set about streamlining the monarchy, renegotiating the Civil List and taking a great interest in affairs of state. Gradually his interest waned, however, as Mrs Simpson and his retreat at Fort Belvedere occupied his mind more and more. Stanley Baldwin even began to suspect that the King's careless treatment of confidential documents might constitute a security risk.

The Duchess of York, meanwhile, was in one sense grateful for the long period of mourning with its consequent lack of public engagements. She went with her family to Eastbourne to shake off the residual effects of her illness. Easter was spent at The Royal Lodge with Queen Mary, who joined in the celebration of Princess Elizabeth's tenth birthday and the thirteenth wedding anniversary of the Duke and Duchess. In May the Yorks, their children and Queen Mary went to Southampton to see the newly completed ocean liner *Queen Mary*, the largest ship in the world. Then there was the Chelsea Flower Show and finally, on 21 July, the end of Court mourning, which was marked by a reception in the gardens at Buckingham Palace, presided over by the new King. In July, too, Elizabeth presented prizes at the London School of Medicine for Women in Brunswick Square, when she quoted the words of Lewis Carroll: 'In the darkest hour of man's despair lies woman's mission.' That was to become something of a motto for her in the difficult years which lay ahead.

At the end of July 1936 the Yorks attended the wedding of the Hon. Jean Elphinstone, Elizabeth's niece, then they toured the North-East of England, paid a visit to the Strathmores at Glamis, and finally went to spend their customary summer holiday at Birkhall, the royal residence near Balmoral Castle. It was at this time that the King of England and the wife of another man were cruising the Adriatic in the yacht *Nahlin* and attracting the attention of the world's Press. David and Wallis returned home in September and the King went immediately to Balmoral. Later that month he was due to open a new hospital in Aberdeen, but he made a transparent excuse and went off to Ballater railway station, near Balmoral, to meet Mrs Simpson, while the Duke of York performed the hospital opening. The Scots never forgave Edward VIII for that 'insult'.

In October Mrs Simpson received her divorce decree and 'The King's Matter' moved towards its climax. At this stage the King was still undecided as to his best course of action. He desperately wanted to marry Wallis but he was keen to remain on the throne as well. He had one chance of being able to achieve both aims, or so his friends thought. He could contract a morganatic marriage with Wallis, by which she would become his lawful wife but not his queen.[1] This solution to the constitutional dilemma was suggested by Esmond Harmsworth of the *Daily Mail* when he entertained Mrs Simpson to lunch. Wallis thought it was a good idea, and the King was ready to clutch at any straw. But Stanley Baldwin, fighting off an attempt by some members of the Cabinet to send an ultimatum to the King threatening the resignation of the Government if he did not end his association with Mrs Simpson, advised that there was no provision in English law for a morganatic marriage. The King insisted that the proposal should be officially examined, and Baldwin consulted both his Cabinet colleagues and the Prime Ministers of the Dominions: the reply was a firm 'No'.

The tide turned irrevocably against the King on 1 December, when the Bishop of Bradford, Dr A. W. F. Blunt, made the speech at his diocesan conference which gave the British newspapers a chance to break their silence. On the same day the Duchess of York was receiving the Freedom of Edinburgh, and in her address she said:

> The honour conferred on me today by the Town Council of Edinburgh is one that I deeply appreciate both as a Scotswoman and as one who has always loved the history and the beauty of the capital of Scotland. Most of the great events in Scottish history have had their beginning or their end in this ancient city . . .

The following day the *Yorkshire Post* published what was taken to be Dr Blunt's attack on the King's relationship with Mrs Simpson, and abdication moved a step nearer.

The substance of what the Bishop said was as follows:

> The benefit of the King's Coronation depends, under God, upon two elements – first on the faith, prayer, and self-dedication of the King himself, and on that it would be improper for me to say anything except to commend him, and ask you to commend him, to God's grace, which he will so abundantly need, as we all need it – for the King is a man like ourselves – if he is to do his duty faithfully. We hope that he is aware of his need. Some of us wish that he gave more positive signs of his awareness . . . His per-

sonal views and opinions are his own, and as an individual he has the right of us all to be the keeper of his own private conscience. But in his public capacity at his Coronation he stands for the English people's idea of kingship. It has for long centuries been, and I hope still is, an essential part of the idea that the King needs the grace of God for his office. In the Coronation ceremony the nation definitely acknowledges that need. Whatever it may mean, much or little, to the individual who is crowned, to the people as a whole it means their dedication of the English monarchy to the care of God, in whose rule and governance are the hearts of kings.

The people of Britain, who knew nothing of their King's desire to marry Mrs Simpson, would not have detected any undertone in Bishop Blunt's speech had they not been led into doing so by the Press. The Bishop himself later said that he had no intention of criticizing the King for his relationship with Mrs Simpson and added that he had never even heard the lady's name.[2] It was Arthur Mann, editor of the *Yorkshire Post*, who first chose to construe what Blunt had said as a reference to the matter that was causing so much concern in royal circles and among politicians. Mann wrote a long editorial telling the whole story of Edward VIII and Mrs Simpson, and circulated it to the London papers through the Press Association. The Fleet Street editors were thrown into confusion as to how they should treat the bishop's 'attack'. The *Morning Post* decided to make no comment; the *Daily Telegraph* carried a report of Blunt's speech but refrained from editorializing; *The Times* reported the address in full and carried a leader congratulating the Duke and Duchess of York on their visit to Scotland. (Geoffrey Dawson, the editor of *The Times*, had decided a few days earlier that it would be no bad thing if his readers were encouraged to distribute their loyalty to the Crown a little more widely; he had apparently already made up his mind that Edward VIII would go.)[3]

By the following day, Thursday 3 December, all caution on the part of the Press had been thrown to the winds. Dawson had written an article under the heading 'King and Monarchy' which discussed what the American newspapers had been saying about 'Wally', admitted that there was a good deal of truth in those reports, and pointed out that the institution of monarchy was far greater than the man who had care of it. The King heard that this article was to be printed on the Thursday morning and on Wednesday evening asked the Prime Minister to stop it. Baldwin pointed out that the Press could not be dictated to by the Government, at which the King apologized and pleaded with him to ask Dawson if he could read the article before it appeared. 'For the sake of peace', Baldwin telephoned Dawson and asked if he could have a proof of the piece; the editor replied that the paper was about to go to press, but later on he sent the Prime Minister a proof. By that time, however, Baldwin had gone to bed, so the first he saw of the leader was when he got his *Times* the following morning. Every other Fleet Street paper had the story of the King's romance on its front page, the *Daily Mirror* leading the way with the bald headline, 'The King Wants to Marry Mrs Simpson'. Such was the furore which greeted Bertie and Elizabeth when they returned to London that they and all the other members of the Royal Family cancelled their engagements.

That same evening Mrs Simpson left London for refuge in France, accompanied by the King's old friend and personal Lord in Waiting, 'Perry' Brownlow.[4] Lord Brownlow feared that Mrs Simpson's flight would serve only to accelerate the King's abdication and during their journey to Cannes persuaded Wallis to issue a statement saying that she was 'willing, if such action would solve the problem, to withdraw forthwith from a situation which has been rendered both unhappy and untenable'. By then, however, Brownlow's premonition had been proved right. King Edward had already told Baldwin that he was going to abdicate.

At this point there was an unaccountable delay in the proceedings. The Prime Minister definitely knew on Saturday 5 December of the King's firm decision to go, yet on the following Monday he told the House of Commons: 'I do not know yet, I cannot know yet, what the King may decide or how he may decide to act.' This was not strictly true, but neither was it a falsehood. Baldwin knew that the King was set on abdication but he did not know how it would be effected or what would happen afterwards. The Duke of York was the heir presumptive, but there were strong doubts in Government circles as to whether he had the strength or was dynamic enough to carry through the enormous task of restoring public and Empire confidence in the monarchy after the shock of an abdication. It is almost certain that there were discussions about the possibility of changing the order of the succession to allow Prince George, Duke of Kent, to become King and his son heir apparent. So for two days Baldwin kept silent and Edward avoided contact with Bertie.

Finally, however, it was decided that the throne would have to go to the Duke of York, and on 7 December Bertie had a long meeting with his brother at Fort Belvedere. Next day – while Elizabeth was confined to bed at the house in Piccadilly with influenza – Bertie joined Baldwin, Prince George and Walter Monckton, the King's intermediary, for dinner with Edward at the Fort and the details of the handover were hammered out. On the 9th Baldwin told the Commons he hoped to make a statement the following day, and on the 10th the Instrument of Abdication was signed. It read:

> I, Edward the Eighth, of Great Britain, Ireland and the British Dominions beyond the Seas, King, Emperor of India, do hereby declare My irrevocable determination to renounce the Throne for Myself and for My descendants, and My desire that effect should be given to this Instrument of Abdication immediately. In token whereof I have hereunto set My hand this tenth day of December nineteen hundred and thirty six, in the presence of the witnesses whose signatures are subscribed.

At 145 Piccadilly Elizabeth, propped up on her pillows, reflected that they would have to take what was coming to them, and somehow make the best of it, while the young Princesses tried to get used to the idea that when people mentioned the Queen it was 'Mummy' they were talking about.

The outgoing King broadcast to the nation on the evening of Friday 11 December. He said:

> At long last I am able to say a few words of my own. I have never wanted to withhold anything, but until now it has not been

constitutionally possible for me to speak. A few hours ago I discharged my last duty as King and Emperor, and now that I have been succeeded by my brother, the Duke of York, my first words must be to declare my allegiance to him. This I do with all my heart.

You all know the reasons which have impelled me to renounce the throne, but I want you to understand that in making up my mind I did not forget the country or the Empire, which as Prince of Wales and lately as King I have for twenty-five years tried to serve. But you must believe me when I tell you that I have found it impossible to carry the heavy burden of responsibility and discharge my duties as King as I would wish to do without the help and support of the woman I love. And I want you to know that the decision I have made has been mine and mine alone. This was a thing I had to judge entirely for myself. The other person most nearly concerned has tried up to the last to persuade me to take a different course. I have made this, the most serious decision of my life, only upon a single thought – of what would in the end be best for all.

This decison has been made less difficult to me by the sure knowledge that my brother, with his long training in the public affairs of this country and with his fine qualities, will be able to take my place forthwith without interruption or injury to the life and progress of the Empire. And he has one matchless blessing, enjoyed by so many of you and not bestowed on me, a happy home with his wife and children.

During these hard days I have been comforted by Her Majesty, my mother, and by my family. The Ministers of the Crown, and in particular Mr Baldwin, the Prime Minister, have always treated me with full consideration. There has never been any constitutional difference between me and them, and between me and Parliament. Bred in the constitutional traditions of my father, I should never have allowed any such issue to arise. Ever since I was Prince of Wales, and later on when I occupied the throne, I have been treated with the greatest kindness by all classes of people, wherever I have lived or journeyed throughout the Empire. For that I am very grateful.

I now quit altogether public affairs, and I lay down my burden. It may be some time before I return to my native land, but I shall always follow the fortunes of the British race and Empire with profound interest, and if at any time in the future I can be found of service to His Majesty in a private station I shall not fail.

And now we all have a new King, I wish him and you, his

people, happiness and prosperity with all my heart. God bless you all. God save the King.

Listening to those words on the wireless in the offices of *The Times*, Geoffrey Dawson, perhaps knowing that they had been framed with the help of Winston Churchill, was heard to say that they sounded as if they were the thoughts of the average bank clerk.

On the evening of 11 December the ex-King took his leave of his family and travelled alone to Portsmouth, where he boarded the destroyer HMS *Fury* and was borne into exile. In the House of Commons the day before there had been talk of 'a King across the Water', recalling that earlier King who had fled England in the night, James II. But if anyone expected an upsurge of loyalty such as had come from the Jacobites he was disappointed. And if anyone else hoped for a sudden rising-up of republican sentiment, his thoughts too were very wide of the mark. During the last days of Edward VIII there had been demonstrations of support for him in the streets, notably from fascists, but they had passed almost unnoticed; in the House of Commons there had been a left-wing move to replace the monarchy with a republican government, but this had been roundly defeated. The striking thing about the Abdication was the way in which the changeover of kings was accomplished with hardly any fuss. As Baldwin said in the lobby of the House of Commons when someone asked what was to be done about the Coronation planned for May 1937: 'Same day. New King.'

And anyone who doubted whether the new King could cope with his unexpected responsibilities and the added problem of living down the scandal of the Abdication reckoned without the new Queen. The newspapers, at any rate, were in no doubt. Eulogies of Queen Elizabeth appeared on the very day of Edward's farewell broadcast. *The Times* said she had been the royal bride 'the public had hoped for' and recalled how 'the heart of the nation warmed towards the gracious Scottish girl with beauty of feature and complexion, a low-toned charming speaking voice, and above all a particularly happy and even radiant expression'. The *Morning Post* commented: 'Like the King's children, she industriously and faithfully gives her services to as many good causes as it is possible for her to help, living laborious days, never sparing herself, and doing it all with such a happy goodwill that she is considered both patroness and very sincere friend.' And when the shy and hesitant King George VI appeared at his Accession Council on 12 December he told the assembled Privy Councillors, 'With my wife and help-meet by my side, I take up the heavy task which lies before me . . .' To emphasize the importance of Elizabeth's role, one of Bertie's first acts as King was to invest his wife with the Order of the Garter.

The first problem faced by King George and Queen Elizabeth was adjusting to their new way of life, and they began the process by doing something that reminded them of former, perhaps happier times: they went to Sandringham for Christmas. Sandringham was the place Bertie always thought of as 'home', the place where he had been born, the place where his father had been happiest, and now he turned to it with relief – a relief tinged with sadness as he remembered that Christmas just a year before, which now seemed an age ago, when he had taken his leave of his father.

Christmas 1936 was a time for taking stock. Bertie had never expected, never wanted to be king and felt that he was in no way as well qualified for the job as his elder brother had been. His first reaction to the news that his brother intended to abdicate had been something approaching panic. Yet Bertie had been accustomed to royal life since birth and had not been unaware of his position as heir presumptive. He knew that as long as his brother remained a bachelor there was a possibility, God forbid, that the Crown might pass into the hands of the Yorks: to Bertie, therefore, the biggest shock lay in the manner of his accession. For Elizabeth, however, the Abdication realized the worst fears which had been in her mind when she had considered Bertie's proposal of marriage. She had been concerned about the loss of privacy and personal freedom involved in becoming Duchess of

York. How much greater was the cost of being queen, especially now that she had two children who would be denied any chance of the normal family life which had been their mother's dearest wish for them.

And yet when the new King and Queen reviewed their position during that Christmas holiday in 1936 they found to their surprise that the situation was not as bad as it had first seemed. Elizabeth, finding strength in her profound faith in God, discovered that she was not afraid, but instead calm and resigned. Bertie felt that he needed time to settle in as king but that he could, given the chance, make amends for what the Royal Family saw as the shame brought upon it by the defecting David, and he realized, too, that now he had a specific role to play it somehow made things easier for him.

Practically speaking, it was less easy for Elizabeth, because she had to win some of the overwhelming regard the people had for the tall, imposing, regal Queen Mary. Her size was no help – as a policeman once lamented when he was trying to keep his eye on her in the middle of a crowd, 'I wish she was not quite so small' – and one of the secrets of her appeal as Duchess of York had been her 'ordinariness': people had felt that she was just like one of them. Now she had to be 'queenly', which meant subduing to some extent her natural gregariousness and ebullience. People close to her began to notice that she walked more slowly and with greater dignity; she waved to the crowds with less obvious enthusiasm; she began to dress more elegantly and less to the dictates of fashion; and she worked hard at appearing more serene and mature and less girlish (she was, after all, only thirty-six years old). But one thing that never changed was her famous smile.

The King and Queen returned to London in February 1937 and were immediately plunged into preparations for the Coronation, which was scheduled for 12 May. It was fortunate that Edward VIII had included the Duke of York in his planning for the event. Bertie was familiar with details of the arrangements and the only change required was provision for the crowning of a queen as well as a king. There was still uncertainty in official circles as to how the public would react to the sudden and unexpected change of monarch, but some of the doubts at least were removed when, on 1 May, eighty thousand people cheered themselves hoarse as King George and Queen Elizabeth appeared at the climax of the football season, the FA Cup Final between Sunderland and Preston North End at Wembley Stadium. Elizabeth presented the Cup to Raich Carter, captain of the winning Sunderland team, and on hearing that Carter had recently married she told him: 'It'll be a grand wedding present.'

Eleven days later came all the pomp and ceremony of the Coronation Service, broadcast by wireless throughout the kingdom and all over the world, and also filmed for the cinema newsreels (the Earl Marshal, who has official responsibility for royal ceremonial, opposed coverage by the BBC's new television service). No one at Buckingham Palace was able to sleep much on the eve of the Coronation. Bertie and Elizabeth were awake by three o'clock in the morning, and the new King was so nervous that he could not eat breakfast.

It was a cold day, with intermittent showers of rain, when at 10.30 in the morning the great golden Coronation coach left the Palace and made its way in magnificent procession to Westminster Abbey. Breaking with the established custom that the Queen Dowager should not attend the Coronation of the new Sovereign, Queen Mary travelled in a carriage with Princess Elizabeth and Princess Margaret: she felt that the circumstances in which her son and daughter-in-law were being crowned demanded a display of royal solidarity which was more important than tradition. Some people who watched the procession on its way to the Abbey say the cheers were louder for Queen Mary and the Princesses than they were for the King and Queen. In her diary Queen Mary wrote: 'Lillibet and Margaret looked too sweet in their lace dresses and robes, especially when they put on their coronets.'

Elizabeth was the first to enter the Abbey, where seven thousand people made up the congregation. For the first part of the long service she was left to her own thoughts, then when her husband had been crowned and installed on a throne to receive homage, she was required to rise and walk to the altar for her coronation by the Archbishop of Canterbury. As she moved forward to take part in the ancient rite she glanced at her daughters in the royal box behind the Chair of Estate in which she had been sitting. When she had been anointed and crowned and had received the sceptre and the ivory rod on which is perched an enamelled dove, she took her place on the throne to the left of her husband's and with him received Holy Communion.

The services over, the King and Queen partook of a light lunch in the canons' room at the Abbey then donned their crowns and re-entered their coach for the long drive back to the Palace. From the Abbey the cavalcade entered Parliament Square then made its way slowly along Victoria Embankment, up Northumberland Avenue to Trafalgar Square and via Pall Mall to St James's Street, turning right into Piccadilly, north into Regent Street and on in a huge semi-circle up Oxford Street to Marble Arch, Park Lane, Hyde Park Corner, and at length through the Palace gates. The last part of the drive, from Hyde Park Corner, took place under the lenses of television cameras making the first ever outside broadcast. It was pouring with rain, but the enthusiasm of the vast crowds could not be dampened and the Royal Family were called to the balcony of the Palace five times. When it was all over the new Queen was so exhausted and so overcome with a feeling of relief that she retired to bed. The strain on her nerves had been so great that it caused her to lose her voice for several hours.

But a short rest was all the King and Queen were allowed. The day after the Coronation they made a triumphal progress in an open carriage through the streets of London. Seven days later they reviewed the Fleet at Spithead and on 24 May they attended a service of thanksgiving at St Paul's Cathedral to mark Empire Day. In June there was a vast review of ex-servicemen at Hyde Park. In royal terms nothing seemed to have changed, in spite of the fact that the throne had had three different occupants within twelve months. Indeed the Abdication, which in a more hot-blooded nation might have provoked revolution or civil war, had merely served to confirm Britain in the short-sighted complacency which characterized the country in the latter part of the 1930s. 'The King's Matter' was reduced in the public mind to the level of low melodrama, with Stanley Baldwin playing the hero, standing up for the good and the right, and Wallis Simpson cast as the villain, the 'scheming woman' who seduced from the path of righteousness the weak-willed and morally uncertain King.

This, as we have seen, was by no means the true picture, but it was the one that satisfied the national conscience and as a result Baldwin retired, a few weeks after the Coronation, with his prestige as high as it had ever been and the gratitude of his country expressed in the form of an earldom.[5] At the same time Winston Churchill, the man who was to tower above every Prime Minister this century, save perhaps one,* had been pushed by the Abdication crisis firmly onto the political sidelines. He had tried through his counsel to keep Edward VIII on the throne. He had been humiliated in the House of Commons when he had pleaded for a relaxation of the pressure that was relentlessly forcing the King's departure. But he had seriously misjudged the mood of the public. The boldness, imagination and the emotional charge Churchill was to bring to his wartime leadership had no appeal to the smug believers in home, hearth and 'peace for our time'.† So Churchill remained fretting on the back benches while the National Government, now in the care of Neville Chamberlain,[6] continued on its uninspired way. It was almost as if King Edward VIII had never existed.

But David did exist, and he was still a source of anxiety to the Royal Family. He and Wallis were married at the Chateau de Candé, near Tours, on 3 June 1937.[7] The marriage ceremony was performed by the Reverend J. A. Jardine, an obscure Anglican clergyman from Darlington, County Durham, who for reasons of his own was prepared to break the rule of his Church.[8] But on the day before the wedding David had received a blow that was

*The exception being Lloyd George.
†Neville Chamberlain's phrase describing the infamous Munich agreement with Hitler in 1938.

to hurt him for the rest of his life. It was a letter from George VI confirming that David would have the title of His Royal Highness the Duke of Windsor – but adding that Wallis would not be known as Her Royal Highness and that no such dignity would be accorded to any children of the marriage. Bertie said he had been forced to take this action and he hoped his brother would not see it as an insult to his bride, but of course that was just how David did see it. At one point he was determined to take legal action in support of Wallis's claim to the title (and indeed the legality of depriving her of the same status as her husband has always been in doubt), but he was advised against this course of action. The story arose that the King had taken his decision under pressure from the Governments of the Dominions, but there is little doubt that he took the lead himself in a situation which baffled the politicians.

As the King pointed out to the Lord Chancellor's office, creating David His Royal Highness the Duke of Windsor would prevent difficulties in the future: a royal duke cannot be elected to the House of Commons and neither can he speak or vote in a debate in the House of Lords. Bertie had not forgotten that at the time of the Abdication there had been much talk among sections of the Press of forming a 'King's Party' to support David and therefore to split the country. As far as Wallis was concerned, the King told Baldwin that if she were given the title of Her Royal Highness it could never be taken away from her, and the Royal Family was by no means certain that her marriage to David would last, bearing in mind her previous marital record. If, as a royal duchess, she were divorced from David and decided to return to England she would still have to be treated as a royal duchess. If David were to divorce Wallis and marry again he would create yet another royal duchess. The title of Her Royal Highness could become meaningless and the monarchy could be made a laughing-stock. So David had to be content with the courtesy title of 'Her Grace the Duchess of Windsor' for his wife.

No doubt the King's decision on the status of the new Duchess of Windsor was influenced by certain personal considerations, too. David nursed the hope that when the fuss caused by his abdication had died down he and Wallis would be able to return to Britain and take some place in royal life, albeit on the fringes. But he underestimated the antipathy which Wallis had aroused in the Royal Family, particularly among the women and specifically Queen Elizabeth and Queen Mary. Elizabeth had disliked Mrs Simpson from the start and had resented the way in which David's obsession with her and her friends had placed a barrier between himself and Bertie. As for Queen Mary, on 3 June she noted in her diary, 'Alas! the wedding day . . .'

In his desire to live in Britain again, David also paid too little regard to the bitter disappointment in him felt by the British people. There were many ordinary homes in which the name of the Duke of Windsor could not be mentioned for years afterwards. And if he really did want to return home, the Duke set about achieving this aim in a very strange way. Within a few months of their marriage he and Wallis were being welcomed to Adolf Hitler's Germany by Dr Robert Ley, who was succinctly described by the veteran American radio correspondent William L. Shirer as 'one of the real Nazi ruffians'.[9] The Duke, Shirer concluded, had been badly advised in making the trip. That was putting it mildly. The Windsors took tea with Hermann Goering and his wife, met Himmler, Goebbels and Hess, and were received by Hitler himself at Berchtesgaden. This apparent endorsement of the Nazi régime by a member of the British royal house, even one in exile, caused an outcry in the world's Press, and it was so vociferous in the United States that the Duke was obliged to postpone a planned visit there. It was no wonder that Bertie and Elizabeth, the two people most affected by David's abdication, were deeply worried in case he might try to re-establish himself in Britain.

Whatever the inner anxieties, however, the King and Queen behaved outwardly as they were expected to. At the beginning of July 1937 they made a state visit to Scotland and, since it was the first time for more than three hundred years that a Scottish Queen had entered Edinburgh, the Scots were beside themselves with joy. One eighty-four-year-old Highlander brought a smile to Elizabeth's face when he told her: 'You're a bonnie lassie. I wish I'd courted you myself.' During the visit the King invested Elizabeth with the Order of the Thistle in St Giles' Cathedral, and she received an honorary Doctor of Laws degree at Edinburgh University.

After Scotland came the turn of Northern Ireland, though the visit brought threats of violence from the rabidly republican Sinn Fein movement. Foreign newspapers received reports of a possible attempt to assassinate the King and Queen, but in the event the only outrages committed during the tour were the burning of a Customs post, the blowing up of some railway wagons and the explosion of a land mine in Belfast. Much to the delight of the Ulstermen the King made a speech at the Belfast Council Chamber. There had been rumours that his stammer had returned as a result of nervous strain caused by the Abdication, but Bertie spoke without faltering and when he had finished he turned in triumph to Elizabeth, who smiled her pride and encouragement to him.

August and September were holiday months at Balmoral, and the King and Queen certainly needed them. Apart from the press of royal duties there was a whole new routine for them to become accustomed to, and one of its main drawbacks was that they had to spend much more time apart than they had been used to. All that remained of their previous life were the family weekends at The Royal Lodge. The King had to spend many hours at his desk going through the papers in the despatch boxes that were brought to him every day. Though the actual role of the queen consort under the British constitution has never been entirely clear, Elizabeth had her own paperwork to do – considering and replying to invitations, dealing with correspondence from the various organizations of which she was patron or president, matters relating to the regiments of which she was colonel-in-chief, and so on – and at the same time her husband consulted her on many matters requiring a royal decision. No one knew the extent of Elizabeth's influence on the King's handling of affairs of state: that influence was always discreet, never overt, and never used on behalf of anyone who wished to steer the King in a particular direction. Any attempt to approach the King through the Queen was invariably rebuffed with the suggestion that the King should be consulted directly. Queen Elizabeth did not fit the image of the conventional 'woman behind the throne'. Her support of the King was important, some say crucial, but it was emotional, not in any sense political.

What Elizabeth found hard to accept when she became Queen was the fact that she could no longer lunch with her friends at the Ritz or Claridges, or go dancing with her husband at the Four Hundred Club, or spend a quiet weekend at some country house – everywhere she and Bertie went they were followed by a considerable retinue, not to mention the detectives who shadowed and guarded them. There were also problems for Elizabeth the mother. She and Bertie had been able to deal with the daunting change in their circumstances, but there was its effect on the children to be considered. Princess Elizabeth, aged eleven at the time of the Coronation, had to get used to the fact that she would be queen one day and had to be trained for the awesome responsibilities that would entail. Princess Margaret, who celebrated her seventh birthday in 1937, had to learn that her big sister had, through no effort or achievement of her own, attained a position to which the younger girl could never aspire. And for both the children there was the shock of moving from the cosy, informal home in Piccadilly to the forbidding pile of Buckingham Palace.

The Queen determined that life at the Palace should be organized so that the chilly, cheerless mausoleum should be as much like a home as possible. There were difficulties. For one thing the Palace, when the new Royal Family moved into it in February 1937, was overrun by mice and furnished with worn relics of Queen Victoria's reign. The place had recently acquired electricity, but this was more of a bane than a blessing since, for example, the lighting was of the most basic kind, often with only a single bulb to illuminate a vast room and the light switch somewhere in the long corridor outside. To the young Princesses, cut off from friends and from almost all the usual pleasures of childhood, the Palace seemed at first more like a prison than their new home. But the Queen never lost sight of the fact that, in spite of their sudden elevation, they were still the same people with the same needs and accordingly she ran Buckingham Palace on much the same lines as she had arranged life at 145 Piccadilly, personally supervising everything from the menus to the sort of flowers that were placed in the rooms of guests. And however much she and the King had to do, Elizabeth retained the tradition of the early-morning romp with the children, though it now had a strict time-limit, and she ensured that for certain fixed periods each day the Princesses could be with their parents.

Changes had to be made in the pattern of Princess Elizabeth's education to fit her for the throne she was to occupy. She was already doing well in French and German, helped by her parents, and to these subjects were added Latin, economics and, later on, detailed instruction on the British constitution. Queen Mary gave her grand-daughter lessons in deportment to refine the Princess's exceptional natural grace of movement, and tuition in music and dancing continued. On top of all that, Elizabeth found she still had plenty of time for her favourite occupation, horse-riding. Both Princesses became attached to the Buckingham Palace company of the Girl Guides and, while the Palace was not exactly homely, there was at least the magnificent garden to explore, which was particularly interesting for Elizabeth because of its astonishing range of wildlife. And when the doors of the Palace closed on the royal events of the day the opportunity remained for a little family fun, charades, parlour games, and sing-songs round the piano such as the Queen remembered from her own childhood. The Strathmore family, too, had their part to play, providing holidays at Glamis and St Paul's Walden Bury that kept Elizabeth and Margaret in touch with the world outside the confines of the Court.

Thus the crowded year of 1937 neared its end. In the autumn the King and Queen toured the industrial districts of Yorkshire and this was followed by the State Opening of Parliament, which caused Bertie a great deal of worry because of the speech he had to make from the throne. (He managed it very well, though with some hesitation owing to his difficulties in following Lionel Logue's breathing exercises while sitting down.) In November there was a state visit by the King of the Belgians and the following month a royal visit to Cornwall. The Queen became colonel-in-chief of both The Queen's Bays and The Black Watch, and received the honorary degree of Doctor of Literature from the University of London. The Public Orator of the University, Professor Harold Butler, said the degree was a tribute to 'one who fills so nobly the high place to which it has pleased Providence to call her. Scotland has given many good gifts to England, but none so valued as that daughter who is now our Queen.'

There were some light-hearted moments, too, like a game of darts at a social centre during a visit to Slough, when in three throws Elizabeth scored two more points than Bertie – 'I think this is a very good game,' she said. And at St Paul's Walden Bury, which had become the home of Elizabeth's brother David and his family, the Queen was upstaged by a child. She had unveiled a plaque commemorating her birth, baptism and coronation at a ceremony in the village church where she had been baptized and afterwards she planted two oak trees in the grounds of the manor house. The little son of David Bowes-Lyon felt that his regal aunt had not planted the first tree properly and he solemnly set about shovelling more earth round its roots, much to the amusement of the Queen.

The year closed for the Royal Family in the traditional manner with Christmas at Sandringham, a season considerably merrier than the previous one had been in the aftermath of the Abdication. The reluctant King and Queen had come through the first twelve months of their reign with heads held high and the monarchy was as stable as it had ever been in spite of the severe shock to the system delivered by Edward VIII. The mood of the nation as a whole was calm, confident, even self-satisfied. The worst years of the Depression were over – though there remained pockets of high unemployment in the older industrial centres like the North-East, Scotland and South Wales, where a man was still expected to keep his family on handouts of about five shillings a week – and the slow climb to prosperity seemed to be well under way. The class war which had seemed to be breaking out in 1926 had not materialized and nothing seemed to conflict with the view of Lord Beaverbrook and his *Daily Express* that the rich and the poor were exactly the same except that the rich had more money. The Government of Neville Chamberlain was dull, plodding and certainly not objectionable and while behind the scenes in Parliament there were furious arguments about whether Britain was in danger from the vulgar dictators on the European mainland, the great mass of people felt that what was happening across the English Channel was no concern of theirs. Material improvement and the middle-class values of godliness, cleanliness and general respectability were of far more importance to the blinkered British. Yet these very attitudes contributed in no small measure to the success of Bertie and Elizabeth in their first year as King and Queen, for the family in Buckingham Palace were accepted as the best possible symbols of the conventional morality.

Acceptance alone, however, does not ensure the survival of a monarchy. There also has to be respect, loyalty and love, and it was in promoting these feelings that Queen Elizabeth was so valuable. She had the task of establishing the popular style of the new reign, while the King was kept busy by the opposing political forces of the 'rearmers' and 'appeasers', the one group keen to show military muscle in the face of threats from Hitler and Mussolini and the other ready to compromise in the hope of avoiding war. Elizabeth set about bringing the Crown to the people with the same lack of formality and lively interest which had become her trademarks as Duchess of York. The nation was delighted to discover that though she was more removed from ordinary folk in rank she remained as close to them in common humanity as she had ever been.

In February 1938 she visited a new community housing project in Westminster, where she chatted with the tenants about their homes, their hopes and their difficulties. Afterwards she wrote to the city council asking that she be kept informed year by year of the council's progress in housing poor people. At a handicrafts exhibition in London organized by the National Federation of Women's Institutes she showed sympathy and understanding to the wife of an unemployed Durham miner – 'I hope things will be much better presently,' she told the woman. In May she went to Norwich to open newly restored cloisters at the cathedral and to unveil statues of the King and herself in their coronation robes. This was serious business, but in the midst of all the ceremonial she took time off to ask for the recipe of the home-made mead with which the toasts were drunk at luncheon with the bishop and civic dignitaries. It was little touches like these which gave people, women in particular, the impression that underneath the grandeur of her royalty Elizabeth was a wife and mother like any other, interested in home and hearth. In a sense she was already becoming the 'Queen Mum'. Certainly her interest in domestic problems, and especially the difficulties caused to families by unemployment, was real enough. In 1938 the King opened an Empire Exhibition in Glasgow and Elizabeth gave the commissioner for the so-called 'Special Areas' of high unemployment in Scotland £40 to enable eighty unemployed men, each with one relative, to visit the exhibition.

It was not only home and hearth, though, that bound Queen Elizabeth so closely to her people. As well as all its other duties and responsibilities the Crown is expected to make a contribution to the cultural life of the nation, and the Queen was not found lacking in this department by the élite minority who cared about such things. (Art, music and literature had very little to do with the lives most people led in the thirties. It must be remembered, for example, that despite the growth of mass education and literacy, there were during that decade never more than about thirty thousand undergraduates in British universities, out of a total population of some forty-five million: higher education was still mainly for the privileged and the wealthy.) In March 1938 the art world greeted with delight bordering on ecstasy Elizabeth's purchase of two paintings by living British artists – 'Chepstow', an impressionistic landscape by Wilson Steer, RA,[10] amd Augustus John's portrait of George Bernard

Shaw.[11] *The Times*, that fearless arbiter of elevated taste, gurgled gleefully:

> Even among those with a genuine taste for painting, the number with the courage of their purely artistic preferences, irrespective of fashion subject, is limited. The majority want a lead. It has been given from a quarter above the social uncertainties and complications upon which a reputation for artistic judgment usually depends. The Queen has decided that contemporary British painting matters – irrespective of subject represented or fashionable tendency in style; and it will be against all experience if, according to their means, the decision is not followed by many of her subjects – to the raising of the general level of taste, and to the practical advantage of good artists, who, less from insensibility to their merits than from uncertainty about the importance of art in life, are apt to be neglected.

That article is a prime example of the sort of rubbish which is written about the activities of the Royal Family even today, when an amorphous kind of 'equality', based apparently on mediocrity, is alleged to be the cure for social ills. The leader-writer of *The Times* was in danger of disappearing up his own pompous rhetoric. He refused to admit the possibility that the Queen may have bought the two pictures simply because she liked them, just as she later bought Beatrice M. Christy's wood engraving of White Lodge because it was a nice representation of the Yorks' first home after their marriage, and the editorial sage also failed to recognize that the decision 'contemporary British art matters' had been made not by the Queen, but by himself. All the Queen had done was to buy a couple of modern British paintings, but because of the peculiar reverence in which the Royal Family is held her purchase assumed the proportions of a significant artistic statement. Indeed if the effect of *The Times* leader was to send people rushing out to buy modern British paintings because the Queen had bought some, it would be unlikely to bolster up 'the courage of purely artistic convictions' but would rather show that the 'art lovers' possessed the sensibilities of a flock of sheep. The tendency to follow where others lead, which does not, of course, afflict only the art world, is a problem for royalty. It is accepted that a member of the Royal Family makes political statements at his or her peril, but it has to be borne in mind that an action which would be perfectly natural and harmless in an ordinary person requires a degree of caution on the part of a royal figure lest it lead to undesirable consequences, such as commercial exploitation.*

However, the state of contemporary British art had ceased to be of much importance, even to *The Times*, by the autumn of 1938. By that time Hitler had annexed Austria and was making territorial demands on Czechoslovakia, and Neville Chamberlain, the Prime Minister, who was committed to a policy of appeasement, decided to go to Munich for a meeting with Hitler. On the very day that Chamberlain was telling his countrymen over the wireless that Britain would not go to war for the sake of 'a quarrel in a far-away country between people of whom we know nothing' – noble sentiments, indeed – Queen Elizabeth was delivering a message of hope from the King to a quarter of a million people assembled on Clydeside to watch the Queen launch the ocean liner named after her. 'This ceremony to which many thousands have looked forward so eagerly, must now take place in circumstances far different from those for which they had hoped,' she said, in the curiously stilted, though correct, grammar of royal speeches. But she added that the King 'bids the people of this country to be of good cheer, in spite of the dark clouds hanging over them, and, indeed, over the whole world'.

On 29 September, two days after the launching, the Queen was boarding a train to London at Ballater station when someone mentioned the grave international situation. Elizabeth said the latest news had greatly heartened her: 'We will all hope that it will lead to a peaceful settlement.' The King had told her that Chamberlain, who had flown to Germany that same day, was confident of reaching an agreement with Hitler. On the 30th the Prime Minister stepped from the aircraft which had brought him

---

*One notable example of this occurred in 1967 when property values in Malta suddenly soared because of a false rumour, cleverly exploited by speculators, that the Queen Mother was having a house built at Madliena.

home, waved a piece of paper in the air and shouted: 'I've got it!' He had made a pact with Hitler which proved to be the death warrant of free Czechoslovakia, and he himself had been the author of the words written on the paper he displayed so enthusiastically:

> We regard the agreement signed last night and the Anglo-German naval agreement as symbolic of the desire of our two peoples never to go to war with one another again. We are resolved that the method of consultation shall be the method adopted to deal with any other questions that may concern our two countries.

One wonders what was in Adolf Hitler's mind when he signed his name underneath those words.

Though the King, his service chiefs and a large number of politicians were by no means convinced that the Munich Agreement had finally averted a European war, it was with a sense of some relief that the Royal Family went to Sandringham to celebrate Christmas 1938. Bertie and Elizabeth could look back on a second satisfying year in their reign, of which the highlight had been their state visit to Paris in July. Elizabeth had dazzled the fashion-conscious Parisians with a series of stunning white gowns designed by Norman Hartnell – 'the best dressed Queen' and 'a portrait by Winterhalter' had been among the approving comments in the home of *haute couture*. There was, however, a sad irony about the success of Elizabeth's white ensembles: they were a mark of mourning for her mother.

Lady Strathmore died at her home in Bruton Street on 23 June 1938. She was seventy-five years old.[12] The royal visit to Paris was postponed for three weeks and during that period the wardrobe of thirty or more dresses required for the various events the Queen would attend in the French capital had to be suitably adapted for mourning. Elizabeth decided that of the three permissible colours – black, purple and white – the latter would be the most appropriate. Elizabeth owed a great deal to her mother. As the obituary notice for Lady Strathmore said, she had 'great fascination and charm . . . an enchanting laugh . . . great cour-

age . . . a power of endurance which never allowed her to give in
. . . great wisdom'. Such were the qualities she had passed on to
her daughter, and they were to prove invaluable to both the
Queen and the country when the time came for the concept of
'peace for our time' to be shown up as the sham that it was.

5

The Palace at War

In June 1939, as Europe was slipping inexorably towards the abyss of war, the people of New York were fascinated to read in their newspapers that the Queen of England was a second cousin six times removed of George Washington. The Portcullis Pursuivant of the Royal College of Arms in London had prepared a genealogical table linking the Queen to the First President through an obscure gentleman by the name of Colonel Augustine Warner, who had arrived in England's American colonies in 1628. Warner's daughter, the table showed, was the grandmother of George Washington, and the colonel's granddaughter by his second daughter was among the ancestors of the thirteenth Earl of Strathmore, grandfather of Elizabeth Bowes-Lyon. This information was particularly welcome to Americans because as they read it Queen Elizabeth was taking the United States by storm.

Bertie and Elizabeth set off for their tour of Canada and the United States from Southampton on 6 May, aboard the liner *Empress of Australia*. (They had intended to travel in the battleship *Repulse*, but the King had decided that in view of the ominous signs of war the battleship should remain with the Fleet.) The voyage across the Atlantic was not without interest, for on the fifth day out of port the *Empress* encountered dense fog and icebergs which for three days kept its speed down to as little as five knots, when the engines were not stopped altogether. Elizabeth told Queen Mary in a letter that during those three days the ship had moved only a few miles, its foghorn bellowing, and it had not been forgotten on board that twenty-seven years before, in much the same location and at about the same time of year, the *Titanic* had struck an iceberg and sunk with the loss of twelve hundred lives. The King added that the situation was not ideal, but at least he got some peace!

The invitation to visit Canada from the Prime Minister, W. L. Mackenzie King, had mentioned only Ottawa, the capital, but the King determined to visit every province of the Dominion, which increased the numbers of people who could see Their Majesties but limited the number of functions in any one place which the royal visitors could attend. Canadians had been deeply attached to Queen Victoria (indeed they still celebrate her birthday as a national holiday) and to Edward VIII, who, as Prince of Wales, had bought a ranch in Alberta: no one could forecast how the people would react to George VI and Queen Elizabeth, particularly in the French-speaking regions of the country. In the event, the crowds who turned out to greet the royal couple were larger than they had seen anywhere else in their travels.

During their visit Bertie and Elizabeth journeyed almost four and a half thousand miles, mostly by train and with frequent stops to gaze at the magnificence of the Canadian Rockies and watch the abundant wildlife of the wilderness. As she had done in Australia and New Zealand during her tour as Duchess of York, the Queen went out of her way to have personal chats with members of the crowds, particularly the children. The Governor-General of Canada, Lord Tweedsmuir (better known, no doubt, as John Buchan, the novelist), wrote that Elizabeth had a talent for attracting the right kind of publicity. She spent ten minutes talking to a group of Scottish stonemasons at the laying of a foundation stone, while the seventy thousand people watching the ceremony wondered what on earth was going on;

133

at another event she disappeared into a crowd of ten thousand ex-servicemen, much to the dismay of the men detailed to guard her. The Canadians loved it, and even the French-speakers were won over when the Queen made a speech partly in English and partly in French. Canada has always suffered from a sort of inferiority complex with regard to its huge North American neighbour, but having a King and Queen they could call their own gave the people a sense of being one-up on the United States, which could muster only an elected president.

But if the tour of Canada was a splendid success, the royal progress through the United States was, in the words of one American newspaper, 'a triumph'. To some extent the United States had disowned Europe after the Wall Street crash of 1929. There was a powerful body of opinion which clung to the idea that America should not become involved with the troubles of the rest of the world, and there were certainly political differences between Washington and London over how to approach the European dictators. Thus the royal visit was something of a delicate manoeuvre. The American President, Franklin D. Roosevelt, was keen to display the historical and contemporary links between Britain and the United States to both his own people and the world, but he had to be careful not to give the impression that America was being pushed into the European cauldron.

An exceptionally shrewd statesman, Roosevelt knew that sooner or later the United States would have to join the inevitable war in Europe. He hoped that from his country's point of view the fighting would come later rather than sooner, so he regarded Britain as the free world's first line of defence against Hitler and Mussolini. But Roosevelt also knew that Britain would not be able to hold the line against the dictators without material help from the United States, and by inviting the King and Queen to visit his country he hoped to reinforce Anglo-American unity in an obvious and emotional way. It all depended upon how the American people – most of whom had never seen a king before, and wanted no truck with royalty anyway – would react.

As it happened, the Americans were fascinated and delighted by their royal visitors. The eight-year-old daughter of Harry Hopkins, Roosevelt's closest adviser who was to become well known to Britons during the Second World War, exclaimed, 'I've seen the Fairy Queen!' – and many adults agreed with her. One paper reported: 'The scene today was one of splendour, and the chief ornament of it was admitted to be the Queen. Her bright colouring and flawless complexion were dazzling, and her naturalness, gay animation and her smile made her a striking figure.' Another journal, more down to earth, said: 'The Queen is a beautiful woman, with a complexion that would knock them dead in Hollywood. Her smile, when she lets it go, as she does frequently, is best of all.' She even captivated a hard-headed Texan member of the House of Representatives, who told her: 'Cousin Elizabeth, you're a thousand times more pretty than your pictures.' What else could she reply but, 'Thank you, sir'?

The Roosevelts were no less entranced by Their Majesties when they visited the President's estate, Hyde Park (no connexion with the English one), overlooking the Hudson River in Dutchess County, New York State. That visit not only led to a firm friendship between one of America's best-loved presidents and one of Britain's best-loved kings, but it also led directly to a great deal of American help and support for beleaguered Britain during the early days of the war that was to follow so quickly.

When the King and Queen left the United States a newspaper commented: 'The King's tour was the Queen's triumph.' Elizabeth said that the 'wonderful tour has given us memories that the passage of time will never dim'. And as they sailed for home from a Canadian port on 15 June there were tears in their eyes, as well as in the eyes of many who watched them go.

Back in Britain the certainty of war had grown considerably, but throughout the summer of 1939 everyone pretended that it would not happen, while at the same time preparations went ahead in case it should. Prophetically, one of Elizabeth's first engagements after her return from America was to present new

Colours to The Queen's Bays and Dragoon Guards, of which she was colonel-in-chief. But the ceremony at Assaye Barracks in Tidworth, Wiltshire, turned out to be more of a family occasion than a military one.

The Queen spent a long time talking to the wives and children of the regiment, those of 'other ranks' as well as officers. Her eye fell upon Kenneth Gosley, at eleven weeks the youngest child 'on parade' – 'Is he a good baby?' she asked his mother. Thomas Sargent, the aptly-named son of one of the regiment's non-commissioned officers, happened to be a year old that day: 'Very many happy returns,' the Queen said. Beautifully dressed in a blue crepe suit and matching 'halo' hat, Elizabeth was accompanied by Regimental Sergeant-Major Dolby when she met the families on a lawn by the barracks guardhouse, and as she and her escort approached the expectant children the tension became too great for the RSM's sixteenth-month-old daughter, Dorothy, who rushed forward shouting 'Daddy! Daddy!' From the safety of her father's arms she watched her ten-year-old sister Evelyn present a bouquet of red and white carnations to the Queen. 'What a lovely family you have,' Elizabeth told the RSM. She could always be relied upon to make people feel important, even proud of themselves, and there was nothing forced or false about her interest. She was never allowed to forget that she was Queen, but at the same time she remembered that she was a woman first, and it was as a woman more than as a queen that she related to ordinary people.

Another event of that summer was, in time, to prove of enormous importance to both the Royal Family and the country. The King and Queen, with their daughters, visited Bertie's 'alma mater', Dartmouth College, among whose cadets at the time was Prince Philip of Greece, the cousin whom Princess Elizabeth would marry. A splendid romantic fiction has grown up that the couple's first meeting was during the visit to Dartmouth and that Princess Elizabeth fell in love at first sight. In fact Elizabeth and Philip had met on a number of previous occasions, such as the Coronation and the wedding of the Duke of Kent, who married Philip's aunt, Princess Marina of Greece, but the encounter at Dartmouth was important in the sense that the more Elizabeth saw Philip, the more she liked him.

As usual the family withdrew to Balmoral for the holiday, and Queen Elizabeth also visited her father at Glamis. While staying at her old home, Elizabeth decided to call on the families of another of her regiments, The Black Watch, who were staying at a special holiday centre in Broughty Ferry, near Dundee. The matron of the centre received a telephone call one morning informing her that the Queen would be dropping in later that day. It was a nice thought on Elizabeth's part, but one can imagine the feelings of the matron and the scenes inside that holiday home when it sank in that the Queen would be there within a few hours.

The summer holiday turned out to be a short one. On 23 August Nazi Germany signed a treaty with the Soviet Union. The following day the King returned to London from Balmoral, as Parliament passed an Emergency Powers Bill which effectively put the country on a war footing. On the 25th Britain signed a mutual assistance pact with Poland. Then, at 4.45 on the morning of 1 September, Hitler's stormtroopers smashed their way across the Polish frontier, and seventy-five minutes later German planes were bombing Warsaw. Poland appealed to Britain for help, and Neville Chamberlain sent a Note to Hitler ('not an ultimatum') demanding the withdrawal of Nazi troops from Polish soil. Hitler ignored this, and on 2 September ten Cabinet ministers insisted that Chamberlain should send an ultimatum to Berlin. At nine o'clock on the morning of Sunday 3 September 1939 the British Government's ultimatum was delivered to the German Foreign Ministry – and two hours later Great Britain (as well as India and the colonies) was at war with Germany for the second time in two decades. Australia and New Zealand followed immediately with their declarations of war; the Canadian Government waited for the Ottawa Parliament to ratify its decision and entered the war on 10 September, four days after South Africa, which had rejected the neutralist approach of its Prime Minister.[1]

On 12 September the problem that faced Bertie and Elizabeth

was one rather closer to home then the Second World War was at that stage: the Duke and Duchess of Windsor arrived at Portsmouth aboard the destroyer HMS *Kelly*. David had been waiting for an opportunity to serve his country and had dashed home to see what he could do for the war effort. But if he expected to be met as the returning prodigal he was disappointed. His old ally, Winston Churchill, who had been appointed First Lord of the Admiralty in Chamberlain's War Cabinet, had sent the *Kelly*, commanded by Lord Louis Mountbatten,[2] to fetch the ex-King, and he had also ensured that a reception party was waiting for the Windsors – a guard of honour, the band of the Royal Marines, and a red carpet. No member of the Royal Family was at the quayside, however, and Bertie had declined even to send a car for his brother.

The Windsors stayed at Hartfield House, the Sussex home of David's friend 'Fruity' Metcalfe, while the King and the Government tried to decide what to do with the Duke. On a personal level, the return of the Windsors was completely ignored by the Royal Family, though David did have a meeting with Bertie at Buckingham Palace (Wallis having been tactfully left behind in Sussex). The talk was friendly and there were no recriminations – indeed David seemed to have forgotten all about the events of December 1936. Bertie told his brother that he could have the choice of being attached either as a civilian to the staff of the Regional Commissioner for Civil Defence for Wales, or as a temporary major-general to the British Military Mission in Paris, which was headed by General 'Wombat' Howard-Vyse. David decided he would prefer the civil defence job. The King, however, later had second thoughts – no doubt bearing in mind the feelings of Elizabeth and Queen Mary if 'that woman' remained in Britain – and sent his brother to Paris. Before the end of September, the Windsors were on their way into exile again.

There now began the period of strange calm known as 'the phoney war', when the feared attacks by the Germans failed to materialize. The winged conquerors of Warsaw were expected daily over London, and the Queen, who had rushed back to the capital from Balmoral immediately after the declaration of war, found herself engaged on royal duties she could never have imagined. She inspected the headquarters of the Women's Voluntary Service for Civil Defence, where she was impressed by the 'amazing spirit and atmosphere', and she was pleased to see that the volunteers were coping 'calmly and cheerfully' with the difficulties of organizing, among other things, the mass evacuation of children from the high-risk urban areas into the countryside. Elizabeth also found herself carrying an extra piece of essential royal equipment – a gas mask. At first she had her mask in the regulation-issue khaki satchel suspended on white webbing from her shoulder, but later on she used a combined handbag and mask-holder, and on one occasion she had the gas mask case made up in purple velveteen to match her coat. Women all over the country were using their gas mask satchels, which were rather neat if not pretty, as handbags.

Elizabeth was well aware that women had an important part to play in the war effort and she naturally felt that she had to give a lead. On 13 September 1939 she sent a personal message to the women workers of the Red Cross and St John of Jerusalem War Organization:

> I have heard from many quarters of the splendid work that is being done by those who are voluntarily giving their services . . . both at home and abroad. The example that they are setting is a real inspiration and encouragement to all of us in these days, which, dark and sad though they be, are brightened by the abundant evidence of the willing response that our countrywomen are making to every call upon their services. As yet our task has only just begun; sacrifices and hardships must inevitably lie ahead of us and much exacting work. Yet the spirit with which our troubles are being faced is such that we need feel no anxiety for the future. To all who are contributing in every sphere and grade of voluntary work to the maintenance of that spirit, I send my best wishes and my heartfelt gratitude. I pray that God may have you in his keeping.

She became Commander-in-Chief of the Woman's Royal Naval Service (Wrens), the Auxiliary Territorial Service (ATS) and the Women's Auxiliary Air Force (Waafs). And she organized and helped her staff at Buckingham Palace to make bandages for the Central Hospital Supplies Service. She told members of the women's section of the British Legion that 'your resolve must have a heartening and encouraging effect upon your menfolk, wherever they may be'.

One of her main concerns was the level of facilities provided for mothers and children evacuated from the areas of large population. Once, on a visit to a reception area for evacuees at Horsted Keynes, near Haywards Heath in Sussex, she came upon a group of little girls playing and went over to one four-year-old who was washing her doll. 'Don't forget to wash behind its ears,' the Queen said. Shortly before Christmas she ate lunch with more than 250 children evacuated to Chichester from South London. Sitting at a long trestle table with a white painted top, she ate meat and vegetable stew followed by jam tarts and with water to drink in green mugs. The meals were prepared by the Women's Voluntary Service at a cost of three-pence per child, which was paid by the families with whom the youngsters were billetted. So impressed was the Queen with the support given to the evacuation programme that in May 1940, when the war had begun in earnest, she sent a personal message to about 350,000 homes in the United Kingdom which had welcomed evacuees. The message, printed on a card eleven inches by seven inches and with the Queen's Arms at the top, read:

I wish to mark by this personal message my appreciation of the service you have rendered to your country in 1939. In the early days of the war you opened your door to strangers who were in need of shelter & offered to share your home with them. I know that in this unselfish task you have sacrificed much of your own comfort, & that it could not have been achieved without the loyal co-operation of all in your household. By your sympathy you have earned the gratitude of those to whom you have shown hospitality, & by your readiness to serve you have helped the State in a work of great value.

There are homes up and down the country where that message, framed and preserved under glass, can still be found today. In 1943 the Queen sent a similar message to families in the Dominions who had fostered British children.

Armistice Day in 1939 seemed to be of particular, if ironic, significance, and the Queen chose the moment to broadcast on the wireless to the women of the Empire:

> I know that you would wish me to voice, in the name of the women of the British Empire, our deep and abiding sympathy with those on whom the first cruel blows have fallen – the women of Poland. Nor do we forget the gallant womanhood of France, who are called on to share with us again the hardships and horrors of war.
>
> War has at all times called for the fortitude of women . . . Their lot was all the harder because they felt that they could do so little beyond heartening, through their own courage and devotion, the men at the front. Now this is all changed, for we no less than men have real and vital work to do. To us also is given the proud privilege of serving our country in her hour of need . . . I know that it is not so difficult to do the big things . . . But these things are not for every woman. It is the thousand and one worries and irritations in carrying on wartime life in ordinary homes which are often so hard to bear.
>
> Many of you have had to see your family life broken up – your husband going off to his allotted task, your children evacuated to places of greater safety. The King and I know what it means to be parted from our children, and we can sympathize with those of you who have bravely consented to this separation for the sake of your little ones . . .

The Dominions had been keen that Princess Elizabeth and Princess Margaret should be sent abroad out of harm's way – Canada was one place suggested. But the Queen would not hear of it. 'The Princesses could never leave without me,' she said, 'and I could not leave without the King – and, of course, the King will never leave.' So the girls were sent to Windsor Castle, which, for the duration of the war, returned to its original function as a fortress.

After the Queen's Armistice Day broadcast, the letters page of *The Times* carried the following tribute: 'The Empire has a new and great asset in a Queen who can broadcast as well as ours can. I have never listened to a broadcast more technically perfect or more moving in its eloquence and its substance . . .' The broadcast also showed the Queen in a new role. Previously she had been a sort of royal ornament, supporting and complementing the position of the King. Now she had a part to play which was peculiarly her own: while the King acted as the standard-bearer for the armed forces, Queen Elizabeth was called upon to inspire and to lead on the home front through whatever horrors were to come. She proved to be particularly well fitted for the task.

'The phoney war' continued through the long, bitter winter of 1939–40, the weather making everyone miserable and the continued lack of activity serving to increase tension. The Royal Family spent Christmas at Sandringham as usual but it was an anxious time and a sad one since once the holiday ended the great, beautiful house was closed up and remained so until the end of the war. Spring came, and so did Adolf Hitler. On 9 April 1940 the Wehrmacht invaded Denmark and Norway. Within three months the Netherlands, Belgium and France had also fallen to the Germans and the crowned heads of Norway and the Netherlands, as well as King Zog and Queen Geraldine of Albania – who had fled from the Italian armies – were refugees in London. (The King of the Belgians and King Christian of Denmark had decided to remain with their peoples under the Nazi occupation.) Nearly 300,000 British soldiers, virtually the entire army sent to defend western Europe, had been rescued from the beaches of Dunkirk, along with 139,000 French troops. It seemed certain that Hitler, having trampled Europe underfoot, would not stop until he had conquered Britain, and fears of an invasion grew daily.

Everyone waited to hear the code-word 'Cromwell' – it meant 'invasion imminent'. Bertie and Elizabeth travelled in an armour-plated car and carried steel helmets and gas masks wherever they went. The King was always armed with a sten gun, while the Queen was never far away from a pistol or a rifle. The two Princesses became virtual prisoners at Windsor, for fear of an attempt to kidnap them by German paratroops. Plans were made for the speedy evacuation of all members of the Royal Family from London if the Germans landed on British soil, though the King was ready to offer his services to whatever resistance organization might be formed and, in the words of his new Prime Minister, Winston Churchill,[3] to go down 'fighting amid the ruins of Whitehall'. As Bertie told his people in a wireless broadcast on 24 May:

> The decisive struggle is now upon us . . . it is no mere territorial conquest that our enemies are seeking. It is the overthrow, complete and final, of this Empire and of everything for which it stands, and after that the conquest of the world. And if their will prevails they will bring to its accomplishment all the hatred and cruelty which they have already displayed . . .

He ended with the words that became so famous: 'Let us go forward . . . as one man, a smile on our lips, and our heads held high, and with God's help we shall not fail.'

With the fall of France in June, the problem of what to do with the Duke of Windsor appeared again, though this time in a more urgent form. David and Wallis had fled from France to Spain and had then moved on to Portugal. Reports reached the British Government that the Germans planned to try to persuade or force the Duke to return to Spain for the time being and to install him as a puppet King of England after a successful invasion. Clearly David had to be got out of Europe, but the prospect of his returning to stay in Britain with Wallis still could not be countenanced. In the circumstances it might have been possible to forgive the Duke for 'letting the side down', but there was a real fear in Elizabeth's mind that if David established himself at home once more his charisma and natural talents as a populist might undermine Bertie's confidence and destroy the effects of all his hard work since the Abdication. As for Wallis, it was to be many years before she was deemed to be acceptable in royal circles.

The British Government had to act quickly, however, before the Nazis got their hands on the ex-King, so Winston Churchill offered David the post of Governor of the Bahamas. The Duke accepted, without relish, and Wallis came to the conclusion that the Royal Family would go to almost any lengths to keep the Windsors out of Britain. On 1 August 1940 David and Wallis sailed for Nassau, where they were to spend nearly five years, chafing at a role which they considered to be beneath them and nursing their resentment at what they regarded as shabby treatment by the British Establishment.

As the Windsors sailed away from the war, the brilliant summer skies over the south and east coasts of England became the scene of the grim duel which has gone down in history as the Battle of Britain. The Nazis' aim was to sweep away the Royal Air Force and to bomb the British into submission. On 6 September three hundred German bombers escorted by six hundred fighter aircraft appeared over London to announce the beginning of the Blitz. Three days later a bomb fell on Buckingham Palace, but did not explode – at least not until 1.30 on the morning of 10 September, for it had a delayed-action fuse. The blast shattered all the windows on every floor at the north side of the Palace, but there was no other damage and no one was hurt. Because the air raids were so severe at night, the King and Queen had taken to sleeping at Windsor and driving to London in their bullet-proof car during the day. They toured the worst-hit areas of the East End, and Elizabeth arranged for beds, chairs, wardrobes and other furniture from Windsor – some of which had been in the possession of the Royal Family since the days of Queen Victoria – to be sent to East End families whose homes had been damaged.

On 13 September a bold Luftwaffe pilot, taking advantage of low rain clouds, flew his aircraft virtually undetected across London in broad daylight, swept up The Mall and dropped six bombs directly on Buckingham Palace. The King and Queen were with Alexander Hardinge in Bertie's upstairs sitting room overlooking the quadrangle. They heard the German aircraft and watched two bombs fall on the far side of the Palace and two more explode in the quadrangle, about thirty yards from their room. It was a narrow escape and they were very shocked, but until the end of the war no one knew how close Their Majesties had been to death. One of the bombs completely destroyed the Chapel, injuring three men working nearby, and one which fell in the Palace forecourt was seen to be of the delayed-action type,

The royal tour of South Africa, 1947. Peter Townsend is in the background,
next to the saluting officer.

The King and Queen with Queen Mary, Princess Elizabeth and the Duke of
Edinburgh on the balcony at the Palace after the Princess's wedding in 1947.

Royal Ascot, 1951: the Queen arrives with Princess Elizabeth in an open carriage.

Left. The King and Queen 'at home' on their silver wedding anniversary.

Mourning for a king: Queen Elizabeth II, Queen Mary and the Queen Mother awaiting the arrival of the body of King George VI at Westminster Hall for the lying-in-state, 11 February 1952.

Off duty: the Queen Mother with one of her favourite corgis at the Castle of Mey shortly after taking up residence there in 1956.

The Queen Mother wears a miner's helmet and white overall for her tour of a Rhodesian copper mine during her visit to Africa in 1957.

The Queen Mother visiting the *Ark Royal* at Devonport in July 1958. She is seen here arriving on the flight deck by helicopter – her favourite form of transport.

Prince Charles and Princess Anne join their grandmother to watch the meet of the West Norfolk Hunt at Hillington in January 1956.

Grandmother's day: the Queen Mother nurses the newly-born Prince Andrew in her garden at Clarence House, as Prince Charles and Princess Anne look on. The photograph was taken on the Queen Mother's sixtieth birthday.

Fishing on the Waikato River, near Auckland, during a tour of New Zealand in 1966.

so lunch was taken in an air raid shelter, lest the bomb should explode.

Immediately after the bombing of the Palace, the King and Queen toured the East End and felt a new bond with their people. Elizabeth uttered perhaps her best remembered words: 'I'm glad we've been bombed. It makes me feel I can look the East End in the face.' There had been a certain amount of resentment among those suffering most in the air raids that while they bore the brunt of the war their rulers did nothing but make fine speeches about courage and sacrifice and dispense sympathy. Those ugly feelings disappeared in the debris at Buckingham Palace. As Bertie and Elizabeth walked among the shattered homes after their own lucky escape, one man whose house had been destroyed called out tearfully, 'You're a good king, sir.'

The Queen had made a fine speech on the wireless, after the fall of France, encouraging Frenchwomen bravely to carry on the struggle against oppression. Now, as Britain felt the full, terrible weight of Nazi power, the Queen led by example as well as words. Much of her time was spent in visiting wounded soldiers, of whom she had gained a good deal of experience in that other, far-off war. Remembering those men she had cared for at Glamis, she told a librarian at a military hospital in Scotland: 'The soldiers sometimes like rather more interesting books than just detective stories and that sort of thing; they even like books on such subjects as astronomy.' As usual she was alive to needs which other people, through ignorance or prejudice, did not always notice. On another occasion, when some wounded Canadian troops wanted to take photographs of her, she thoughtfully went to stand by a window where the light would be better. She was always beautifully dressed, always sympathetic and cheerful, and always where she was needed most. In a special royal train of three carriages she accompanied the King on missions of comfort to Wales, the West Country, the North, wherever the bombing had taken its heaviest toll. She toured anti-anticraft batteries in remote areas, and usually inquired closely into the kind of recreational facilities provided for the men who manned the guns. She tramped round armaments factories and called at Civil Defence centres. A poem in tribute to her, written by a woman in Chicago, was published in the *Daily Colonist* of Victoria, British Columbia, and later appeared in English papers:

> Be it said to your renown
> That you wore your gayest gown,
> Your bravest smile, and stayed in town
> When London Bridge was falling down . . .

The German invasion of Britain never took place. The Royal Air Force was not swept from the skies. The Blitz, the worst of which was over by the spring of 1941, did not destroy the fighting spirit of the people, for 'This was their finest hour'. But if there was a sense of pride arising from the proof that Britishers were equal to anything Hitler could throw at them, it was soon followed by the realization that Britain was under siege and would remain so until she could actually take the offensive against Germany and its ally Italy (which had entered the war in June 1940).

Winston Churchill, who had become a virtual dictator, saw that there would be no peace unless total victory were achieved, and total victory meant total war, the channelling of all resources – human, mechanical and financial – into the single aim of beating the enemy. The position was equally clear to President Roosevelt of the United States, who was well aware that the resources Britain could muster were no match for those at the disposal of the Germans, with the whole of Europe under their domination. Roosevelt was in no position to render military assistance to Churchill, indeed he had constantly to reassure his people that American troops would not become involved in the war, but his adroit moulding of public opinion by inviting the King and Queen to the United States in 1939 had prepared the way for him to provide other forms of badly needed aid for besieged Britain.

The response of the United States was not entirely governmental, however. A vast 'Bundles for Britain' campaign appealed to the natural generosity of the American people, and they responded magnificently. When a huge selection of gifts from the United States was placed on display in London in February 1941 Queen Elizabeth confessed herself 'delighted and touched', and shortly after her birthday that year she made a special wireless broadcast to Americans:

> It is not our way in our dark days to turn for support to others, but even had we been minded so to do your instant help would have forestalled us. The warmth and sympathy of American generosity have touched beyond measure the hearts of all of us living and fighting in these islands. We can, and shall, never forget that in the hour of our greatest need you came forward with clothes for the homeless, food for the hungry, comfort for those who were sorely afflicted. Canteens, ambulances and medical supplies have come in an unceasing flow from the United States. I find it hard to tell you of our gratitude in adequate terms, though I ask you to believe that it is deep and sincere beyond expression.

At the same time, the Queen was at pains to point out that Britain was very far from despairing:

> Through these waiting months a heavy burden is being borne by our people. As I go among them I marvel at their unshakable constancy. In many cities their homes lie in ruins, as do many of those ancient buildings which you know and love hardly less than we do ourselves. Women and children have been killed, and even the sufferers in hospitals have not been spared; yet hardship has only steeled our hearts and strengthened our resolution. Wherever I go I see bright eyes and smiling faces, for though our road is stony and hard, it is straight, and we know that we fight in a great cause.

Elizabeth spoke particularly of the work the women of Britain were doing, with 'magnificent courage and amazing endurance': serving in the Armed Forces, toiling on the land, driving lorries and ambulances, cooking, ciphering, typing. She had a special word for the nurses, who 'in the black horror of a bombed hospital . . . never falter and, though often wounded, think always of their patients and never of themselves'.

It was a splendid broadcast, and it was received ecstatically in the United States, where cinema audiences would burst into a riot of applause when the Queen's picture appeared in newsreels. The *New York Sun* said the message was 'so happily phrased that it could not fail to stir an emotional response in all who heard it'. Much was made of the fact that Elizabeth had written the speech herself, consulting only her two secretaries. The *Sun* commented: 'This was just as well. This was women's business: it required no clumsy hand from the Cabinet to carry it forward. Her Majesty evidently needs no politician to tell her what, in such matters, is diplomatic. Her brief address was as tactful as it was gracious.' In London *The Times*, always keen to have the last word, added a footnote to the broadcast in its leader column:

> The true import of these phrases is that when the Queen speaks of and for the working women of Britain, she has every right to speak as herself one of them. Very little of her ceaseless activity gets into the newspapers. It is impossible to put into print the qualities of head and heart which give a vitalizing power to her public life. The Queen's 'job', like the King's, demands unrelaxing energy and sincerity . . . it would be well for the future of the world if our enemies could quickly realize . . . the genuine and indivisible unity which binds together the highest and the humblest in our land . . .

There is little doubt that the broadcast produced a far deeper response among Americans than did Churchill's meeting with Roosevelt during the same month, August 1941. When the United States was finally forced into battle the following December the seeds that flowered into the Grand Alliance had, on an emotional level at least, already been planted in American soil.

But Elizabeth was not about to leave it to others to provide aid and comfort for her embattled people. At the height of the Blitz she herself had provided money for the first of a series of convoys which became known as 'Queen's Messengers' and carried food and emergency supplies to badly bombed towns and cities, like Coventry and Plymouth. She gave the first eight lorries a personal send-off. 'The message which I would entrust to these convoys,' she said, 'will not be one of encouragement, for courage is never lacking in the people of this country. It will rather be one of true sympathy and loving kindness.'

The King and Queen knew precisely what their subjects were suffering: not only had they experienced bombing themselves but they also lived on the same meagre rations as the rest of the population – for instance, four ounces of butter per person per week; between one and two ounces of cheese; two ounces of tea; twelve ounces of sugar; two ounces of sweets; one egg per fortnight (children under the age of five and expectant mothers received more). Tinned food, cereals and condensed milk were rationed by an elaborate system of personal points, and the Ministry of Food was full of suggestions to help people to stretch their small allowance of meat, or preferably to do without meat altogether. As the country's 'chief housewife', Elizabeth was naturally interested in these culinary experiments, not all of which were successful, except in the sense that they made people laugh. At a Ministry of Food exhibition in May 1941 the Queen was asked by an American newspaper reporter whether she had ever eaten one of the Ministry's less felicitous meatless dishes, Woolton Pie,[4] an unpalatable concoction (described as 'dry and uneatable') of carrots, parsnips, turnips and potatoes covered with white sauce and pastry. 'Yes I have,' Elizabeth told the journalist, adding with a smile and just a touch of acid, 'Have you?'

First-hand experience of wartime life at the Palace was gained by Eleanor Roosevelt, the wife of the American President, when she visited London as a guest of the King and Queen shortly after the first troops from the United States arrived in Britain. Mrs Roosevelt noted that the food she was served was just the same as she might have received in any home or canteen throughout the land – though she thought it rather bizarre that the Palace meals should be presented on plates of gold or silver. The President's wife also found the Palace extremely chilly, often with only a single-bar electric fire to heat a huge room which lacked proper windows because of the bombing. It was hardly surprising that both Bertie and Elizabeth were suffering from heavy colds. 'My goodness, it's been cold at Buckingham

Palace,' was the Queen's heartfelt comment when the war ended.

In the winter of 1941–2 there was little prospect of the war ending. British forces had been pushed out of Greece and Crete and were suffering reverses in the strategically important Middle East; merchant shipping had been badly mauled by German U-boats, with losses in a single month reaching nearly three-quarters of a million tons; the bombing of German towns and industrial centres had failed to produce the spectacular results expected by high-ranking officers of the Royal Air Force. Yet in 1941 two events occurred which later proved to be crucial to the outcome of the war. In June, Hitler tore up his treaty with Joseph Stalin and invaded Russia, expecting complete victory before the winter. On Sunday 7 December the Japanese took care of their end of the Axis that intended to dominate the world when they sank a large part of the American fleet in a surprise attack on Pearl Harbor and brought the United States into what was now a global conflict. Hitler reacted in characteristically idiosyncratic fashion by declaring war on America, an unnecessary display of bravado which helped to ensure his downfall. Winston Churchill told President Roosevelt: 'This certainly simplifies things. God be with you.' Thus Britain, the United States and the Soviet Union joined forces against common enemies and in so doing took the first step towards shaping the world of the late twentieth century.

Things got worse before they began to improve, however. The Germans had failed to conquer Russia before the snows came and had been checked for a while, but then in the summer of 1942 they began to make rapid advances again. Earlier that year the Japanese had forced the British base at Singapore to surrender and had occupied Hong Kong, Burma, the Phillipines, Indonesia, Malaya and the Pacific islands of Guam, Midway and Wake: they now threatened India and Australia. In the Middle East the British forces suffered a series of setbacks culminating in the capitulation of the thirty-thousand-strong garrison at Tobruk in June 1942. Meanwhile, in London, the annual exhibition of the Royal Academy opened in May as if nothing untoward were happening, and the Queen bought two paintings – 'Martigues', by Arnold Mason, and Sir Walter Russell's 'Yachts in the Cutting, Blakeney'. If *The Times* thought anything about these particular purchases and their effect on art appreciation, it kept its views to itself: newsprint was far too precious.

Apart from the gloom that followed the misfortunes of early 1942, the war had a personal blow in store for the Royal Family. Bertie and Elizabeth were snatching a brief holiday at Balmoral in August that year when news came that the King's youngest brother, Prince George, Duke of Kent, who was serving as an air commodore in the Royal Air Force, had been killed on active service. Bertie and Elizabeth were deeply shocked. George had spent a few days with them at Balmoral before setting out to inspect British bases in Iceland, and only a month earlier they had attended the christening at Windsor of his younger son, Prince Michael. The aircraft carrying the thirty-nine-year-old Duke to Iceland had taken off from a Scottish airfield on 25 August and, in appalling weather, had crashed into a mountain after only thirty minutes in the air. The loss of his brother affected the King 'most poignantly', as Winston Churchill put it, and Bertie feared he would break down during the funeral service, which took place at Windsor on 29 August. Afterwards he could not settle until he had seen the place where his brother had met his death, and he made what he referred to as 'this pilgrimage' on 14 September, when he personally thanked the rescue teams who had recovered the Duke's body and those of his party.

Towards the end of the year, though, there was news to raise the spirits of the King and the whole nation. General Montgomery and the Eighth Army in North Africa defeated General Rommel's hitherto invincible Afrika Korps at the Battle of Alamein and three days later Anglo-American troops took part in their first invasion of the war when they landed at Casablanca, Oran and Algiers and began the push that reached its climax the following year, with the invasion of Italy, the Allies' first foothold in mainland Europe. In Russia an entire German army was smashed at the bitter battle of Stalingrad and the Soviet generals were preparing for a major offensive in the spring. In the Pacific the Americans were regaining ground island by island after defeating the Japanese in the decisive Battle of Midway. Winston Churchill's prophesy that victory would become possible once the United States became involved in the war was beginning to be fulfilled. By Sunday 16 May 1943, celebrated as Empire Youth Day, Queen Elizabeth was able to tell two thousand young people gathered for a rally in the gardens of Buckingham Palace:

> Today our hearts are filled with thanksgiving for the great events which have marked the past weeks, and for the success which, under God's guidance, has crowned the endurance and courage of countless men and women from all parts of the Empire . . . It is for you, the youth of this country, to show that you, too, are ready to think of others before yourselves and to dedicate yourselves anew this afternoon to the ideal of service.

A month later the King left London to visit his victorious armies in North Africa and during his absence Elizabeth held an investiture at the Palace, the first Queen to do so since Victoria. Appropriately enough the Victoria Cross was among the decorations conferred on this occasion. It went to Wing Commander Guy Gibson, leader of the RAF Dambusters, the squadron which carried out perhaps the most daring air raid of the war, when bombs which bounced on water were used to breach the Moehne and Eder dams in the industrial heartland of Germany. Thirty-three other Dambusters were decorated by the Queen that day.

But the sudden reversal of fortunes in favour of the Allies brought difficulties for Britain in its wake. The country had a greater proportion of its manpower under arms than any of the other combatants, and all its women who could be mobilized for the services or for war work had been called upon. In 1943, therefore, under the strain of the new efforts and sacrifices required to make possible the final victory, Queen Elizabeth found herself once more rallying the women who were trying to make sure that some vestiges of normal life remained. As joint president (with Queen Mary) of Sandringham Women's Institute, Elizabeth addressed the national conference of the WI at the Royal Albert Hall in London:

> Today our villages are sadly empty, the young men are away fighting for the land they love so well, and the girls, too, are away on their war work. The great responsibility of carrying on rests with older women, and how gallantly they are doing this, shouldering every sort of job with a grand and cheerful spirit. Today the place of the countrywoman is more important than it has ever been before. Despite all the wartime difficulties, it is she who must care for the workers who are growing our food, use her skill to make the most of that food, bring up her children to love and defend those values for which we are fighting, and guide them to love and cherish the beautiful country of which we are so proud.

And still the Queen set an example to all of her sex, taking an active interest in anything that might help to sustain her weary people through the hazards and trials that continued to test them to the limit. She began to tour the gardens which were springing up on bomb sites in response to the severe shortage of vegetables, and there were always the wounded, military and civilian, to be visited. When she went to a hospital in Lewisham, South London, to see thirty-two children injured in an air raid which had destroyed a school, the Queen took with her a bunch of bananas brought back from Casablanca by Lord Louis Mountbatten for Princess Elizabeth. The Princess had insisted that the fruit should be given to the bombed children, and when the Queen entered their hospital ward she told them: 'I've brought you something rare – guess what it is.' Bananas had not been seen in Britain since the outbreak of war, and one four-year-old girl was far from certain about the one handed to her. 'Do I have to eat it?' she asked the Queen anxiously.

Elizabeth's remarkable ability to encourage, inspire and comfort people through the greatest war in history depended in large measure upon her own deep religious faith, and as the vision of the victory of freedom over oppression began to assume tangible form in 1943 she felt that she should share her unshakable conviction with others in a personal attempt to prevent the short-sighted cynicism engendered by war from souring the peace that would ultimately follow. Accordingly, in a message to the women of the Empire, she used her considerable talents as a broadcaster to propound a theme which was to become constant in her speeches for several years.

> I feel that in the thinking and planning which we are doing for the welfare of our country and the Empire, we women as homemakers have a great part to play and, speaking as I do tonight from my own dearly loved home, I must say that I keenly look forward to a great rebuilding of family life as soon as the war ends . . . In these last tragic years many have found in religion the source and mainspring of the courage and selflessness that they needed. On the other hand, we cannot close our eyes to the fact that our previous Christian heritage is threatened by adverse influences. It does indeed seem to me that if the years to come are to see some real spiritual recovery, the women of our nation must be deeply concerned with religion, and our homes are the very place where it should start; it is the creative and dynamic power of Christianity which can help us to carry the moral responsibility which history is placing upon our shoulders . . .

The broadcast was well received, its noble sentiments and obvious sincerity much appreciated. But Christianity could not turn back the clock. The war had unleashed forces which would change the world with bewildering speed and the peace would be more challenging and in some respects more dangerous than the hostilities. Christianity itself would have a fight on its hands.

In the meantime, though, there was still the Second World War to be won.

6

Joy and Grief

The war entered its final phase on 6 June 1944, when troops from Britain, her Empire and the United States landed on the beaches of Normandy and for the first time faced the full might of Hitler's armies. Two days earlier victory in Italy had been assured with the capture of Rome by the Allies. There was still a long way to go and the Germans had some nasty surprises in store – jet aircraft, flying bombs and rockets which foreshadowed the modern guided missile – but luck was on the side of the invaders and, with a few notable exceptions such as the disastrous landings at Arnhem, everything went right for them. By 25 August Paris had been liberated and the Russians were pushing back the Germans amid bitter fighting on the eastern front. The Wehrmacht withdrew from Greece in December 1944 and within four months the remaining German forces in Italy had surrendered, the Allies had crossed the Rhine, the Russians had entered Berlin from the east, and both Hitler and Mussolini were dead. Finally, on 7 May 1945, Germany surrendered unconditionally.

Attention then turned towards the Far East, where the Japanese were still doggedly holding out and, so the Allies estimated, could continue to do so for at least another eighteen months. The obliteration of Hiroshima and Nagasaki by the horrific new

155

atom bombs changed everything, and Japan capitulated in August, although the formal surrender did not take place until early the following month. On 15 August King George VI broadcast to the Empire which he was soon to see disappear. 'The war is over,' he said. 'Those four words have for the Queen and myself the same significance, simple and immediate, that they have for you.' But he pointed out that the cost of the war still had to be counted. 'We have spent freely of all we had,' he said – Britain was virtually bankrupt – and added that the consequences of 'this terrible war' would be felt 'long after we have forgotten our rejoicings of today'.

One consequence of the war had already been felt by Winston Churchill. A few weeks after the victory in Europe, Churchill announced the resignation of the National Government and formed a caretaker administration composed mainly of Conservatives while preparations were put in hand for a general election. Party politics were back. Polling took place on 5 July but because of the vast number of voters serving abroad with the Armed Forces the result could not be announced until the 26th: it was a Labour landslide by an overall parliamentary majority of more than one hundred seats. Churchill, the great war leader, was out; Clement Attlee,[1] the leader of the Labour Party, was Prime Minister.

The King was sorry to lose his trusted adviser and friend, but the will of the people had been clearly expressed. Wars are not between peoples but between ideologies and systems of government, therefore a régime which wishes to indulge in war has to persuade the people it rules that they will be better off when victory is achieved than they would be if they allowed the opposing system to win. In 1945 the people of Britain were eager to claim their reward for the sacrifices they had made during the Second World War, and many remembered bitterly how the promise of a land fit for heroes had not been fulfilled when they had re-elected their war leader in 1918. Attlee's Labour Party promised homes, jobs, a welfare state and public ownership of industry and services and managed to convince the electorate that it could provide all these things. Churchill's Conservatives also offered social reforms but made it sound as if they were secondary to the maintenance of Britain's glory as an imperial and world power. Too many people had had too much of glory; what they wanted was comfort and security, so they voted Labour. The days of empire were gone, the day of 'the common man' had arrived, and with it came radical changes in British society which presented a new challenge to the monarchy.

Queen Elizabeth herself had unconsciously prophesied one of the greatest postwar shifts in the balance of society when, addressing women Civil Defence workers in London at the end of 1944, she had said:

> I believe strongly that when future generations look back on this most terrible war they will recognize as one of its chief features the degree to which women were actively concerned in it. I do not think it is any exaggeration to say that in this country, at any rate, the war could not have been won without their help. That is a thought which gives me pride as a woman . . .

The thought was to provoke a good deal more than pride, however. Before the war women, though they had with great reluctance and after much pain been granted the right to vote, were still second-class citizens, dependent to a large extent on the whims of the men who were considered to be their masters. The importance they assumed during the war gave women a new view of their own potential, demonstrating that most things men could do they could do at least as well, and it ensured that they would not be content to return to their traditional secondary role. When the Queen thanked the women of Britain for their magnificent wartime achievements she could not know that the movement for female emancipation would grow steadily during the next thirty years – until women gained, in theory at least, equality with men under the law – and that it would contribute to the development of a so-called 'new morality' which would cause upsets even in the Royal Family.

The sexual revolution was not, however, in the minds of Bertie and Elizabeth in the summer of 1945, as they enjoyed their first postwar holiday at Balmoral and, like many other people, considered the future. They had reigned for almost ten years,

157

but most of that period had been spent in the abnormal and extreme circumstances of war which had burst upon them just as they were becoming accustomed to the roles history had unexpectedly chosen for them. Now they had to settle down to a life which was to become more public than ever, owing to the tremendous advances in the field of communications which had been byproducts of the war. At another level they had to steer the monarchy through a changing relationship with what had once been the British Empire but was now becoming a Commonwealth within which a number of countries – including Canada, Australia, India and Burma – were demanding if not outright independence (as in the cases of India and Burma) at least a substantial devolution of power towards themselves: two years later the King, instead of signing himself George RI,* would become simply George R.

On top of all this the King and Queen had to consider the future of Princess Elizabeth who, like her mother, had had her youth interrupted by war but had been denied the character-forming opportunities granted to Elizabeth Bowes-Lyon in 1914–18. In 1942 the Princess, as all sixteen-year-old girls were required to do, had registered for war work, hoping that she might become a volunteer nurse. The King, however, refused to countenance any idea of that sort and it was not until the spring of 1944 that he allowed Elizabeth to 'do her bit'. She joined the Auxiliary Territorial Service, which taught her to be a military driver, but she was hardly out of the training period when the war in Europe ended. She was nineteen years old, heir to the throne, and she had missed virtually all contact with ordinary life. The King and Queen hoped they would now have a chance to rectify that deficiency.

But the immediate priority was to put Britain back on its feet. Bertie and Elizabeth had brought the monarchy closer to the people than it had ever been, and they intended to work closely with their subjects in the huge task of national reconstruction. The Queen toured rows of prefabricated houses built to provide temporary accommodation[2] for bombed-out families and often

* *Rex et Imperator* – King and Emperor.

she would knock on a door to greet the startled tenant with the words, 'May we come in?' To emphasize that life was going to be better than it had been before the war, there were exhibitions of new furniture and the latest domestic gadgetry – Elizabeth saw a forerunner of the modern, thermostatically-controlled, automatic electric oven and pronounced it 'almost too good to be true'. And somewhere in Britain today is a woman who was christened Elizabeth because she was born at the very moment when the Queen arrived to visit a newly built wing of Queen Charlotte's Hospital in Hammersmith, west London.

One symbolic sign of revival was the refitting of the great liner *Queen Elizabeth*, which the Queen had launched on Clydeside in the fateful summer of 1938 and which, having been used as a troopship during the war, was in 1946 dressed up to fulfil her original purpose. The Queen and Princess Elizabeth spent seven hours in the ship as it underwent speed trials. At one point the Queen took the helm and, directed by the navigator, altered the ship's course. 'How remarkably easy the wheel is,' she said to the quartermaster, adding as he took the helm again, 'I hope I'm giving the ship back to you in good condition.'

The ship was certainly in better condition than Britain. The Labour Government was determined to do better than its predecessors in the twenties, but the odds were heavily weighted against Attlee and his men.

First, the country was desperately short of money. The lease-lend agreement with the United States, negotiated early in the war to allow Britain to buy American goods on credit, ended in August 1945. The Government obtained a loan from Washington of nearly a billion pounds, but by 1947 that was almost gone, largely frittered away. The word 'austerity' began to be heard, and the man who made it his own as Chancellor of the Exchequer was Sir Stafford Cripps, himself a very austere figure of whom Churchill said, 'There, but for the grace of God, goes God.'[3] Imports were cut, expenditure on the armed forces was reduced, there were cutbacks in the building programmes for houses and factories, and taxes were increased to the tune of £200 million.

The second major problem was shortage of food, which was not helped by the import reductions. Meat was very scarce, potatoes were put on ration and even bread was rationed (which had not been the case during the war) after the failure of the 1945 harvest. Various schemes were conceived to supplement the British diet. The Ministry of Food tried hard to popularize whalemeat and a South African species of fish called snoek. Some people ate and enjoyed whale steaks, but the ten million tons of snoek which were imported seem to have vanished into legend: perhaps it was just the name, or maybe snoek really was as awful as it sounded – it is difficult to know because no one appears ever to have tasted it. Then there was the Overseas Food Corporation, a £20 million extravaganza otherwise known as the Groundnuts Scheme, which aimed to produce vegetable fat in Tanganyika. The least said about that comedy of errors the better.[4] It was to be a long time before the British would see the end of ration books. Even clothing was still rationed, the allowance being sixty-six coupons per year, with something like a shirt requiring eight coupons and an overcoat sixteen. It was the age of 'Make Do and Mend', and a lady called 'Mrs Sew-and-Sew' who told housewives how to perform miracles with old clothes.

One problem the Government – and the Royal Family for that matter – did not need at such a time was the Duke of Windsor. David had resigned as Governor of the Bahamas and visited London several times during 1946 to try to persuade the Government to make him a sort of extra ambassador to the United States, charged with the task of furthering Anglo-American relations and co-operation but with no diplomatic duties. He was content to resume his life in France, but he hoped that if he could work for his country in some semi-official capacity Wallis and he would eventually be accepted in London. Again his hopes were dashed: the Government flatly rejected him, and his family was not prepared to suggest anything. So David and Wallis settled down once more in exile, with a house in Paris leased to them by the French Government at a nominal rent and a country house which they bought forty-five miles from Paris.

By a special concession the French authorities exempted the Duke from income tax on the huge fortune he retained and, outside Britain at least, the Windsors lived a sort of sham royal life in an apparent attempt to realize dreams of what might have been.

Meanwhile a less controversial, though by no means straight-forward, royal romance was proceeding well. Princess Elizabeth and Prince Philip of Greece were engaged to be married, though it was to be some months before the public knew about this. Elizabeth and Philip had kept in constant touch with each other since their meeting at Dartmouth College in 1939. They were both great-great grandchildren of Queen Victoria and were therefore cousins,[5] and it was by virtue of this kinship that they were able to remain close during the war, when Lieutenant Prince Philip was serving with the Royal Navy and getting himself mentioned in despatches. Philip spent several periods of leave at Windsor, during which the King and Queen noted that young Elizabeth was becoming more and more attached to him, captivated by his good looks, his dynamic energy, his ready wit and his abundant sense of fun. By 1941 his Greek royal relatives – who included George VI's sister-in-law, Princess Marina, Duchess of Kent – had placed Philip firmly on the list of prospective husbands for the future Queen of England, although it was not until some time later that he was viewed as a serious suitor by Elizabeth's parents. Indeed it is likely that he did not see himself in that role while there was every chance of his being killed.

The turning point in the relationship came during Christmas at Windsor in 1943, when Philip was there on leave, and the young couple's love was obvious to all who saw them. Of course, there was no question of marriage, for Elizabeth was not yet eighteen and knew little of life and less of men. When George VI was approached by King George of Greece on the matter of a possible marriage between the latter's cousin, Philip, and Elizabeth, the King replied that while he liked and respected the young naval officer there could be no question of discussing a betrothal while Elizabeth was so young and inexperienced.

There the matter rested until Philip was given a shore job by the Navy at the end of the war: he thus became, of course, much more available to Elizabeth. The King, who was very possessive towards his daughters, played his last card when he began giving balls at the Palace so that Elizabeth and Margaret could meet a wide range of young men (as long as they were Guards officers). He had nothing against Philip, who was in any case perfectly eligible as a partner for the future queen, but he did not look forward to losing his daughter so soon after he was at last able to spend more time with her than the early years of kingship and the war had allowed, and he also appreciated the steadying influence Elizabeth had on the more wayward Princess Margaret, who was destined to become the chief target of the monarchy's critics.

Princess Elizabeth, however, was independent of mind and strong of will . . . and she was in love. When Philip formally proposed to her in the summer of 1946, she first accepted him and only then went off to tell her parents. The Queen was delighted. She liked Philip and saw that he was essential to her daughter's happiness. The King could raise no objection. Princess Elizabeth was a sensible young woman who knew her own mind and was not likely to change it once it had been made up. Philip had the right qualifications. But there were certain difficulties. Philip was a foreigner, and the British people were not over-fond of foreigners at the time, tending to blame them for the war. Worse, he was a member of the Greek royal family, who were at the centre of a bitter civil war which had already brought Britain a great deal of political embarrassment through her military intervention. Worse still, he had strong German connexions. The King advised the young lovers that no official statement about their betrothal should be issued for the time being, though he told them kindly that they could consider themselves engaged as long as they kept quiet about it.

There was a second reason in the King's mind for delay. He, the Queen and the two Princesses were due to go on a flag-waving tour of South Africa, where the Afrikaners had grumbled under British rule ever since the Boer War and where there were threats of secession from the Commonwealth. Since it was the first time they had all been abroad together, the King did not want an outsider in tow, even if he was going to join the family. Thus the engagement was kept so secret that Palace spokesmen positively denied it when questioned by the Press, which had of course noticed the growing attachment between Elizabeth and Philip.

The South African tour took place in February 1947 and happened to coincide with the very worst of that appalling winter in Britain, which upset the King as he felt he should be at home suffering with his people. It was the worst winter for half a century. At one point sixteen degrees of frost were reported in London. Transport came to a standstill, so that what little fuel the country did have in stock could not be moved to power stations and gasworks. The King suggested to his Prime Minister that the tour should be cut short, but Attlee replied that no useful purpose would be served – and in any case everyone could see that after six years of war the weary King would benefit from some sunshine. So the tour went on and proved to be a great success. It was a further thirteen years before the people of South Africa opted for the status of a republic and withdrawal from the Commonwealth. During the royal visit there was one amusing incident in the East Rand, when the Queen found herself having to use her umbrella to fend off a huge Zulu who had rushed out of a crowd and was seemingly intent on attacking the royal party. In fact the tribesman was merely trying to give a ten-shilling note to Princess Elizabeth as a present.

When the Royal Family returned home the snow and ice and the severe flooding which had come with the thaw were past, but the ordeal of waiting went on for Princess Elizabeth and her unofficial fiancé. Philip had by then become a naturalized Briton, having taken his mother's surname of Mountbatten (she was the sister of Lord Louis),[6] but there were residual doubts as to how the public, and particularly the more xenophobic sections of the Press, would react to him as a future prince consort. So it was not until the ground had been carefully prepared and the newspapers had been primed that the announcement was made. It came on 10 July 1947:

> It is with the greatest pleasure that the King and Queen announce the betrothal of their dearly beloved daughter, the Princess Elizabeth, to Lieutenant Philip Mountbatten, RN, son of the late Prince Andrew of Greece and Princess Andrew (Princess Alice of Battenburg), to which union the King has gladly given his consent.

The wedding took place at Westminster Abbey on 20 November, on which day it was announced that Philip Mountbatten had become a Knight Commander of the Order of the Garter, Baron Greenwich of Greenwich and Duke of Edinburgh.[7] Princess Elizabeth was created a Lady of the Garter. Once again a royal spectacle became a morale-booster when there was little else to celebrate.

The arrangements for the wedding were almost identical to those for the marriage of Princess Elizabeth's parents nearly twenty-five years before, though there were concessions to both austerity and the feelings of the bride and bridegroom. The elaborate wedding breakfast of 1923 was translated into a twenty-minute, three-course meal (filet de sole Mountbatten, perdreau en casserole – meat with new potatoes and beans – and bombe glacée Princess Elizabeth), and this time the speechifying was kept to the minimum. The *Daily Express* commented: 'It was the Queen's personality which had shaped the entire wedding . . . It was the Queen who . . . finally decided the details of the wedding gown . . . She was the one, it seems, on whom everyone relied to make the tedious decisions . . .' Rationing was still very much in force, of course, and a hundred clothing coupons had gone into the Princess's gown, while twenty-five each had been allotted to her bridesmaids. But all the tedious decisions brought their reward when the Queen, dressed simply in apricot brocade, watched with joy and pride the splendid ceremony in the Abbey. Afterwards the King wrote to Princess Elizabeth, 'I have watched you grow up all these years with pride under the skilful direction of Mummy, who as you know is the most marvellous person in the world in my eyes . . .'[8]

As well as assuming responsibility for arranging Princess Elizabeth's wedding, the Queen pursued with unabated enthusiasm a full programme of royal duties in 1947. There was a service at Westminster Abbey for the Mothers' Union, of which the Queen had become patron; there was a visit to Perth to receive the freedom of the city on behalf of her regiment, The Black Watch, and a trip to York to inspect the King's Own Yorkshire Light Infantry. In September came the Edinburgh Festival and the 'Enterprise Scotland' Exhibition, designed to publicize industry north of the Border, and there was a host of other functions and personal appearances. At one engagement, a celebration marking the twenty-fifth anniversary of the Bible Reading Fellowship, Elizabeth spoke, as she had done during the war, of the need for Christian principles to underwrite the new and better life for which everyone hoped. Addressing herself to what the Archbishop of Canterbury, Dr Geoffrey Fisher,[9] had described as a storm-tossed generation in which far too many people had no roots of faith, the Queen said:

> These are challenging days in the history of the world. A new era is struggling to be born, and what is it to be? We in our nation and the Empire are called to give a moral lead to the world and we can only do this if we are true to our great Christian tradition.

The following year, in May, she outlined some of the specific problems of the new age when she took part in the centenary celebrations of the pioneer educational establishment for women, Queen's College in London:

> We live today in a technical society, and the problems which it has created affect every aspect of our physical lives. I feel, however, that we must not allow ourselves to be obsessed by the purely material complexities which confront us. They affect, also, our personal and national relationships. In the past men and women were mainly preoccupied by the affairs of family or local life: events and ideas taking shape abroad seemed remote and impersonal. Now the whole world is, as it were, our village. Owing to the development of communications, words spoken today far across the world are delivered, in banner headlines, for all to read tomorrow morning. Thus we find ourselves brought into the midst of world affairs, and at a time of great confusion and chaos.

As a result our minds are nowadays exposed to so much that is new and perplexing that they may become numbed if they are not trained to judge what is thrust before them.

Elizabeth had even developed her own formula to cope with the situation:

> The knowledge of facts or events is of no value if the mind is insufficiently trained or self-disciplined to understand them, to pass judgment on them, and finally to act quickly, boldly and clearly upon that judgment. Therefore I would like to name the qualities which I believe we need as the three Ds – the elder brothers of the three Rs: first, discernment, the ability to judge between the false and the true, the essential and the unessential; second, decision, the power to turn judgment into action; and third, design, the art of giving practical form to a plan of action.

And this was the daughter of a little-known Scottish earl, the woman who had hesitated before agreeing to marry the King's son, who had been more or less dragged onto the throne of England at a time when many people, including her husband, were afraid that it would collapse. If anyone doubts the con-tribution Elizabeth Bowes-Lyon made to the survival and development of the British monarchy, or her influence on the way in which it has adapted to rapidly changing conditions in society and the world, the speech I have just quoted should go some way towards answering those doubts. As Duchess of York she had endeared herself to the nation by her humanity, warmth, sincerity and, above all, by her interest in people. As Queen she displayed all those qualities but added to them an extraordinary ability to lead, in both a practical and an emotional sense. As one important tribute to her achievements put it:

> She has desired to find her sphere of service in the intimacy of human relationships and understanding. She speaks to all men and women on the level of common experience. She is never afraid to challenge the over-sophistication of the age in which she lives; she ignores the cynics and pessimists and holds up for admiration the things that are lovely and of good report.[10]

The great pity is that during the past thirty years or so too many people have been too ready to take notice of the cynics and the pessimists.

In spite of the fact that, as she said herself, she had never been to school, Elizabeth took a personal interest in education, and particularly the education of women. For a girl who never went to school she also collected an impressive number of honorary degrees from universities, and with one of them she conferred upon women the status of full members of Cambridge University. When she received her honorary Doctor of Law degree at Cambridge in October 1948, an all-male tradition was broken by her address to the Senate. Her message, though, was for women:

> All that is best in womanhood is needed today – gentleness and a ready sympathy, courage, hatred of cruelty, and an instinctive love for the young, the weak and the suffering. By your residence at Cambridge you can add to these natural endowments the grace of a well-trained mind, full of purpose, empty of prejudice. The torch of learning has been handed to you. Bring the light into your homes, which are the cradles of Christian citizenship, and shine it upon your children and all whom you meet.

The amazing woman who spoke those words came to the throne, by what proved to be one of the happiest accidents in history, at the very time when it needed her most. Queen Elizabeth, and through her King George VI, were Britain's first modern monarchs. Had Prince Bertie not married Elizabeth Bowes-Lyon it is possible that he would not have become King after the Abdication (bearing in mind the doubts expressed about him in 1936 and the influence of his remarkable growth in self-confidence and stature during the previous thirteen years of his marriage to Elizabeth). If Bertie had acceded to the throne without Elizabeth at his side, it is likely that his approach would have been nearer to that of his father, while his shyness and the difficulties he experienced because of his stammer might well have proved to be a barrier between him and his people.

As it was, King George VI and Queen Elizabeth metaphorically brought the throne down from its dais and out into the streets: they were objects of loyalty and love not simply because

167

these were due to them but also because of their direct and personal relationship with their people. Queen Victoria was worshipped from a distance, and her grandson, George V, was almost as remote. Had this distance between Crown and country been maintained, it is not hard to imagine what would have happened to the monarchy in 'the age of the common man' – there have been plenty of examples in other countries. On the other hand, a populist approach is not enough by itself. Edward VIII was one of the most popular royal figures of all time, but there were aspects of his character which, had he reigned for what might have been expected to be his natural term (leaving aside the question of his choice of wife), could have harmed the institution of monarchy in Britain.

Between them King George VI and Queen Elizabeth had the courage, strength, self-discipline and dedication to guide the Crown through a difficult period, and Elizabeth's contribution can be seen partly in terms of the wide range of her public activities, from the perceptive speeches to undergraduates and academics to the tap at the prefab door and the gentle inquiry, 'May we come in?' People at all levels of society saw her not only as their Queen but also as their friend. When a woman in Bristol was driven to despair by the desperate housing shortage after the war, she wrote to the Queen. It was one of thousands of letters Elizabeth received each year, but she took the trouble to write to the woman's local council suggesting that here was a case of special need, and the woman was given priority on the council's housing list. That woman knew she had a good neighbour in Buckingham Palace.

The year 1948 was a notable one in the life of Queen Elizabeth. She celebrated twenty-five years of marriage and also welcomed her first grandchild. But at the same time she received the first warning of the widowhood that was approaching with tragic speed.

The silver wedding anniversary of the King and Queen was an opportunity for their people to show how completely the reluctant monarchs had won their hearts. The Archbishop of Canterbury, Dr Fisher, summed it up at a thanksgiving service in St Paul's Cathedral: 'The nation and the Empire bless God that He has set such a family at the seat of our royalty.' Thousands of people jammed the streets of London as the King and Queen drove from Buckingham Palace to the cathedral in a state landau surrounded by the splendid uniforms of the Household Cavalry, and many a throat was hoarse from cheering after Their Majesties' twenty-two-mile drive through the capital following the service. In the evening Bertie and Elizabeth both made wireless broadcasts. The Queen said:

> I am deeply thankful for our twenty-five years of happiness together, for the opportunities we have been given of service to our beloved country and for the blessings of our home and children . . . There must be many who feel as we do that the sanctities of married life are in some way the highest form of human fellowship, affording a rock-like foundation on which all the best in the life of the nation is built. Looking back over the last twenty-five years and to my own happy childhood, I realize more and more that wonderful sense of security and happiness which comes from a loved home . . .

The happy royal home was further blessed on 14 November 1948 when Princess Elizabeth's first child was born – to the joy of everyone a boy, a future king. Recalling the embarrassments of his wife's two confinements, the King instructed the Home Secretary that his attendance would not be required, and the tradition which had survived since the days of James II was finally buried. But as Princess Elizabeth awaited the birth of His Royal Highness Prince Charles Philip Arthur George at Buckingham Palace, her father was suffering the early effects of mortal illness.

The war had left the King a weary man. Though only fifty-two years old, he looked much older, worn and tired. But it was not simply fatigue which struck him down in the autumn of 1948, it was a condition called Buerger's disease, a severe degeneration of the arteries in the legs, the victims of which are almost always heavy smokers. Like his father, George VI smoked a great deal, forty or fifty cigarettes a day, but he was not destined to see his seventieth birthday, as George V had done: three conditions connected with his smoking would kill him within four years. The earliest symptoms were cramps in the King's legs, which became very painful during the family's customary summer holiday at Balmoral in 1948. Bertie naturally consulted his doctors and on 12 November was told that he had a dangerous obstruction in the circulation of his right leg – there was a possibility that gangrene might set in and the foot might have to be amputated.

This news the King and Queen kept to themselves. Princess Elizabeth could not be told when her confinement was imminent and in any case no public announcement could be made since a royal tour of Australia and New Zealand was planned for early the following year. As far as the tour was concerned, however, the King's doctors were adamant: on 23 November it was announced that, on medical advice and with the concurrence of the Prime Ministers of Britain, Australia and New Zealand,

> His Majesty has agreed to cancel all his public engagements over a period of some months. This decision involves the indefinite postponement of the visit to Australia and New Zealand which the King and Queen had undertaken to pay, with Princess Margaret, during the first half of next year. Their Majesties wish to express to the people of Australia and New Zealand their profound regret and bitter disappointment . . .

The seven doctors treating the King advised him to take a complete rest, which meant that the Queen had to fulfil many of his public duties, during which she maintained a dignity, calmness and cheerfulness which was admired by all who knew how anxious she was about the health of her husband. At first the rest cure seemed to work but shortly after the Christmas holiday at Sandringham the doctors decided that they would have to operate to save the King's right leg. Bertie was furious, suspecting that he had been forced, against his wishes, to take a rest under false pretences. Elizabeth and the doctors calmed him down and on 12 March 1949 he underwent surgery to sever the nerves controlling the circulation to his leg. Afterwards he had to spend a good deal of time resting, but he was able to undertake some engagements in the summer and after the holiday at Balmoral – where he felt somewhat disgruntled because the operation had restricted his sporting activities, cutting out riding altogether – he seemed to be very much better. By the autumn of 1949 it was considered appropriate for Princess Elizabeth, who as heir to the throne had to be close at hand during her father's illness, to accompany the Duke of Edinburgh to Malta, where the Duke was taking up a naval appointment.

A year passed, and in the course of it war broke out once more, the Labour Government in Britain received the first warning of its impending downfall, and the Royal Family welcomed the arrival of another new member. There was particular pleasure for the King and Queen in the birth of Princess Elizabeth's daughter on 15 August 1950: the infant princess was baptized Anne Elizabeth Alice Louise, her first name being the one to which George V had objected so strongly when the Yorks had wanted to give it to their second child. But there was no pleasure for the Government of Clem Attlee in the result of the general election in February 1950 when, in the largest percentage poll in the country's history,[11] Labour's huge majority of five years earlier was cut to a mere eight seats. The people of Britain were tired of austerity, worried about a 30 per cent devaluation of the pound against the dollar,[12] and frightened by the prospect of further nationalization (the Bank of England, civil aviation, the coal mines, wireless and cables, transport and the gas industry had already come into public ownership and, prompted by its powerful Keep Left group, Labour had a long list of other industries suitable for treatment). There was no pleasure either for anyone when, on 25 June, the Korean War began with the invasion of South Korea by communist forces from the North. Fear of the 'Red Menace' was at its height on both sides of the Atlantic, and Britain entered the Korean War on America's coat-tails.

The King, meanwhile, was progressing well – so much so that the postponed visit to Australia and New Zealand was rescheduled for 1952. By May 1951, however, when he opened the wonder of the decade, the Festival of Britain, it was clear to everyone that Bertie was a sick man. In June his doctors diagnosed a catarrhal inflammation of the right lung and the King cancelled a visit to Northern Ireland. Queen Elizabeth went to the province alone, to be welcomed in Belfast by her brother-in-law, Lord Granville,[13] by the Prime Minister, Sir Basil Brooke, and by thousands of cheering Ulster people. In Dublin, though, there were protests against the visit by members of the Anti-Partition Association and a member of the Dail, the parliament of the Irish Republic,[14] said that no member of the Royal Family had the right to set foot on Irish soil while British troops occupied part of the country. The 'Irish Question', which had bedevilled British politics for centuries, was far from settled. In a little more than a decade the blood spilt in Northern Ireland would rob the province of its own government and send British soldiers to patrol its streets.

The holiday month of August came, and Bertie and Elizabeth retired to Balmoral. The King was able to indulge in a little shooting, but he was losing weight at an alarming rate and towards the end of the holiday he was afflicted by a sore throat. By the middle of September, after the King's chest had been X-rayed and samples of his lung tissue had been taken, it was clear to the doctors that he had cancer. He was not told, but Elizabeth was: she was consulted before any medical bulletins were issued so she could make certain that no alarm was caused to the public. On 23 September the King had an operation to remove his left lung, having been informed that there was a blockage in his bronchial tube. He appeared to recover completely, though he was much thinner, looked even older and had some difficulty with his voice. But the Queen knew that it was only a matter of time.

Still she had to carry on with the royal round and, despite the dreadful knowledge that gnawed at her, she had to reassure people wherever she went that the King was making good progress. She also had to keep up her husband's morale, since she knew what ailed him and he did not, though it is almost certain that he knew death was not far off. Her courage never faltered, and later Winston Churchill paid tribute to her as 'that valiant woman with the famous blood of Scotland in her veins'. In November 1951 the Queen herself became ill with a cold. It had happened at so many times of crisis in her life – shortly before the death of George V, during the climax of the Abdication – and now when her husband was dying. This time, however, she was out and about within a couple of days. It would never have done for the King and Queen to be on prolonged sick leave at the same time.

Of course Bertie and Elizabeth went to Sandringham to celebrate Christmas 1951, the King cheered by the return to power in that year's autumn election of his old friend Winston Churchill. They returned to London in January to bid farewell to Princess Elizabeth and the Duke of Edinburgh when they set off on a journey round the world: the Australian tour could not be put off again, and if the King could not go who better than his daughter to take his place? The whole family went to the theatre on the eve of the departure – they saw *South Pacific*. On 31 January the Princess and her husband were on their way to East Africa, the first stage of their tour, while the King and Queen went back to Sandringham, where Princess Margaret and their two grandchildren, as well as a few friends, awaited them.

It was late in the shooting season but the King enjoyed plenty of sport, going out – protected by a waistcoat that was heated electrically – after hare and waterfowl. He went out shooting on 5 February while the Queen and Princess Margaret enjoyed a cruise on the Norfolk Broads. On that Tuesday evening Princess Margaret entertained the company by playing the piano, then everyone listened to the news on the wireless to keep abreast of the progress of Princess Elizabeth. After dinner the King retired to his room and at eleven o'clock he was sitting up in bed reading when a servant took him some cocoa. At midnight one of the watchmen saw the King close his bedroom window, and some time between then and 7.30 the following morning he died of a coronary thrombosis, just a little more than a month after his fifty-sixth birthday. It was perhaps fitting that his death should bear such a striking similarity to the death of his father, in the same place, at the same time of year.

Princess Elizabeth and the Duke of Edinburgh were in Kenya. The Duke broke the news of the King's death to his wife at the Sangana Hunting Lodge in the Aberdare Forest game reserve, where the couple were taking a short break from their tour,* and preparations began immediately for their return home. By the afternoon of 7 February Queen Elizabeth II was in London receiving the homage of her eighty-four-year-old grandmother, Queen Mary. Next day the new Queen joined her family at Sandringham and walked with her mother and sister behind her father's coffin as it was borne to the church of St Mary Magdalene, across the park from the house. On 11 February the King's body was taken by train to London for his lying-in-state and four days later George VI was buried at Windsor. Among the mourners in St George's Chapel was the Duke of Windsor, the man who had pushed Bertie and Elizabeth onto the throne. The Duchess of Windsor was not present.

The King's widow, henceforth to be known as Queen Elizabeth the Queen Mother, bore her grief with the dignity and fortitude which had come to be expected of her, though doctors and members of her family feared that she might be bottling up too much emotion. 'I wish Queen Elizabeth would break down. This incredible self-control will take its toll,' a royal physician said.[15] But the Queen Mother did not break down. She had never wanted to be queen, yet having become one she adhered strictly to the code of faultless behaviour which she felt was incumbent upon a queen. In this she modelled herself on Queen Mary, for whom the blow of George VI's death was 'one of many that, over the long years, fate has struck in vain endeavour to weaken a brave and gracious spirit'.[16]

The Queen Mother, though, was much easier to identify with than the stiff and aloof Queen Mary and it was probably no exaggeration when one commentator claimed that in February 1952 millions of people wished that they could share the widow's weight of grief. Nor was it presumptuous to suggest, as did *The Times*, which prides itself on its special relationship with the monarchy, that the Queen Mother could perhaps take solace

*The Lodge had been a wedding gift from the people of Kenya.

in the knowledge that no king in British history had owed more to his wife, although it is unlikely that Elizabeth's thoughts ran on such lines. Three things were uppermost in her mind: she had lost a beloved husband; the nation had lost a fine king; her task now was to fill the gaps his death had left in the lives of both the Royal Family and the country. The new Queen would in time stamp her own personality upon the institution of monarchy, helping it to adapt to the changing needs and wishes of its people, but there would always be room for the contribution only the Queen Mother could make, providing a unique link between the new world and the old.

On 18 February, three days after the King's funeral, she issued a personal statement:

> I want to send this message of thanks to a multitude of people – to you who, from all parts of the world, have been giving me your sympathy and affection throughout these dark days. I want you to know how your concern for me has upheld me in my sorrow, and how proud you have made me by your wonderful tributes to my dear husband, a great and noble king. No man had a deeper sense than he of duty and of service, and no man was more full of compassion for his fellow-men. He loved you all, every one of you, most truly. That, you know, was what he always tried to tell you in his yearly message at Christmas; that was the pledge that he took at the sacred moment of his coronation fifteen years ago. Now I am left alone to do what I can to honour that pledge without him. Throughout our married life we have tried, the King and I, to fulfil with all our hearts and all our strength the great task of service that was laid upon us. My only wish now is that I may be allowed to continue the work that we sought to do together. I commend to you our dear daughter. Give her your loyalty and devotion: in the great and lonely station to which she has been called she will need your protection and your love. God bless you all, and may He in His wisdom guide us safely to our true destiny of peace and goodwill.

Unaccountably, it was not until after the statement had been published that an omission was noticed. There was no mention of Queen Elizabeth II's consort, or of her two children. Palace officials hastily set the record straight by informing newspaper editors that the reference to the new Queen should have read: 'I commend to you our dear daughter; give her your loyalty and devotion. Though blessed in her husband and children, she will need your protection and your love in the great and lonely station to which she has been called.' The oversight made no difference to the main sentiments expressed in the Queen Mother's message, however. In the early days of her widowhood it was to be the memory and the example of her husband that sustained her, both privately and in her public life.

But if, in the optimism that greeted the beginning of the new reign, it was assumed that the Queen Mother would now take a back seat, that assumption was quickly shown to be wrong. In a tribute to Elizabeth on her fiftieth birthday, the view had been expressed that 'there is nothing left for time to add to the affection' in which the Queen was held.[17] The years following the death of George VI were to prove that statement utterly untrue. Though the title of Queen Mother is not one favoured in royal circles – Elizabeth's staff have always referred to her simply as Queen Elizabeth – she was obliged to adopt it because of possible confusion with her daughter, and since she did her popularity has actually increased. The mother image is an extremely potent one in Britain – the mother country, 'mother of the free', the mother of parliaments – and the love and respect shown to Elizabeth was never so marked as when to millions of people throughout the world she became 'The Queen Mum'.

7

A New Life

National grief at the death of King George VI was deep and sincere. People were stunned at the news: one small boy found himself gazing in wonder at the sight of hundreds of silent men in overalls clustered round a factory loudspeaker which normally relayed such wireless frivolities as *Workers' Playtime*. But as always it was a matter of 'le roi est mort – vive le roi', or in this instance 'vive la reine'.

The accession of Queen Elizabeth II was accompanied by a great resurgence of pride and self-confidence among the British. It was the dawn of a new age – a 'new Elizabethan age', people called it – anticipating a return to prosperity and a flowering of native talents in both technology and the arts. For once, this confidence was not misplaced. Under the Conservative Government of Winston Churchill, though not, strictly speaking, because of it, the balance of international trade turned in Britain's favour and the foundations of the so-called consumer society were laid. Prices remained fairly stable, industry began the process of regeneration free of the kind of controls the Labour Government had wanted, unemployment began to fall and the end of food rationing was in sight.

Against the background of this exciting new mood, the Queen

177

Mother was engaged in the sad business of winding up the life she had known for the past sixteen years. It is never easy for the bereaved partner of a happy marriage to become accustomed to life alone, but in the case of a king's widow there are added difficulties. The monarchy is a sort of family business in which the Sovereign is chairman and managing director, and for reasons of security and efficiency it is necessary for the monarch to, in the Duke of Edinburgh's phrase, 'live above the shop'. Thus the Queen Mother, having moved unwillingly into Buckingham Palace in 1937, found herself in 1952 almost equally reluctant to move out, since the place held so many memories of her beloved Bertie. For more than a year she remained in the first-floor suite of rooms where she and the King had spent the most momentous years of their married life, while the new Queen and her family occupied the Belgian Suite below. Then in May 1953, just a month before the Coronation, the Queen Mother and Princess Margaret moved into Clarence House, St James's, which had been the home of Princess Elizabeth and the Duke of Edinburgh after their marriage.

The Queen Mother was less affected by the handing over to her daughter of Balmoral Castle since it meant that she returned to Birkhall, where she and Bertie had spent their summers before the Abdication, and she still had her much-loved Royal Lodge, the scene of some of her happiest days with her husband and children. She decided, however, that she also needed a real home of her own, a place where she could regain some of the peace and privacy she had been obliged to give up in 1936. Within a few months of the King's death she bought the decaying sixteenth-century castle of Barrogill, in the far north of Scotland, and set about creating the first entirely private home she had known since childhood.

In the meantime the Queen Mother was honouring the promise she had made to continue the work she and the late King had begun together. As the four-month period of full Court mourning neared its end she threw herself headlong into a programme of public appearances, visiting Scotland, addressing the anniversary festival of the Toc H Women's Association,[1] presenting prizes at the Royal College of Music, calling at the famous Biggin Hill RAF station with Winston Churchill, attending the ballet at Covent Garden.

As early as May 1952 she was to be found at the controls of a new Comet jet airliner when she took over from the pilot during a proving flight across Europe. Flying the latest type of civil aircraft was no mean achievement for a woman who, to this day, has never driven a car, and the Queen Mother thought the occasion worthy of a telegram to the members of No. 600 (City of London) Squadron Royal Auxiliary Air Force, of which she had become honorary air commodore during the war. 'I am delighted to tell you,' the telegram said, 'that today I took over as first pilot of a Comet aircraft. We exceeded a reading of 0.8 Mach at 40,000 feet. Thoughts turned to 600 Squadron. What the passengers thought I really wouldn't like to say.' An association with some regiment or organization is no mere formality to the Queen Mother. There was no need for her to send that message to her squadron, but she knew they would appreciate it. And though she was no longer in Buckingham Palace Elizabeth was still ready to play the good neighbour. When disastrous floods struck the East Coast early in 1953, she was the royal visitor who travelled round supporting and cheering up the people worst affected.

On 2 June 1953 the new Elizabethan age came officially into being with the Coronation of Queen Elizabeth II. So marked was the national feeling of optimism, so strong the urge towards self-assertion, that Coronation celebrations of one sort or another continued for the best part of twelve months. For the Queen Mother it was an occasion tinged with nostalgia and perhaps a little sadness as she recalled the great events of her own life which had taken place at Westminster Abbey: her marriage in 1923, her own coronation in 1937 and ten years later the wedding of her elder daughter. The Queen Mother, with Princess Margaret, rode to the Abbey in a glass coach and took her place in the front row of the Royal Gallery, only the second queen in the long history of the British monarchy to watch the crown being placed on the head of her child. One observer noted: 'In she came, glittering from top to toe, diamonds every-where . . . the Queen Mother playing second lead as beautifully as she had played the first . . . She is the only woman I ever saw who can always slow up naturally when she sees a camera.'[2] By the Queen Mother's side in the gallery sat the four-year-old Prince Charles, listening intently to his grandmother's explana-tion of the ceremonies. When the services had ended sharp-eyed members of the congregation noticed that the little Prince disappeared rather suddenly behind the rail of the gallery – he was searching for his grandmother's handbag, mislaid on the floor.

The year of national rejoicing, however, was not without its sad and unpleasant moments for the Queen Mother. A little more than two months before the splendour of the Coronation another, less happy procession had been seen in the streets of London – the cortège of Queen Mary, who, having outlived her husband and three of her sons, died at the age of eighty-seven on 24 March 1953. It was a blow to the Queen Mother, coming so soon after the death of her husband: the two great foundations upon which she had built her royal life were now only memories. And within a few days of the Coronation she found herself at the centre of a public scandal which revived painful memories of 1936 and must have made Elizabeth wish that she still had Bertie by her side. Princess Margaret wanted to marry a man who was divorced.

The roots of the love affair which was to cause so much anxiety stretched back to 1944, when a handsome, dashing RAF fighter pilot, Wing-Commander Peter Townsend, was appointed Equerry to King George VI. As he left the Regency Room at Buckingham Palace after being interviewed by the King, Townsend – thirty years old, married and a father – met for the first time Princess Elizabeth, then aged seventeen, and the fourteen-year-old Princess Margaret, who was soon to fall under the spell of the good-looking war hero. Townsend was the perfect equerry for the King. He had experienced both the stress of isolation as a fighter pilot and the responsibilities of a station commander; he was courageous, loyal and knew his duty; and nerves tempered by war were unlikely to crack under one of the King's famous outbursts of temper.

Gradually Townsend became not only an invaluable member of the Household but also a friend of the King, and indeed of his family. As Princess Margaret grew older the King, perhaps rather thoughtlessly, encouraged her friendship with Townsend. He had always been indulgent towards his younger daughter and at the same time he was worried that Margaret would be lonely without her sister Elizabeth, who, it was becoming obvious, would marry Philip as soon as she could. At this time Townsend had no relationship with Princess Margaret other than as the daughter of his master. In 1950, however, the situation began to change when strains appeared in his marriage. His position on the King's staff, originally a temporary one, was made pemanent: he was promoted to the rank of group-captain and appointed assistant Master of the Household. His new responsibilities, and the fact that he was the King's trusted friend as well as his servant, meant that Townsend began to spend more and more time away from Adelaide Cottage, the grace and favour residence in the Home Park, Windsor Castle, where he lived with his wife and two sons.

Matters came to a head in 1952. The King died and Townsend obtained a divorce on the ground of his wife's adultery. On the one hand the Group-Captain was the man to whom the widowed Queen and her younger daughter turned for support, and on the other hand he found in Princess Margaret a sympathetic listener as he mourned the collapse of his marriage. When the Queen Mother appointed Townsend Comptroller of her Household, he and the Princess began to spend a good deal of time together. Margaret was no longer the adolescent hero-worshipper but a lively young woman of twenty-two. She had become the centre of a sparkling social group known to the Press as 'the Margaret set' (echoes of her Uncle David's socializing in the twenties and thirties). She was seen at parties and clubs with a whole range of eligible escorts and the papers were full of speculation as to whom she might marry: would it be the Earl of Dalkeith, the Marquis of Blandford, Lord Porchester, the Hon.

Peter Ward, or Colin Tennant, heir to Lord Glencomer? In truth, she had chosen Peter Townsend, and he was beginning to fall in love with her.

Had King George VI lived things would have been different. He would have told Townsend, in a firm and fatherly way, to abandon any idea he might have of marrying the Princess. He would have prevented the couple from being alone together, even from seeing each other if necessary. It would have been cruel, perhaps, but on this point the King would not have given way to his daughter's wishes, and that would have been far less cruel in the long run than what actually happened. As it was, the Queen and the Queen Mother were stunned when Princess Margaret and Townsend declared their love for each other after a holiday weekend at Sandringham, but their natural self-discipline and royal training made them retain their composure, while their instinctive humanity made them treat the couple kindly. (Sources close to the Royal Family say there was no truth in the story which circulated at the time that the Duke of Edinburgh was openly hostile to Townsend.)

The first sign of the disaster to come was given by Sir Alan Lascelles, the Queen's temporary Private Secretary (he had worked in that capacity for George VI). When Townsend told Sir Alan of the situation the Private Secretary was deeply shocked and told the Group-Captain that he must be mad to think that anything could come from a relationship between himself and Princess Margaret. That was hardly encouraging, but worse was to follow. On the day of the Coronation the Princess was seen talking animatedly to Townsend in the Great Hall of Westminster Abbey, and she was photographed laughing with him as she brushed some fluff from his uniform. It is not difficult even for cynical newspaper reporters to see when two people are in love, and for the next few days the public prints were full of the story.

On 14 June *The People*, one of a number of Sunday papers of the day which based their appeal on being salaciously puritanical, asked the question that was guaranteed to embarrass the Crown: was Princess Margaret contemplating marriage with Group-Captain Townsend, a man not only divorced but also a member of a royal household? This time there was to be no conspiracy of silence among the Press such as there had been in 1936. The Queen and the Queen Mother were placed in an extremely difficult position. They did not want to see a confrontation like the one which had developed between Edward VIII, his family and Parliament. They loved Margaret and did not want her to be hurt, either by a public outcry or by losing the man she loved. They understood and sympathized with her feelings – after all, the Queen herself had been committed in love at a tender age, while the Queen Mother had always wished nothing for her children so much as a happy life. Yet both the Queen, who would have to give her consent to the marriage, and the Queen Mother, to whom the Princess naturally turned for guidance, thoroughly disapproved of divorce and were therefore logically opposed to the idea that Margaret should marry Townsend. A further problem was the Princess herself: she had always been strong willed and she was accustomed to getting her own way. Any heavy-handed attempt to direct the course of her life was bound to cause trouble.

It was Winston Churchill who suggested what seemed to be the perfect solution when his advice was sought. The Prime Minister had once risked his political future by giving aid and comfort to Edward VIII and he had learnt the bitter lesson of 1936. He counselled that it would be folly to defy the teaching of the Church of England so soon after the sacred rite of the Coronation, but he pointed out that in two years' time the decision would no longer rest with the Queen – Princess Margaret would have attained the age of twenty-five and, under the terms of the Royal Marriages Act, would be theoretically free to marry anyone as long as she gave the Privy Council twelve months' notice of her intention. It only remained to secure the Princess's agreement to a delay of two years, and to remove Townsend from the Queen Mother's Household. Churchill's advice was accepted with relief. In two years anything might happen . . . the Princess might meet someone else, someone more 'suitable'. Townsend was despatched to Brussels as air attaché at the British embassy and, though the separation was painful, Princess Margaret agreed under the impression that at the end of it no obstacle would be placed in the way of her marriage. 'They gave us hope,' she said later. That hope would soon be roughly snatched away.

As Peter Townsend prepared to take up his appointment in Brussels, the Queen Mother and Princess Margaret left London for Southern Rhodesia, where they were to attend celebrations marking the centenary of the birth of Cecil Rhodes,[3] who had secured the territory for Britain in 1889. They flew in a Comet of British Overseas Airways by way of Rome, Beirut and Khartoum to Salisbury, the Rhodesian capital, where they were greeted by seven thousand children. On 2 July the Queen Mother and the Princess travelled to Bulawayo and took tea on the way with some of the country's leading white settlers. Next day the Queen Mother opened the Central African Rhodes Centenary Exhibition before an audience of twenty-five thousand people. She said the exhibition showed the 'wonderful progress' which had taken place in Central Africa: 'The whole development has been that of a tiny white community surrounded by primitive Africans growing into a young and flourishing nation.'

It was at that time not yet clear that Rhodesia, like many other countries in Africa, was living on borrowed time, with the white minority maintaining the attitudes of an empire which no longer existed. For the time being the Africans were content to live under the paternalistic rule of the British. Twenty thousand of them cheered one of their chiefs as he welcomed 'the mother of our gracious Queen and British Empire, in which space and distance have become of small account when words and works may encircle the globe as does the sun, so that no part of the Empire may brood in darkness'. But in the African townships there were some men who suggested that the 'wonderful progress' the Queen Mother had noted was more for the benefit of the white colonists than for the native population who, because they were regarded as primitives, were accorded only second-class citizenship in the land which had once been their own. Independence movements were already growing and in time they would become an important force in big-power politics. Britain would learn, as other imperial powers had done before her, that it is easy to build an empire, harder to maintain it and even more difficult to dismantle it with honour when it becomes a political and economic embarrassment. When the political game was going badly, however, the British Government could always play the royal card, and the Queen Mother in particular was to find herself spending a good deal of time in Africa as colonies were transformed into 'emergent nations'.

The Rhodesian tour of 1953 was an arduous one. From Bulawayo the Queen Mother and Princess Margaret went on to Gwelo and Umtali, where a group of children presented the Queen Mother with a large doll which had a variety of costumes and a miniature suite of furniture – gifts for Princess Anne, who was then approaching her third birthday. On 10 July Princess Margaret was taken ill with a cold and flew back to Salisbury, while her mother motored two hundred miles to Fort Victoria, rejoining her daughter two days later. The relentless pace of engagements was maintained with the opening of a hospital, the laying of the foundation stone for a new multi-racial university, a tour of an African village, a visit to a tobacco auction, garden parties and a ball for fourteen hundred guests at Government House in Salisbury. The Press corps who followed the royal party were amazed at the Queen Mother's endurance and the way in which she kept alive her interest in what she saw. However, the strain of the visit and the variable weather which accompanied it took their toll and the Queen Mother was laid low with a chill when she returned home.

She was sufficiently recovered by 6 August, however, to receive the freedom of Inverness 'in recognition of a life devoted to the service of the nation and of the Commonwealth and Empire, and as an expression of the loyalty and affection which the Highlands and their capital have always felt for all members of the royal family'. (Presumably the 'always' was a slight case of hyberbole: it is hardly likely that many Highlanders felt much affection for the House of Hanover, for example.) During her visit to the Highlands the Queen Mother made several trips to

Barrogill Castle to see how the work of restoration and renova-
tion was progressing, and when she returned to London it was
to receive the freedom of the City in an impressive ceremony at
Guildhall. 'All of us to whom London means home,' the Queen
Mother said, 'must find pride in the progress of reconstruction
which we see around us. Slowly but surely the wounds and
scars of war are being healed again and London is assuming her
fair mantle of dignity and grace.' She said that in accepting the
freedom of the City she pledged herself anew 'as long as I shall
live to the service of our people, our country and our Commonwealth'. As the years passed, she never lost sight of that promise.

Early in 1954 came invitations for the Queen Mother to visit
the United States and Canada that autumn, but she had plenty
to keep her occupied before then – visiting Norfolk, the West
Country, Leeds, Lancashire, Wiltshire and Scotland, including
Barrogill Castle, where electricity and new bathrooms had
recently been installed. She left for the United States on 20
October aboard the ocean liner named after her, landing in New
York, twelve hours late because of bad weather, on the 26th. 'I
am delighted', she told the official welcoming party, 'to find
myself once again in New York and among its kind and friendly
people, for ever since our happy visit in 1939 I had always hoped
that one day I might be able to come back.' She unveiled a
portrait of the Queen for members of the Canadian Club in the
city, visited the Metropolitan Museum of Art, saw a show on
Broadway and lunched with the Pilgrims of the United States.
At one function it was raining as the Queen Mother left and
Walter Gifford, formerly the American ambassador in London,
held an umbrella over her. 'Just like dear old London, isn't it?' he
said, then added hastily, 'That wasn't meant to be an unkind
remark.' The Queen Mother retorted: 'No – just a little crack!'
She visited Eleanor Roosevelt, widowed like herself, and
attended celebrations at Columbia University for the bicenten-
ary of the granting of the university's charter by King George II.
Columbia bestowed upon her an honorary Doctor of Laws
degree, noting her various abilities and talents in the citation to

'a noble Queen, whose quiet and constant courage in time of great stress sustained a nation and inspired a world; in hazardous days, finding her station beside her husband, George VI, and with her devoted people; a gifted musician, accomplished linguist and understanding student of the arts'.

Anglo-American relations were not without their tensions in 1954 as the administration of President Dwight D. Eisenhower pursued what appeared to be a worldwide crusade against communism while the British Government was committed to a policy of international co-operation which included the Soviet Union, communist China and their satellite states. The Queen Mother drew attention to these differences when, during a dinner given by the English-Speaking Union at the Waldorf Astoria in New York, she boldly dipped her toe into the chilly waters of politics:

> We in Britain are perhaps too much disposed to judge American policy by the making of it, which frequently takes place in an atmosphere of considerable clatter. We do not always wait as confidently as we should for the final results, which are apt to be moderate, generous and wise. Similarly, people in the United States are inclined to misinterpret British policy, because we go about it in our own quite different way.

The purpose of the dinner, though, was to mark a development in Anglo-American co-operation, the foundation by the English-Speaking Union of a permanent fellowship fund in memory of George VI. The Queen Mother found the tribute to her late husband 'wonderful and moving' and said that the King would have approved as warmly as she did of the idea of taking young people from Britain on scholarships to the United States 'to learn something about your country and its traditions and about yourselves and your institutions'.

After New York it was on to Washington – 'this beautiful city', the Queen Mother said – and a meeting with President Eisenhower, 'whom all Europe recognized as a great commander and whom the King and I knew as a true friend of Great Britain'. At the White House, where the Queen Mother was received by President and Mrs Eisenhower, she was told by the

Secretary of State, John Foster Dulles, 'I know all this has served to make abundantly clear the regard in which you are held, and, I may say, the affection with which the people look to you and your family.' With Mamie Eisenhower the Queen Mother visited the world famous Smithsonian Institution and the Mellon art gallery. Leaving Washington, she went to Annapolis, state capital of Maryland, then on to Richmond, Virginia, and Williamsburg, the former capital of the British colony of Virginia, where a painstaking attempt was being made to recreate the colonial city as an historical showplace.

On 12 November the Queen Mother flew to Ottawa and, though the night of her arrival was bitterly cold, several thousand Canadians were waiting to greet her when she stepped from her aircraft. As she had done in the United States, she recalled her visit with the King in 1939 – 'during the darkest days of the war my husband and I often recalled those happy times and found comfort in the recollection'. She made speeches in French as well as in English and followed the usual course of official openings, tours and receptions, then she returned to New York to begin her voyage home in the liner *Queen Mary*. 'You have won the hearts of all Americans', she was told by the American chief of protocol, as she prepared to board the ship.

Summing up the Queen Mother's visit to the United States, *The Times*, never shy about drawing morals for those not privileged to view the world from its own lofty peak, commented:

> It would have been unimaginable in 1854 that Queen Victoria's mother should drive with the President down Constitution Avenue with her banner of arms flying beside the Stars and Stripes, and should kneel to pray in George Washington's stall at Williamsburg. The reason would not have been that Anglo-American relations were then particularly unfriendly, but that the monarchy itself was still a barrier of estrangement. It is so no longer; it is becoming a link of understanding between the peoples . . . This has not come about by any automatic stream of tendency; it has been brought to pass, against the grain of history, by the personal qualities of the men and women who have occupied or stood close to these two highest secular eminences of

the modern world; and among them on the British side no one has done more, by the unconcealable warmth of her love for humanity, than Queen Elizabeth the Queen Mother. She is able to speak for the Commonwealth straight to the hearts of friendly peoples, at a level of feeling the politicians cannot reach.

What the newspaper was saying, in effect, was that in the Queen Mother Americans discovered the very opposite of their stereotype of the English as 'stuffy, snobbish, snooty and unapproachable'. One New Yorker, Edward L. Bernays, put it succinctly:

> She appeared to have the very American characteristics we all hold dear. In the Queen Mother Americans discovered to their delight warmth, sincerity, frankness, democratic bearing, interest in American institutions, and a vigour that no one imagined a Queen could have. Undoubtedly she has been a most potent symbol for Britain in this country, not excluding ambassadors, generals and prime ministers.

When the Queen Mother returned home after her triumph in the United States, however, it was not her abilities as an ambassador that were required, but all her skill as a mother. Princess Margaret was still determined to marry Peter Townsend.

With Townsend out of the country and the Rhodesian tour of 1953 behind her, Princess Margaret apparently settled down into her old social life and the doings of 'the Margaret set', who drank pink champagne and danced until dawn, once more attracted the attention of the gossip columns. By the summer of 1954 it was rumoured in the Press that the Princess was about to become engaged to her old friend Colin Tennant. What the newspapers which spread that story did not know was that Princess Margaret and Townsend were still very close and that even as the engagement rumour was circulating Townsend was in London meeting the Princess, with the knowledge of the Queen and the connivance of the Queen Mother. The lovers spent two hours together at Clarence House and agreed that a further year's separation was not too high a price to pay if at the end of it they could marry without hindrance.

The fateful year of 1955 came, and royal life went on much as usual. Early in the year the Queen Mother was elected Chancellor of London University, a post which gave her great pleasure and satisfaction, and she lent her support to a conference called by the National Federation of Women's Institutes which began the 'Keep Britain Tidy' campaign. She cancelled many of her engagements in March because of an attack of influenza, but the following month she was fit enough to make her first flight in a helicopter when she visited her Royal Auxiliary Air Force squadron at Biggin Hill. (The helicopter later became her favourite form of transport.) May found her in Caithness opening a huge regional water scheme and in June she attended a service at Westminster Abbey to honour the tenth anniversary of the signing of the United Nations Charter. But behind all this activity she had the nagging worry about what was going to happen when Princess Margaret became free, in theory at least, to marry Peter Townsend.

The crucial date was 21 August, Princess Margaret's twenty-fifth birthday. The Royal Family were gathered at Balmoral, where the Queen Mother had organized a sale of work at Crathie Church in which the main attraction was the stallholders – the Queen, the Duke of Edinburgh, the Queen Mother, Princess Margaret, Prince Charles and Princess Anne. Three thousand people attended the sale, but the figure was more than trebled the following day, Sunday the 21st, when the Royal Family attended morning service at the church. Among the crowd were a number of newspaper reporters anxious to gain some inkling of what was in Princess Margaret's mind now that she no longer needed her sister's permission to marry.

Townsend returned to London on 12 October and met Margaret on the evening of the 13th at Clarence House. The Press was on the verge of frenzy. All that royal spokesmen would say in response to repeated inquiries was 'No comment' and 'No announcement concerning Princess Margaret's personal future is at present contemplated', which served to convince the newspapers that Princess Margaret's personal future was soon to be settled. Meanwhile, at their first meeting for more than a year, the Princess and Townsend simply rejoiced in being together again, but it gradually dawned on them that their two years of heartache had been in vain. They were still not free to marry without causing an unholy row. One sentence in the Royal Marriages Act had been overlooked: the part referring to members of the Royal Family over the age of twenty-five said that a marriage could be contracted without the Sovereign's consent and after twelve month's notice to the Privy Council, *'except that both Houses of Parliament shall declare their disapprobation thereto'*. In a way the situation was worse than it had been in 1953 because the decision was now out of the hands of the Queen and rested instead with the people of Britain, through their Members of Parliament (though it must be remembered that what Members of Parliament do and say does not always reflect the wishes of the people who elected them).

Winston Churchill, the man who had suggested delay in the first place, had retired as Prime Minister and had been succeeded by Anthony Eden. Though sympathetic to the emotional side of Princess Margaret's problem, since he had himself remarried after a divorce, Eden had to warn the Queen that Parliament would not stand idly by if the Princess persisted in her plan to marry Townsend – she might well have to give up her royal functions, renounce her royal rights and lose her income from the Civil List annuities, which at the time was £6,000 a year and due to rise to £15,000 on her marriage (assuming that the marriage was 'suitable', naturally). The Queen is constitutionally bound to accept the advice of her Prime Minister and, since the delay had absolved her of any legal responsibility in the matter, she could do nothing to help her sister, though it is said that her attitude was more flexible than that of the Queen Mother, who could not bear the thought of another 'defection' from the royal ranks.

Princess Margaret and Townsend tried to escape for a quiet weekend in the country. They went to Allanbay Park, near Binfield in Berkshire, the home of the Queen Mother's niece Jean (daughter of Lady Elphinstone) and her husband, Major John Wills. Escape from the Press was impossible, however, and the house was soon virtually under siege by newspapermen, some of whom even hired aircraft to maintain their surveillance. After the weekend the couple were pursued back to London while newspaper editorials, churchmen, politicians, everybody and his brother held forth on the subject of what the Princess ought to do. It began to look as if the argument of 'royal duty' might carry no more weight with Princess Margaret than it had with King Edward VIII; she might indeed be prepared to renounce her royalty, and the income it provided, in order to marry the man she loved. But there was still the religious argument. The Church of England did not recognize the marriage of divorced people; the Queen was bound to uphold the laws of the Church; the Queen Mother had long preached the virtues of a Christian life. Could the Princess ignore all that? Still she agonized.

Then, at a Cabinet meeting on 18 October, Lord Salisbury, Lord President of the Council, Conservative leader in the House of Lords, and a leading lay member of the Church of England, let it be known that if there were any attempt to persuade Parliament to approve Princess Margaret's marriage he would resign. The Prime Minister knew that Salisbury meant what he said – after all, he had resigned with Eden in 1938 in protest at the Munich agreement – and the Government could not afford to lose him, or the support of the influential body of Tory opinion which he represented (indeed, Salisbury had been one of the men who had secured Eden's appointment as Prime Minister, in the days before Tory leaders were elected). Eden advised the Queen that Princess Margaret would have to give up everything she had known and even face the possibility of living in exile, at least for a time, if she married Townsend.

The position of religious leaders was that the time had come to make a stand against the rising tide of divorce in Britain. That view was by no means confined to Anglicans. The chairman of the Methodist Conference, Dr Leslie Weatherhead, felt obliged to comment on the affair. Even if the Princess were to renounce her royal rights and privileges, he said, 'her example does not make it easier to uphold the ideal of Christian marriage in a land in which divorce is already too lightly regarded, homes too readily broken up and children too thoughtlessly deprived of the mental security of having two united parents . . .' They were sentiments with which the Queen Mother heartily agreed, and she also believed that although it was important to find happiness in life, that could not be achieved by doing something which one knew to be wrong, or by shirking one's duty. On the afternoon of 18 October the Queen Mother took tea with Princess Margaret and Townsend at Clarence House. She was as kind and affectionate as ever, but she could not help her daughter to reach her decision – she could only hope that she knew Princess Margaret well enough to trust her to take the 'right' course.

Naturally, *The Times* could not remain silent on the matter, and on 24 October it offered its own sonorous guide for the Princess's conscience, saying that whether she liked it or not Princess Margaret was the sister of the Queen,

> in whom her people see their better selves reflected, and since part of their ideal is of family life, the Queen's family has its own part in the reflection. If the marriage which is now being discussed comes to pass, it is inevitable that this reflection becomes distorted. The Princess will be entering into a union which vast numbers of her sister's people, all sincerely anxious for her lifelong happiness, cannot in all conscience regard as a marriage . . .

In the light of hindsight, this was going too far. Princess Margaret was not only the Queen's sister, she was also a young woman in love with a man who, even in terms of the contemporary view of divorce, was 'the innocent party'. The *Daily Mirror* was probably nearer the truth for most people when it said that it did not matter very much whom the Princess married. But in 1955 the narrow morality, based on Victorian hypocrisy, which has tortured the English conscience to a greater or lesser degree for more than a century, remained largely unquestioned and *The Times* editorial carried a great deal of weight.

Princess Margaret and Townsend met on the evening of the 24th, the day on which *The Times* published its leader. Townsend had already decided what should be done. He had hardly slept the previous night and he had come to the conclusion that the horror must end. At Clarence House that evening he handed Princess Margaret a piece of paper on which he had jotted down suggestions for a statement which he thought she should issue. The Princess read his notes and agreed with what they said. A great feeling of relief swept over the couple. Their ordeal would soon be over.

On 26 October the Queen Mother spent the day in Reading, where she was opening a new technical college. She felt more lighthearted than she had for weeks. But the furore in the Press continued. For some reason, it was thought inopportune to publish Princess Margaret's statement immediately (indeed, there has been a good deal of criticism of the advice the Queen received during this period). On Thursday 27 October the Princess went to see the Archbishop of Canterbury, Dr Fisher, and told him of her decision. Then she and Townsend went to spend the weekend with friends in Sussex, returning to London separately on the 31st. On the evening of their return, the Princess's statement was issued:

> I would like it to be known that I have decided not to marry Group-Captain Townsend. I have been aware that, subject to my renouncing my rights of succession, it might be possible for me to contract a civil marriage. But mindful of the Church's teaching that Christian marriage is indissoluble, and conscious of my duty to the Commonwealth, I have resolved to put these considerations before others. I have reached this decision entirely alone, and in doing so I have been strengthened by the unfailing support and devotion of Group-Captain Townsend. I am deeply grateful for the concern of all those who have constantly prayed for my happiness.

This outcome brought a certain amount of sanctimonious pleasure to those who had opposed the marriage. *The Times* responded predictably: 'All the peoples of the Commonwealth will feel gratitude to [Princess Margaret] for taking the selfless, royal way which, in their hearts, they expected of her.' The stiff upper lip had triumphed again. Princess Margaret met Peter Townsend once more in 1958, when the Queen Mother invited him first for tea and later for lunch at Clarence House. Again the newspapers were roused to hysteria, assuming that since the Queen was away at the time, Townsend was acting behind her back (though in fact the Queen knew about the meetings). The couple have not seen each other since then. In December 1959 Townsend married a twenty-two-year-old Belgian girl, Marie-Luce Jamagne, and they now have three children. As for Princess Margaret, the Queen Mother had hoped that taking the path of duty would lead her towards true happiness: it was ironic that, twenty years later, the Princess should attempt to find happiness through divorce – and doubly ironic that, although the official view of the Church of England had not changed in the meantime, hardly a voice was raised in protest.

With the end of the Margaret–Townsend affair, public attention turned away somewhat from the Royal Family and concentrated on politics, where there were plenty of causes for concern – the growing nuclear arsenals of the United States and the Soviet Union, the Suez crisis of 1956,[4] and the revolution in Hungary which was crushed by Russian troops. Thus 1956 may be seen as a fairly quiet year in the life of the Queen Mother, though not an unremarkable one. In March she went to Paris for the first time since her visit there, as Queen, in 1938. The main purpose of her trip was to open a Franco-Scottish exhibition, which celebrated seven centuries of friendship and co-operation between the two countries. 'Being Scots, I love France as all my countrymen have done,' the Queen Mother said in the speech she made, in French, at the opening of the exhibition.

Shortly after her return from France she was to be found at Aintree watching her own horse, Devon Loch, run in the Grand National. She had loved horses since childhood and had shared her husband's pleasure in his fourteen thoroughbreds, but it was not until 1949 that the thrill of owning a racehorse was brought home to her when, for the first time, she watched one of Bertie's horses pass the post in first place. Encouraged by Lord Mildmay,[5] perhaps the best amateur National Hunt jockey of the postwar period, she decided to revive the old racing tradition of the Bowes-Lyons 'over the sticks'.

Of course, she had an ally in Princess Elizabeth, who had always been passionate about horses, and the two went into partnership to buy a steeplechaser called Monaveen, which according to legend had once pulled a milk cart. At Hurst Park in February 1950, Monaveen romped home to win the George Williamson Handicap by fifteen lengths, and since then the Queen Mother's racing colours – pale blue shirt with buff stripes and pale blue sleeves, and a black cap with gold tassell – have been permanent features of National Hunt racing. More than fifty horses have raced under those colours, and at the peak of her ownership in the 1960s the Queen Mother had sixteen 'chasers in training during one season. She suffered an early setback when Monaveen, having won more than £3,000, broke a leg in his second season and had to be shot, but horses like The Rip, Game Spirit, Devon Loch, Inch Arran, Black Magic, Three No Trumps and Sunnyboy later made her one of the most successful National Hunt owners in the country.

The Queen Mother soon won the respect of racing men when she showed that she was not going to be the sort of owner who would sit back and collect the prizemoney, leaving all the responsibility to professionals. Major Peter Cazalet, her trainer for almost twenty-five years, would find her at his Fairlawne stables in Kent, in all weathers, dressed in wellington boots, thick overcoat and headscarf to watch her horses at their early morning gallop. She rapidly became an expert and insisted on being consulted as to when and where her horses would run – if she thought the going was too hard for a particular horse on a particular day, that horse did not run. The Cazalet family became personal friends, and each year when the December meeting was held at Lingfield, the Queen Mother would go to Fairlawne for the weekend, spending much of her time chatting to jockeys and stable lads. It was a blow when Cazalet died in 1973, but most of the Queen Mother's horses were taken over by an equally successful trainer and old racing friend, Fulke Walwyn. Others went to Jack O'Donoghue, who was impressed by their royal owner's sense of sportmanship: 'Win or beaten, she's always the same. "There's always another day," she says.'

Nor were the Queen Mother's interests in National Hunt racing restricted to those of an owner. She became patron of the National Hunt Committee and a staunch supporter of the National Hunt Jockeys' Association. When foot and mouth disease caused racing to be banned in 1968 she attended a special theatre performance to raise money for racecourse staff deprived of their living by the ban, and when the jockey Doug Barrett was killed by a fall during a meeting at Newcastle in the early 1970s, the Queen Mother sent a gift to be auctioned so that some money could be given to his family. During the 1960s she entertained scores of racing people each year at Clarence House and when, in 1969, Master Daniel became her two hundredth winner, she invited her steeplechasing friends to a celebration at the Savoy Hotel.

One racing prize always eluded the Queen Mother, however: the Grand National. Her best chance came in 1956, and so it was that the entire Royal Family assembled in the Royal Box at Aintree on 24 March, hoping to see Devon Loch make history by becoming the first royal horse to win the National for half a century. The jockey, Dick Francis,* rode brilliantly and Devon Loch jumped magnificently. At the run-in, with a mere fifty yards to go, the Queen Mother's horse was six lengths out in front and the spectators had already begun to cheer what looked like a certain winner. But suddenly the crowd gasped as Devon Loch stumbled, fell and sprawled on the turf as Francis struggled to remain in the saddle. Another horse, E.S.B., went into history as one of the luckiest winners of the Grand National and the Queen Mother – with the philosophical comment, 'That's racing' – dashed down to the unsaddling enclosure to comfort the distraught jockey and the dumbfounded Peter Cazalet. To this day no one knows exactly why Devon Loch collapsed, but whatever the reason the horse passed into steeplechasing legend.

But any disappointment at the Grand National was more than compensated for in June 1956 when, at long last, the Queen Mother was able to move into her very own Scottish castle.

*He is now a successful writer of racing thrillers.

Barrogill dates from 1567 and looks like the setting for a novel by Sir Walter Scott. The building was begun by the fourth Earl of Caithness, George Sinclair, but he soon ran out of money and left his son, a man of evil reputation, to complete the work. The castle remained in the Sinclair family until the latter part of the nineteenth century, when it was sold to an Englishman. It was in an advanced state of decay when the Queen Mother came upon it in 1952. She bought it partly out of love for Scottish history and a desire to save this little piece of it, and partly because of its marvellous position, overlooking the magnificently stormy waters of the Pentland Firth and surrounded on its three landward sides by woods. As she explained when she received the freedom of nearby Wick shortly after taking up residence at the castle:

> When on one of my first visits . . . I found the castle . . . with its long history, its serene beauty and its proud setting, faced with the prospect of having no one able to occupy it, I felt a great wish to preserve this ancient dwelling. It is too common an experience to find that once a house becomes deserted its decay begins and it is a happiness to me to feel that I have been able to save from such an unworthy fate part of Scotland's heritage.

And because the old Earls Caithness were also known as Lairds of Mey, she revived the historic name and rechristened her retreat the Castle of Mey.

The Queen Mother spent £40,000 on securing the building against the wild weather of Caithness, modernizing it (including the provision of central heating, a very welcome refinement in that chilly part of the world), and carrying out an ambitious programme of decoration. She was keen to retain the ancient character of the castle and one of the ways in which she achieved this was to leave many of the floors uncovered or to lay only coconut or rush matting, though the bedrooms were provided with fitted carpets so that they should not be too spartan. The colours she chose were essentially feminine – aquamarine, rose, coral pink – while the furniture, some of it brought from her other homes and some bought from the renowned London salerooms of Sotheby's and Christie's, embraced every style from Queen Anne to Victorian. For her sitting room the Queen Mother chose a tiny, low-ceilinged chamber in the main turret of the castle and made it bright, chintzy and homely, adding an unexpected but highly appropriate touch with a tartan rug in front of the fire.

Out of doors she worked hard on the walled garden so that in the summer it became a riot of colour – clematis, wallflowers, hollyhocks, roses, marigolds and many more. Gardening was always one of her passions and her expertise was officially recognized in 1961 when she was presented with the Victoria Medal of Honour by the Royal Horticultural Society. The medal is awarded to horticulturists of special merit and the number of holders at any one time is limited to sixty-three – the number of complete years in Queen Victoria's reign. In awarding the medal to the Queen Mother, the council of the Royal Horticultural Society said that it was 'deeply conscious of the great contribution to horticulture in this country made by Her Majesty Queen Elizabeth the Queen Mother, by the interest, encouragement and enthusiasm that she has shown over the years, backed by a wide knowledge and love of plants'. A tribute more widely acclaimed was the naming of a rose for her, Elizabeth of Glamis.

The important thing about the Castle of Mey was that there the Queen Mother could be herself. It became commonplace for Caithness folk to see her dressed in an old raincoat and felt hat walking along a beach by the castle with her dogs, or standing in her waders in the icy waters of the River Thurso fishing for salmon, and indeed catching some of those most wily fish. At Clarence House, Birkhall and The Royal Lodge there were always the intrusions of queendom, but at Mey the Queen Mother found that she could give free rein to the part of herself that only she knew.

8

Public Property

'We can't do without her,' Queen Elizabeth II is said to have replied to a suggestion that the Queen Mother should become Governor-General of Australia or Canada. Certainly in the first two decades after her husband's death the Queen Mother was never out of the public eye for very long, and one of the striking things about her career during those years was the enormous amount of travelling she did.

Britain in the 1950s and 1960s was a nation in search of a place in the world. She had entered the Second World War as a great imperial power but by the time the conflict ended the Empire was slipping away. First India then Burma became independent republics; Palestine was transformed into the state of Israel; Eire, which had retained its links with Britain though it had become a republic in 1937, was declared the sovereign republic of Ireland in 1949. These countries were to be followed over the years by Sudan, British Somaliland, South Africa, the Southern Cameroons, the Maldive Islands, Aden and Pakistan. Within the Commonwealth that replaced the Empire, Britain could not demand the loyalty of her colonies but had to earn it, and from a trade point of view it was important that she did so, particularly as more and more of those colonies pressed for self-government. There was also the matter of British influence in the world, which had declined in the face of the financial resources and armed might of the two superpowers created by the war, the United States and the Soviet Union.

But Britain had one advantage not enjoyed by the super powers – a monarchy, to which people throughout the world could respond on an emotional level which could never be reached by an elected head of state from a foreign country. Of course, the number of trips abroad the Queen could make were limited by her domestic commitments and her direct involvement with government, so it was the Queen Mother who, in the fifties and sixties, became Britain's ambassador extraordinary. She was uniquely fitted for this role: she had been Queen before the war, in the days to which older people were already beginning to look back with nostalgia.

The Queen Mother's serious globe-trotting began in the summer of 1957, when she went to Rhodesia and Nyasaland, which had been joined together in a federation.[1] During her fourteen-day tour she was installed as the first president of the University College of Salisbury; she went down a copper mine, wearing a miner's helmet and a white coat; and she received the homage of hundreds of African chiefs, who called her *Mambo Kazi*, 'Big Mother'. In an address to the chiefs the Queen Mother stressed the need for continued co-operation between Africans and white settlers and she even produced an apt metaphor for the occasion. 'When one ox pulls this way and the other that, nothing is achieved,' she said. 'It may even be that the yoke is broken. But when all bow their yokes the plough moves and the work for the harvest has begun.' That message may have expressed the hopes of the British Government but it did not appeal much to Africans whose thoughts had turned away from oxen and towards the cars, big houses and elegant way of life enjoyed by most of the white settlers in their countries. It would not be long before Africa would feel the full force of a violent 'wind of change', in the phrase used by Harold Macmillan.[2]

Macmillan the unflappable, 'Supermac' as he came to be known, succeeded to the premiership in 1957, taking over from

Anthony Eden, who had retired in poor health and with his political reputation damaged by the Suez debacle of the previous year. He was to preside over several years of economic stability and growth which produced the slogan 'You've never had it so good'. Under Macmillan's benign eye the stage would be set for the naked commercialism of the 1960s which brought with it the so-called 'permissive society'. In 1957 there was already a sign of a certain change in attitude appearing in the Royal Family: the Duke of Windsor was invited to attend the dedication of a memorial to Queen Mary at Marlborough House, and for the first time the Duchess of Windsor came with him. After twenty years the wounds of the Abdication were beginning to heal.

The following year, the Queen Mother was off on her travels again, this time to tour Australia and New Zealand. She left London in January 1958, setting the royal pace once more by becoming the first member of her family to fly round the world. She went first to Canada, where in heavy rain she undertook a twenty-mile drive through Vancouver. From there it was on to Honolulu then to Suva, in Fiji, where this time she was obliged to drink the *kava* from which Bertie had so gallantly protected her in 1927. When she swallowed some of the bitter-tasting concoction she realized what her husband had suffered and only partially drained the cup, but wild cheering from the spectators and official prompting encouraged her to drink the rest as custom demanded. On 2 February she arrived in New Zealand to an enthusiastic welcome and a compliment from the Prime Minister, Mr Nash, who told her: 'You are not only Queen Mother but also queen of mothers.'

The tour was very much a sentimental journey for the Queen Mother, and she spoke often of the late King. In Australia she found herself once more in Canberra, now grown to a city of forty thousand people. The keynote of the visit was informality and official functions were kept to a minimum. It was here, perhaps, that the royal 'walkabout' began to develop as the Queen Mother mixed freely with the crowds. This was not without its dangers: in Brisbane she decided to take a closer look at the horses of her mounted police escort and there was a mighty gasp from the spectators as one of the animals lunged forward to nibble a bouquet of orchids and greenery which had just been presented to the Queen Mother – but, calm as ever, she neatly sidestepped and gently stroked the horse's nose.

Certainly it was an endurance test for a woman approaching her fifty-eighth birthday. The weather in Australia varied from torrential rain to intense heat (twenty-one women collapsed in a temperature of 86 °F when the Queen Mother visited Sydney), but she remained cool, elegant, smiling and always ready for a quick chat with some of those who had waited patiently to see her – though when she had to shake hands with 250 people in the course of one reception there were protests from her entourage. There was also a difference of opinion between the organizers of the tour and the Queen Mother's staff over the question of how informal she could afford to be. One Australian official made it known that spectators would be discouraged from attempting to stop the Queen Mother to present her with flowers, but a member of her Household said the Queen Mother had been distressed because she had been unable to stop and accept bouquets and was worried that people who had gone to the trouble of preparing flowers might be disappointed. The Australians were determined that people should be on their best behaviour, and when the Queen Mother visited the University of Melbourne tight security measures were in force to prevent students from getting up to any pranks. This did not go unnoticed. 'It's a pity,' the Queen Mother said, 'that the students are so quiet. Unless they reach an uncomfortable stage, a students' rag is fun.' Then as an afterthought she added, 'Flour bombs are a little uncomfortable, of course.'

Her visit to Tasmania proved that even royal tours do not always go as smoothly as they might. There was a fifty-mile-an-hour gale blowing; at Launceston the public address system broke down in the middle of her speech; at Hobart two fire engines with sirens howling raced through the royal procession; then at Government House the wind blew off the hats of women formed up in ranks to meet her. 'I enjoyed it all,' the Queen Mother said.

What she saw in Australia evidently impressed her, for at a 'welcome home' banquet given by the City of London at Guildhall in March 1958 she said:

> One little family I saw in Australia had left their home near us in Scotland only two years ago. The father had found a job he liked, the son loved the hard but rewarding life on a sheep station, the daughter was at a good school, and the mother was happy because of the great kindness they had received on all sides. I mention this as an example of the opportunities which await those who seek them in this rewarding land.

That wistful little speech seems to indicate that a governor-generalship would not have been unwelcome.

But the Queen was right – the Queen Mother was too valuable to be tied down in one place. In April 1959 she visited Rome, where she unveiled a memorial to Scottish soldiers and a statue of Lord Byron, then called on the Pope. This last courtesy upset some of the Queen Mother's countrymen, notably the Free Church of Scotland, and a quaintly worded statement of explanation was issued from Clarence House. It said in part: 'You will no doubt realize that a courtesy of this nature does not imply or reflect any views as to the political or religious opinions of the heads of state visitant.' The Free Church was not exactly mollified, for it replied dourly: 'The fact remains that the claims of the Pope as head of the Roman Church and sovereign ruler of the Vatican City are so closely interwoven that recognition of the one will be regarded as recognition of the other.' The attitude of the church seems to have been somewhat less Christian than that of the Queen Mother who, during a visit to the Capitol, found her way suddenly blocked by a woman who carried a small child and shouted for 'bread and work', and later expressed her concern for the woman, then under arrest. A slightly mystified Mayor of Rome promised that the woman would be dealt with leniently.

Later in the year it was politics rather than religion that threatened to cast a shadow over another visit to Africa by the

Queen Mother, this time to Kenya and Uganda. The tour provoked protests by Kenyan nationalists who wanted an early end to the state of emergency declared by Britain during the Mau Mau campaign of terror against whites, which was then receding.[3] Kenyans were called upon to boycott functions the Queen Mother attended, though an African nationalist member of the legislative council made it clear that it was the British Government to which the protest was addressed and that Kenyans had nothing against their royal visitor: 'If the Queen Mother does not find a warm welcome from Africans in Kenya, we hope she will understand it is because of the prevailing circumstances – it must not be taken as a sign of discourtesy or disloyalty.' It was not taken as anything at all, since the royal card proved once more to be stronger than anything in the political hand, and very few people heeded the call for a boycott. And to the Masai tribe at least, the Queen Mother assumed the proportions almost of a goddess. When she visited the tribal capital of Narok she told a vast gathering that 'I hope you will be blessed with good rains' – and within half an hour there was a thunderstorm and a heavy downpour. It is not every royal visitor who can claim to be a rainmaker.

The Kenyan visit was one of the few occasions on which the appearance of the Queen Mother attracted political protests, though she herself was not afraid to comment on political issues, as she demonstrated during her tour of the United States in 1954 when she referred to misunderstandings between policymakers on opposite sides of the Atlantic. When the National Health Service came into being in 1948 the Queen Mother told officials and local councillors at the opening of a new hospital in Gateshead:

> The added duties shouldered by the state do not absolve us from the practice of charity or from the exercise of vigilance . . . we cannot afford to relax our personal efforts . . . The English way of progress has always been to preserve good qualities and apply them to new systems . . .

During the famous 'stop-go' economic policies of Harold Mac-

205

millan's Conservative Government in the early 1960s she spoke of 'a chilly wind blowing down Whitehall', and the politically-inspired building boom of the same period provoked a mild rebuke for 'massive and sometimes boxlike modern buildings which spring up almost overnight'.

Of course, politics inevitably came into the Queen Mother's visits to Northern Ireland, and in a sinister way, with violently-worded protests from the republican Sinn Fein movement and fears of attacks by the Irish Republican Army. But she was not to be frightened by threats, such as the one which caused widespread alarm when she went to Darlington, in County Durham, to attend the quatercentenary celebrations of the Queen Elizabeth Grammar School. A few days before she was due to arrive in Darlington, a local newspaper received an anonymous letter which threatened, 'Acid attack on Queen Mother if visit not called off.' It was suspected that the threat came from members of the Campaign for Nuclear Disarmament, the political bogeyman of the day,[4] and five schoolboys who were known or believed to have connexions with the movement had their fingerprints taken by the police, amid a blaze of publicity. But the Queen Mother went ahead with her visit as planned and no attack materialized. 'It looks as if the acid threats were a hoax,' a senior police officer said afterwards. His royal visitor had refused to consider that they might be anything else.

It was not unnatural that schoolboys should have been thought to be responsible for the acid threat during the Darlington visit, for the second half of the twentieth century has been remarkable for the amount of attention paid to the thoughts, feelings and actions of young people, which have provoked envy, disapproval, anger and even fear among their seniors. During the fifties and sixties phrases like 'teenage rebellion' and 'youth protest' became commonplace as British society looked on with dismay at the procession of so-called youth movements which seemed to appear from nowhere and as suddenly faded away. The violence of the Teddy-boys was followed by the beards, sloppy sweaters and jazz language of the Beatniks; a change of fashion brought the Mods, with their neat suits and winkle-picker shoes, and as a reaction to them the leather-clad Rockers and their motorcycles; then came the Hippies and flower-power and drugs and dreams of love and peace, followed by the Yippies (who knows what they stood for?) and later by the Punks, who displayed all the violence of their Teddy-boy ancestors and an even more outrageous appearance.

But the body of young people who, over the years, have attracted more sustained criticism than any other have been students, who have been variously regarded as ungrateful recipients of the privileges extended to them by a benevolent state, as worthless parasites and as dangerous revolutionaries. The Queen Mother, though, was not among the critics, and as Chancellor of the University of London from 1955 she was in a strong position to become one of the stoutest defenders of students. She once said that undergraduates 'are all too often in the headlines of the newspapers today and, of course, attract a good deal of attention on the radio and television' – but all students wanted to do was to get on with their work, and in spite of 'all the difficulties with which they are faced they continue to discharge their vital obligations'.

The Queen Mother somehow managed to embody the kind of virtues which are usually described as old fashioned, in the best sense of the term, and yet to remain in close touch with a modern world which many of her generation found bewildering or frightening or simply so appalling as to be not worth thinking about. It is easy enough for older people to pick out the faults in a society very different to the one in which they grew up, but the Queen Mother displayed a rare insight by trusting young people to rectify those faults, instead of blaming the new generation for creating them. In a speech to a thousand graduates at the annual degrees ceremony of London University she developed a theme about which she had begun to speak in the closing years of the war and which, in the 1970s, would prompt the great E. F. Schumacher[5] to write his brilliant book *A Guide for the Perplexed* in an attempt to knock some sense into a chaotic world. She spoke of the need for a firm spiritual base at a time of rampant materialism when science is treated as a religion and technology as a cure for all human ills:

> The problems which confront us today in this modern atomic age are so complicated as to be bewildering. In the breathless pursuit of technical mastery we must not lose sight of something even more precious, the true purpose of education, which is surely the making of human beings by the training of three aspects of man – body, mind and character. The ages in which the world has made some of its greatest advances are those in which men of piety and vision have caught sight of levels higher than those in which the world is moving. Do not, therefore, in today's tumult, lose sight of the ancient virtues: service, truth and wisdom . . .

That speech was made in 1960, the year in which the Queen Mother, of course, celebrated her sixtieth birthday. Two events made it a particularly happy year for her. On 19 February Queen Elizabeth II gave birth to her third child, Prince Andrew, and a week later it was announced that Princess Margaret was engaged to be married. After the drama of the Townsend affair the Princess had been more or less left alone by the Press and when in 1958 she began to form an attachment to a dashing young photographer called Anthony Armstrong-Jones, nobody seemed to notice. Indeed, when her engagement to Armstrong-Jones was announced the romance was greeted as a well-kept royal secret. The wedding took place at Westminster Abbey on 6 May 1960. It drew the largest crowds in London since the Coronation, and the happiness of the Queen Mother to see her second daughter married, in her thirtieth year, was plain to all: Armstrong-Jones was charming and considerate, as well as handsome and personable, and he did not seem to mind the sort of background hovering which was expected of him on royal occasions; he got on well with his wife's family, and even took up shooting to keep the Duke of Edinburgh company though he was not too keen on killing animals.

After the marriage Princess Margaret seemed to blossom into a mature and beautiful woman. Nevertheless, critics of the monarchy still tended to single out the Princess for their attacks. A number of Members of Parliament complained at the cost of

The Queen Mother is greeted by King Frederik and Queen Ingrid of Denmark as she arrives in Copenhagen for the wedding of Princess Benedikte of Denmark in 1968.

Sampling a strawberry at the Chelsea Flower Show in 1969.

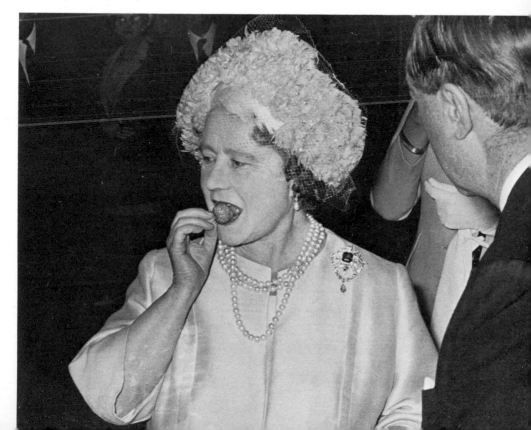

Never mind the weather: the Queen Mother with the Duke of Edinburgh at the Badminton Horse trials in 1971.

The best-loved grandmother in the world.

Stepping out at the North of Scotland Gundog Association trials in 1973.

Prince Charles and Prince Andrew photographed with their grandmother on her seventy-fifth birthday.

Event of the year: the wedding of Princess Anne at Westminster Abbey, 14 November 1973.

Mother's day: the Queen Mother, President of the Royal College of Music, receiving the honorary degree of Doctor of Music from the Queen, who is patron of the college.

Sharing a joke with workmen at the National Theatre shortly before the completion of the building.

Royal charade: Princess Margaret, the Queen Mother and the Queen pose as milkmaids for a spot of homely fun at Balmoral.

A smiling Queen Mother pats her horse Sunnyboy after he had become her three-hundredth National Hunt winner at Ascot in February 1976.

A birthday wave from Clarence House, August 1978.

the wedding, which was £25,000, and there was further grumbling about the fact that the happy couple had been given the use of the Royal Yacht *Britannia* for a six-week honeymoon cruise in the Caribbean. The Queen Mother, however, put in a good word for her daughter when she visited Kensington shortly after Princess Margaret and her husband had moved into grace and favour accommodation at Kensington Palace. The district had a long and intimate connexion with the Royal Family, the Queen Mother said:

> Queen Victoria was born here and the statue of the Prince Consort is near. A new link is even nearer at hand for my daughter has just moved into her first married home a few hundred yards from here. The kind of welcome you have given me assures me of the friendliness she may expect from her many new neighbours.

As it turned out, friendliness was something Princess Margaret would find in short supply during the next few years.

Five days after her daughter's wedding the Queen Mother was in the Federation of Rhodesia and Nyasaland once more. Upwards of sixty thousand Rhodesians lined her ten-mile route from Salisbury airport to the centre of the city, and the government of the colony presented her with six beautiful emeralds from a Rhodesian mine. Other souvenirs she took home were a dozen specimens of wild flowers from Mount Zomba in Nyasaland – these were for her private collection, which has been called one of the most comprehensive in the world. When she left the Federation on the last day of May, the Queen Mother reviewed the British South Africa Police in Salisbury and told them: 'The spirit of courage and enthusiasm which created this great country I have felt to be as strong as ever. My prayer is that with growing understanding and good will you will build a future in which all can live in peace and happiness.' That was the last time she saw Rhodesia, but she would live to see it ruled by an illegal white régime and racked by an internal war brought about by the attempt to build its future as the African state of Zimbabwe.

It was during that tour of Rhodesia and Nyasaland in 1960 that a curious piece of gossip about the Queen Mother began to circulate. The New York *Daily News* somehow picked up a story that the Queen Mother was preparing to marry again, and the 'prospective bridegroom' was identified as her seventy-four-year-old Treasurer, Sir Arthur Penn. A few British papers carried this incredible tale, and for once in her life the Queen Mother lost her temper with the Press. She instructed Colin Black, the press officer for the African tour, to issue a statement saying that the marriage report was 'complete and absolute nonsense'. That was her last word on the subject, Black told reporters, but he added that 'in fact Her Majesty used a stronger word'. Not for nothing had she been married for more than twenty-five years to a seafaring man.

And so the Queen Mother reached her sixtieth birthday. She celebrated it quietly, as she has always preferred to mark anniversaries, spending the morning at Clarence House with her grandchildren – Prince Charles, Princess Anne and the infant Prince Andrew – and going to Kensington Palace for lunch with Princess Margaret and her husband, the Queen and the Duke of Edinburgh. Afterwards she flew to the Castle of Mey for a holiday in peace and privacy.

But at the age of sixty she was very far from being a retired Queen; she remained a dynamic royal personality as much in demand by the people she served as she had ever been, full of energy, still ready to face any new challenge, to travel the world and to exhibit wherever she went unfailing courage and indomitable optimism. Her fitness and powers of endurance were remarkable. In 1961 she broke a small bone in her foot after an accident at The Royal Lodge, but she refused to cancel her engagements. At Vickers-Armstrong's shipyard on Tyneside she arrived in a wheelchair to launch the liner *Northern Star* and was wheeled onto the launching platform, which had been specially lowered. She even dispensed with the wheelchair a few days later when she attended a reception at Lancaster House for two hundred American teachers visiting Britain through a government exchange scheme – with her foot in bandages, she limped across the lawns then sat with her leg resting on a stool for a handshaking session which lasted for more than an hour.

The Queen Mother's foreign engagements in 1961 were restricted to a tour of Tunisia, but the following year there was a full-scale visit to Canada. The Black Watch (Royal Highland Regiment) of Canada, of which the Queen Mother had become colonel-in-chief, was celebrating its centenary, and at a spectacular ceremony before eighteen thousand people at McGill University she presented new colours to the regiment. In her address she recalled the capture of Montreal from the French in 1760, when the victorious British commander, Sir Jeffrey Amherst, had marched into the city with two battalions of the Royal Highland Regiment at his back. 'The virtues of hardihood, courage and honour crossed the sea from Scotland and made new history in helping to build this great country,' the Queen Mother said. But she did not forget the sensibilities of French-Canadians, some of whom would, within a decade, be seeking the independence of Quebec province from 'English-dominated' Canada. At City Hall the Queen Mother spoke French when she replied to her official welcome by the French-Canadian mayor. Later she visited Ottawa, where the Mayor, Charlotte Whitton, said the Queen Mother had stirred to 'unwonted demonstrations' the mass of Ottawans who were 'usually comparably moved only by encounters in football and hockey, or the excitement of our monster bingos'. The Queen Mother was still making history: her journey to Canada was the first time a member of the Royal Family had travelled in a commercial airliner, along with fare-paying passengers, on a normal scheduled flight.

Nineteen sixty-three was another year spent mainly at home, though the Queen Mother paid a private visit to France and in May toured the Channel Islands for four days. The Channel Islanders were in a state of high excitement as they prepared to receive their royal visitor, but then it was realized that building work on a women's college in Guernsey could not begin in time for the Queen Mother to lay the foundation stone as planned. Nothing daunted, the Guernsey education council obtained

211

£100 from the island parliament and used the money to build on the site a wall in which the Queen Mother could plant the stone, which was later incorporated into the college building.

The next setpiece tour had been scheduled for February 1964, when the Queen Mother was due to make a thirty-thousand-mile trip taking in Canada, Australia and New Zealand. But just a week before she was to depart she suffered a sudden attack of appendicitis, and on 3 February she was taken to King Edward VII's Hospital for Officers, where she underwent a thirty-minute operation for the removal of her appendix. Next day a medical bulletin reported that 'Her Majesty's condition after the operation is satisfactory', and within a fortnight she was back home at Clarence House, having been 'a model patient' in the eyes of the nursing staff. After spending a few weeks in convalescence at The Royal Lodge, in the company of Princess Margaret and her husband, the Queen Mother left London by air for Kingston, Jamaica, where she was to join the Royal Yacht *Britannia* for a three-week cruise in the West Indies – but before she went she could not resist calling at Buckingham Palace to see her latest grandchild, Prince Edward, born to the Queen on 10 March.

The Australian tour had been postponed until 1966, and on 23 March that year the Queen Mother arrived in Adelaide, where she was to attend the leading arts festival in Australia, of which she was patron. One person in particular was very glad to see her: Prince Charles had gone to Australia three months earlier to attend Timbertop school, the bush annexe of Geelong grammar school in the state of Victoria, and the Queen Mother was his first visitor. They spoke to each other on the telephone the day after the Queen Mother's arrival and a week later they went off into the Snowy Mountains on a weekend fishing trip. The Queen Mother spent sixteen days touring Australia then went to spend Easter in Fiji, where she became the first royal visitor to be cheered by the islanders, breaking their ancient tradition of remaining silent in the presence of royalty.

After the break the Queen Mother toured New Zealand, though this was more in the nature of a holiday than an official visit. She spent as much time as she could fishing, but for once the fish did not rise to the royal command. At the end of a two-day stint on North Island which produced only one rainbow trout weighing two pounds the Queen Mother was heard to mutter, 'It would have been better to get one out of the deepfreeze . . .' In Christchurch, later in the tour, the citizenry was outraged when a fence at Addington racecourse was daubed with slogans saying 'Oppose British Royalty' and 'Queen Mother Go Home'. An eighteen-year-old youth was fined £40 for helping to paint the slogans, a penalty which seems to have been rather excessive but which no doubt reflected the royalist sympathies of the conservative New Zealanders – and the offender did display a certain narrow-minded nastiness when he offered as an excuse for his action the opinion that New Zealanders should not have to 'pay for some rich woman who lives overseas'.

On her way back to Britain the Queen Mother delighted a crowd gathered to see her during a brief stop in Honolulu when she did a hula-hula dance, no mean feat for a woman of almost sixty-six. Yet within a few months she was back in the King Edward VII Hospital undergoing surgery to clear what was described as 'a partial obstruction' in the abdomen. The public knew nothing about her illness beforehand, indeed on the very day she entered hospital she had attended a function held by the Women's Voluntary Service at St James's Palace. The operation, carried out by a team of six surgeons, took place on the morning of 10 December 1966, precisely thirty years from the date of the abdication of King Edward VIII. Gifts, flowers and telegrams of good wishes came from all over the world and the Prime Minister, Harold Wilson, sent a 'get well soon' letter on behalf of himself, Mrs Wilson and members of the Government. The Queen Mother remained in hospital over Christmas, returning to Clarence House on 29 December. Her first appearance in public came on 22 January, when with the Queen and other members of the Royal Family she attended morning service at the parish church of Fletcham, near Sandringham.

A major abdominal operation is a severe strain for anyone at the age of sixty-six and the doctors advised the Queen Mother to take a long rest. This meant a particular frustration for her: she had to relinquish her appointment in 1967 as Lord High Commissioner to the General Assembly of the Church of Scotland, the office her husband had filled almost forty years before. But she did not exactly take things easy. Four months after her operation she toured the West Country then sailed in the *Britannia* to France to visit Normandy on the twenty-third anniversary of the Allied invasion in 1944. The mayor of the little town of Graye, near Arromanches, presented her with a photograph of George VI which he had taken during the King's visit shortly after the D-Day landings.

By now the Queen Mother's globe-trotting days were almost over, though in the summer of 1967 she spent a fortnight touring the eastern provinces of Canada and she visited the country again in 1974. But she could still show the young royals a thing or two about travelling in style, as she proved in 1975 when she became the first member of the Royal Family to make an official flight in Concorde, the Anglo-French supersonic airliner, on her way to spend a week in Iran at the invitation of the Shah.

Indeed, the Queen Mother has been a shining example in so many ways to the generations of the Royal Family who have followed her. Looking back with affection to her own childhood among a large and happy family, she was delighted when she reached her sixties and seventies to find herself surrounded by a growing throng of royal children – nephews, nieces, grandchildren and finally her first great-grandchild. She revelled in having the youngsters round her at Clarence House or for weekends at The Royal Lodge and holidays at Birkhall. There would be cakes for tea, spirited games, story-reading and sing-songs, just as there had been in another age at St Paul's Walden Bury and Glamis. The Queen Mother would even do conjuring tricks for her young visitors, the favourite being one in which she passed six coins apparently through the back of her hand and into her palm, an illusion she learnt from Prince Charles.

But in the midst of all the fun the Queen Mother still managed to imbue the children with a sense of what life required of them both as members of the Royal Family and as people. The late Prince William of Gloucester[6] once said: 'If I let myself down – say I got into a mess of some sort – my first thought would be that the Queen Mother would feel that I had let her down. I have always felt like this, even as a young child. It isn't that she ever said anything, it's a sort of indescribable sense of dedication she gave me.' He added: 'I can't tell you what the Queen Mother means to all of us. You only had to be loved by her – and to love her yourself – to know that, no matter what, you could never let her down.'[7]

One person to whom this special relationship has been very important is the Prince of Wales. Prince Charles is said by people close to the Royal Family to be regarded as the best possible heir to the throne that anyone could want and to have inherited the Queen Mother's unflagging self-discipline, common touch – which many felt was lacking in Queen Elizabeth II during her early years on the throne – and irrepressible sense of fun. His grandmother's is the tempering influence between the some-times too-serious dedication of his mother and the occasionally obvious irritability of his father.

Like the Queen Mother, Prince Charles always seems to be at ease in public, always ready to chat with people near him and usually in touch with what the 'man in the street' is thinking. On an entirely personal level the Queen Mother is proud of the fact that she taught Prince Charles fly-fishing and made him what she describes as the only member of the Royal Family besides herself who is an expert angler. She also introduced him to the pleasures and mysteries of gardening when he was a small boy by buying him a set of miniature tools so that he could help her with the splendid garden at The Royal Lodge. (On at least one occasion, though, she felt that she had to apologize for her grandson, albeit in fun. Visiting Rugby School in 1961 she was presented with a Rugby football for the Prince: 'I'm sorry to say my grandson has been rather fond of soccer,' she confessed.)

But over the years the member of the Royal Family who seems to have needed the Queen Mother most has been Princess Margaret. In 1960 it looked as if the future of the Princess was settled at last and the following year the seal appeared to be set on her happiness when she gave birth to her first child, Viscount Linley, and her husband was created Earl of Snowdon. In 1964 the Snowdons' second child, Lady Sarah Armstrong-Jones, was born – in the same year as the Queen's third son, Prince Edward – but five years later Princess Margaret and her husband were living separate lives.

There is said to have been some dissension between the couple during their honeymoon, when Princess Margaret accepted a site for a holiday home on the Caribbean island of Mustique as a wedding gift from her old friend Colin Tennant, to whom gossip had once had her engaged. Apart from that, the marriage was dogged by ill-natured criticism, such as that which followed Lord Snowdon's appointment to a £10,000-a-year job as a photographer with the *Sunday Times* Colour Magazine. It was suggested that he had been given the job simply because he was married to Princess Margaret, though this was quite untrue: the magazine was being masterminded by Snowdon's old Cambridge friend Mark Boxer, who needed a good photographer, which Lord Snowdon clearly is.

The real trouble began, however, in 1967. Snowdon had taken a cottage near Handcross, in Sussex, and word circulated that Princess Margaret disapproved of it. The newspapers sensed a serious rift, and made much of the fact that Snowdon had gone off to Japan by himself to take pictures for the *Sunday Times*. The rumours reached such a pitch that Snowdon called a Press conference on his return to deny them. His statement was not entirely believed, and it was noted that in March 1967 Princess Margaret visited Mustique while Colin Tennant was there – she was making arrangements to collect her wedding present. In 1968 Princess Margaret went on holiday by herself, which drew more speculative comment, and though she later had a vacation with her husband he did not accompany her to the wedding of the Aga Khan in Paris that autumn: she went with Patrick, Earl of Lichfield, that other titled photographer who is also the Princess's cousin. The Snowdons were still married, still living together at Kensington Palace, but more or less separated. Princess Margaret began to spend a lot of time with her mother, mainly in the peace of The Royal Lodge. Once more the Queen Mother was caught up in her younger daughter's emotional problems.

From 1969 onwards the Press had a field day with the Snowdons, much to the distress of the Queen Mother and the Queen. It was like the Townsend affair all over again. There were reports of a romance between Lord Snowdon and Lady Jacqueline Rufus Isaacs, the daughter of the Marquis of Reading, whose home is near Snowdon's cottage in Sussex. The publicity infuriated both the Royal Family and the Readings and, possibly as a result of pressure to patch things up, Princess Margaret and her husband were photographed on holiday together in the West Indies during the early part of 1970. The newspapers, however, turned their attention to yet another new 'Margaret set', frequently mentioning names like Tim Tollemache and Dominic Elliot. The public scrutiny intensified in 1972 when both Elliot and Lord Lichfield spent time at the holiday home Princess Margaret had had built on Mustique. The Princess was now forty-two, apparently putting on weight and looking extremely miserable most of the time. The following year she met the young man who was to bring the full weight of Fleet Street's opprobrium down upon her head and his own. His name – Roddy Llewellyn.

By 1975 Snowdon's name was being linked with that of Lucy Lindsay-Hogg, who had worked with him on filming in Australia for a BBC television series, while Princess Margaret's friendship with Llewellyn had not developed unnoticed. In the spring of 1976 came the statement that the Press had been waiting for – some people might almost say hoping for:

> Her Royal Highness the Princess Margaret, Countess of Snowdon, and the Earl of Snowdon have mutually agreed to live apart. The Princess will carry out her public duties and functions unaccompanied by Lord Snowdon. There are no plans for divorce proceedings.

The Princess spent more and more time with the Queen

Mother and was often to be found staying at Clarence House. Then in the spring of 1978 the relationship between the Princess and Roddy Llewellyn became almost daily fare for newspaper readers. Llewellyn, seventeen years younger than Princess Margaret, had by then launched himself on a career as a pop singer, which seemed to infuriate the anti-Margaret brigade more than ever. On 10 March 1978 a Labour Member of Parliament and noted critic of the monarchy, William Hamilton, stood up in the House of Commons and said that £30,000 should be deducted from the annual £55,000 Princess Margaret received from the Civil List. Everyone knew that the List was at that time being revised and that the Princess would receive an increase in the normal course of events. Hamilton said later: 'If she thumbs her nose at taxpayers by flying off to Mustique to see this pop singer chap, she shouldn't expect the workers of this country to pay for it.' Another Labour MP, Dennis Canavan, asked a parliamentary question of the Chancellor of the Exchequer, Denis Healey:

> In respect of the many letters from all over the country I have forwarded to you, will you include in your Budget measures to increase public expenditure in favour of deserving cases, such as pensioners, children receiving school meals, and stop all unnecessary expenditure for the over-privileged, including the £1,000-a-week pocket money which we give to a parasite like Princess Margaret?

At the instruction of the Speaker, Canavan later withdrew his 'parasite' remark, but the fat was really in the fire.

Pressure began to mount for Princess Margaret to withdraw from public life, and royal embarrassment grew. By 6 April the newspapers were reporting that Margaret had been given an ultimatum, some said by the Queen others by the Duke of Edinburgh (who had been unfairly cast as the heartless brother-in-law at the time of the Townsend scandal). The Queen was alleged to have told her sister that she must either give up Llewellyn or leave public life. The Duke of Edinburgh was reported to have told the Princess that she was wrecking the reputation of the Royal Family. Through it all the Queen Mother stood by her younger daughter as it was decided that Princess Margaret must end her unhappy marriage. On 10 May 1978 a statement was issued from Kensington Palace in time for publication in the evening papers:

> Her Royal Highness the Princess Margaret, Countess of Snowdon, and the Earl of Snowdon, after two years of separation have agreed that their marriage should formally be ended. Accordingly Her Royal Highness will start the necessary legal proceedings.

At the time, Princess Margaret was in hospital suffering from gastro-enteritis and a liver infection.

The newspapers next day showed just how much times had changed since the Townsend furore, and even complimented the Royal Family. 'Princess Does The Right Thing' said the *Daily Mail*. Divorcing her husband allowed her to take up her full royal role again without being subjected to a constant barrage of criticism, and it also permitted Snowdon to go his own way.[8] Indeed, there were even royal precedents – Princess Marie Louise in 1900, Princess Victoria Melita in 1901. And at a time when something like one marriage in four in Britain was ending in the divorce courts there was no reason to disagree with the verdict of the *Daily Mail*: 'Princess Margaret and Lord Snowdon are observing the formalities . . . the formalities of the 1970s.' Even *The Times*, that self-appointed guardian of the conscience of Edward VIII in 1936 and of Princess Margaret in 1955, was sympathetic this time: 'All that may reasonably be asked of the rest of the Royal Family' – other than the Queen and her heir, that meant –

> is that in their private life they should act within the broad limits of customary conduct among the people of this country. Divorce does now come within these limits. There is no longer the sense of social shock that there used to be over the break-up of a marriage. It is increasingly regarded as a matter for commiseration rather than criticism . . .

There is no doubt that the real commiseration for Princess Margaret came from the Queen Mother, playing as usual the role of mother with as much skill and understanding as she brought to that of Queen. She had made sure that the Royal Family is, on the personal level, a close family – a family that sticks together in a crisis – and she always believed that on the public level a royal family must keep its finger on the pulse of the nation. There could be no doubt that divorce, robbed of its stigma of 'guilt' by the law reforms of 1962, had become part of the British way of life, and the Queen Mother has proved many times her sensitivity to changes in the British way of life. On top of that she wanted her children and her grandchildren and her great-grandchildren to be happy people, so it was she who stayed at Princess Margaret's side during the last dreadful days of the scandal, who appeared with her daughter at public functions after the Princess had recovered from her illness and the decree nisi had been granted, and who was photographed smiling with Margaret at the Badminton Horse Trials in the summer of 1978, when it was all over. There were no constitutional difficulties attached to the divorce, and from the religious point of view it has to be remembered that the Church of England does not forbid divorce, but merely insists that a divorced person cannot remarry in church, so for the Queen Mother, though she could not rejoice at the situation, it was a matter of putting her daughter's happiness first.

The break-up of Princess Margaret's marriage marked an important stage in the relaxation of royal attitudes which had been going on for some years. Already, in 1965, the Queen had visited the Duke of Windsor while he was recovering from an eye operation. Later the Duke and Duchess of Kent, Prince William of Gloucester and Princess Alexandra had visited the Windsors' Paris home. In the spring of 1972 the Queen herself, with the Duke of Edinburgh and the Prince of Wales, called on the Windsors during a state visit to France. Eight days after the Queen's return home the Duke of Windsor died, on 28 May 1972. The Queen gave her permission for him to be buried at Windsor, and it was during his funeral service at St George's Chapel that the Queen Mother laid aside the bitterness she had felt for more than thirty years. Standing alone at the end of the solemn rites was the grieving widow, the Duchess of Windsor, 'that woman' who many years before had been left in no doubt of the antipathy towards her felt by the then Duchess of York. The Queen Mother moved over to where the Duchess of Windsor stood and gently placed a hand on her arm. In that moment came recognition that though the Duke of Windsor had turned his back on a throne, by so doing he had gained a loving and devoted wife who was now left to mourn him. Love, devotion and mourning were emotions the Queen Mother understood very well.

9

Business as Usual

The 1960s were years of transition for the Royal Family, marking the continuation of the efforts to 'democratize' the monarchy which had been started by Edward VIII, in the brief time allowed to him, and carried on by King George VI and Queen Elizabeth. Edward VIII had moved too quickly, people had been shocked, and one of the reasons for the ready acceptance of George VI had been the resemblance between his approach to kingship and that of his father. As a result the changes in the style of monarchy during his reign proved to be on an emotional level rather than a practical one, a fact emphasized by the violent reaction to Princess Margaret's marriage plans in 1955, three years after the death of the King. When she came to the throne Queen Elizabeth II gave herself pause to, as it were, learn the job then, when the time was right, she deliberately started the process which has now gone so far as to have allowed the divorce of Princess Margaret and the official description of Princess Anne after her marriage as 'Mrs Mark Phillips'. By 1960 the time was right. The playwright John Osborne spoke of the monarchy as 'the gold filling in a mouth of decay', and as economics became the dominant theme of politics and almost everything else some people were questioning whether the Crown was worth its price. Others wondered whether it was morally justifiable to maintain the position of a head of state by right of birth rather than election.

The nation as a whole was in a mood for change, hard evidence of which came with the Labour victory of 1964 which made Harold Wilson Prime Minister.[1] The old distinctions between the man in the overalls and the white-collar worker were being eroded; the aristocracy was being challenged by the rise of a so-called 'meritocracy', an upper class who had succeeded by their own efforts and saw themselves as being all the better for that. In the circumstances it was felt that the Royal Family had to earn their position in life, and in this Queen Elizabeth II concurred. Her children had been sent away to school and now they were encouraged to play as much of a part in everyday life as they could. On a more subtle level, the image of the monarchy was changed by the release of a mass of publicity about the private people behind the public faces, until in the end the nation was treated to a long television documentary showing the leading members of the Royal Family at work and play. They turned out to be people just like the rest of us.

Of course, in her own quiet way, the Queen Mother had been proving for years that she was a person just like the rest of us – and indeed that fact cannot be denied. Unlike her children and her grandchildren, she had been moulded by an early life spent far away from palaces and the rules of behaviour which apply only to royal offspring. True, it had been a privileged upbringing but it had none the less left her many steps closer to the 'level of petty life', in Walter Bagehot's phrase, than her elder daughter could be. Hers was a position that most people felt had already been earned.

As the swinging sixties gave way to the sour seventies there was no sign that the Queen Mother had any intention of doing anything but continuing to earn her keep. During the year in which she celebrated her seventieth birthday she carried out 211 official engagements, including forty-seven audiences, as well as pursuing her various private interests like the 120-acre farm she owns at Longgoe, near the Castle of Mey, where in 1964 she had fulfilled a long-cherished dream by establishing a herd of pedigree Aberdeen-Angus cattle. And there was still her horse-racing, which reached a peak of achievement in February 1976 – at Ascot, appropriately enough, considering the royal connexions with that course – when the jockey Bill Smith rode her horse Sunnyboy to victory in the Fernbank Hurdle, her three hundredth winner. A member of the Queen Mother's Household admitted that Her Majesty had had to put some work 'in cold storage' in order to be present on that important day, and after the race there was champagne for Smith and the trainer, Fulke Walwyn. The Queen Mother told the jockey: 'I'm so thrilled, and especially delighted that it should happen at Ascot. Thank you so much.' Smith said he would have been heartbroken if he had not won. As it was, 'It's the greatest day of my career. I'm honoured.'

By that time the Queen Mother had only about half a dozen horses in training and had cut down on the number of race meetings she attended. But she continued to take the big decisions concerning her horses, inspecting personally any animals she might want to buy, and kept up to date through the racing information service known colloquially as 'the blower', which had been wired into Clarence House. Having reduced the number of her appearances on the course she fell into the habit of watching steeplechasing on television, and woe betide anyone who interrupted that harmless pastime. But she has never been known to lay a bet, and indeed she clearly did not become interested in racing for the prize money, though she has won her fair share. Horses are never sold when they grow too old or infirm to run (Devon Loch, for instance, spent his twilight years in the tranquil meadows of Sandringham), so that any winnings do not lead to a profit.

As far as the Queen Mother's official activities are concerned, it is probably fair to say that in recent years they have been moved gradually nearer to the sidelines of royal life and most often concern organizations of one sort or another with which she is connected as president or patron – and there are more than three hundred of them. Nevertheless she remains a Counsellor of State, as she was during the reign of George VI, and Privy Councils are sometimes held at Clarence House. In 1974, during the last weeks of the Conservative Government led by Edward Heath, with a miners' strike in progress and a three-day working week spreading chaos throughout the land,[2] it was the Queen Mother who was called upon, during the absence abroad of the Queen, to call meetings of the Privy Council and approve the dissolution of Parliament before a general election.

But a good deal of her time, both official and unofficial, has been devoted to the arts, work which was recognized in 1974 when she was presented with the principal award of the Royal Society of Arts, the Albert Medal. Events like the King's Lynn Festival, organized by her old friend and lady-in-waiting Ruth, Lady Fermoy, and the Aldeburgh Festival owe much to the Queen Mother's patronage. She has taken an interest in the King's Lynn Festival for more than twenty-five years, and even knows the names of the scene-shifters. Through Aldeburgh she became a great friend of the late Benjamin Britten,[3] who, to celebrate the Queen Mother's seventy-fifth birthday, set to music seven poems by Robert Burns which he presented to her in an album with his original score. A public performance of the songs was given by the tenor Peter Pears, friend of both Britten and the Queen Mother. One of her favourite musical places is Covent Garden where, after a ballet performance, she likes to stand and gaze at the auditorium emptied of the audience. She simply loves the building and was the inspiration behind a fund which raised money to pay for an extra row of candelabra to be placed between the Grand Tier and the Amphitheatre: the Queen Mother thought that part of the house looked rather bare.

Her interests, however, have not been confined to the higher spheres of culture. She has attended every Royal Variety Performance since the 1950s and for more than thirty years she has been patron of the Variety Artistes' Benevolent Fund. At one notable Royal Variety Performance in 1961, the great Maurice Chevalier brought the house down by singing 'You Must Have Been a Beautiful Baby' directly to the Queen Mother, ending with the words, ' 'Cos Majesty look at you now!' On another occasion, after watching the comic dancer and impressionist Billy Dainty, the Queen Mother admitted that 'I had to dry my hanky out. There were tears in my eyes – he's such a funny man.' As a special tribute the Royal Variety Show of 1978 was dedicated to her. The Queen Mother was invited to choose her favourite performers, but she preferred to restrict herself to dropping broad hints, and the programme reflected the great days of variety between the wars. Top of the bill was the legendary Gracie Fields, who, at the age of eighty-one, sang her equally legendary song 'Sally'. The comedian Arthur Askey, who is the same age as the Queen Mother, was also in the cast. The Queen Mother told him, 'I really shouldn't say it, but this was the best Royal Variety I've ever seen.' That was hardly surprising, considering the person to whom the whole show was dedicated.

The Queen Mother grew up in the country and at heart she remains a countrywoman, never happier than when she is walking her dogs on the beach or in the woods near the Castle of Mey, or tending her gardens there or at Birkhall and The Royal Lodge – she once described herself as 'the only member of the Royal Family who knows anything about gardening'. But of necessity it is London and Clarence House round which most of her life revolves. Unlike her other homes, Clarence House is no beauty, being rectangular and rather box-like, its cool, clean Regency lines smothered in cream paint and the whole looking somewhat incongruous next to the venerable pile of St James's Palace. But there is, of course, much more to the house than the stroller through St James's can see. Behind the stout wooden gates there is a gravelled drive leading to a pillared portico which gives onto a small hall. From the hall three steps lead to what is known as the lower corridor, which is notable for its pair of Regency crystal chandeliers, its display of Worcester china and the huge paintings which adorn its walls, including one of King George VI bestowing the Order of the Garter on the present Queen.

On the ground floor of the building are the morning room, the library – where the Queen Mother is sometimes found eating lunch among her books – and the dining room, with its Spanish walnut table, round which some dozen people can be seated, and its splendid eighteenth-century marble chimney-piece. The ceiling of the dining room is one of the few remaining examples in Clarence House of the work of John Nash, who built it for the Duke of Clarence. The walls of the room are panelled and into the panels are set portraits of Clarence and his family. On the west side of the building at ground level are the Queen Mother's sitting room and the double drawing room, which was originally designed by Nash as two rooms. The drawing room contains a portrait of Queen Elizabeth by Augustus John, begun in 1940 but never finished because of the Blitz. There are also portraits of Queen Victoria and of Lady Strathmore and her two sisters during their childhood, as well as views of the countryside in the neighbourhood of Sandringham. The room contains a grand piano and a television, which the Queen Mother sometimes watches in the evenings.

The Queen Mother's sitting room is approached by the Queen's Corridor, hung with portraits and also with paintings by L. S. Lowry (whose work the Queen Mother liked long before he became fashionable), Sisley, Matthew Smith, Augustus John and others. The main feature of the sitting room itself is a large mahogany desk which contains, apart from a mass of stationery and other office equipment, a gallery of small, framed photographs of the people who have been nearest and dearest to the Queen Mother throughout her life: King George VI, children and grandchildren, parents, brothers and sisters. On a wall behind the Queen Mother as she sits at her desk are some shelves containing a series of flat wicker baskets, each one labelled with the title of a member of her Household. To her right, by the window, is a small table on which stands a cream telephone. Immediately in front of her, on the desk, is a gilt and crystal screen in three sections of which the central one holds the royal letter paper on which each day's engagements are typed. By her right hand is a piece of china like a bon-bon dish which

227

contains a pile of pens and pencils, and beside that is a silver paper-knife. The chair by the desk, like all the others in the room and the couch, is covered in blue silk.

The sitting room is the nerve-centre of the Queen Mother's 'firm'. Her working day begins at about ten o'clock in the morning and sometimes does not end until eleven o'clock at night. As well as keeping in touch with the organizations she patronizes she receives scores of invitations and mountains of other mail, and she maintains an extensive private correspondence. To help her she has seven ladies-in-waiting, her lord chamberlain, comptroller, private secretary, press secretary, two equerries, three extra equerries, clerk comptroller, chief accountant and two clerks. She has always taken a personal interest in the welfare of the members of her Household and her staff. She never passes a servant without a word of greeting, and before she moved into Clarence House in 1953 she insisted that the staff quarters should be modernized, notwithstanding the fact that £50,000 had been spent on the building to prepare it for occupation by Princess Elizabeth and the Duke of Edinburgh after their marriage. The Queen Mother often lunches or dines with her Household, and on a summer day she likes to join them in the garden for tea.

Of the Queen Mother's other official homes her favourite is The Royal Lodge (King George V always insisted on the capital 'T' and Bertie agreed with him). The centrepiece of the house is the great banqueting saloon dating from the Regency. Under a ceiling twenty feet high this room measures forty-eight feet in length and almost thirty feet in width, and by comparison the rest of the house is modest in proportions. Two wings were added by the Duke and Duchess of York in the thirties, one to provide bedrooms, bathrooms and sitting rooms for themselves and the other to form the nursery and accommodation for guests. Servants' quarters were constructed above the garage and in the grounds an open-air swimming pool was built. One special attraction of The Royal Lodge for the Queen Mother is that it remains basically unaltered from the days when she and Bertie first lived there. The same cannot be said of Birkhall, the small Queen Anne house near Balmoral Castle, to which the Queen Mother added a new wing in 1958. In any case Birkhall is now somewhat less important in her life since she has her retreat in Caithness, the Castle of Mey.

It was when she first occupied Mey that rumours of the Queen Mother's retirement began to be heard. The thought was revived ten years later, when she was believed, wrongly, to be having a house built in Malta. Retirement, however, never seems to have been part of the Queen Mother's plans. In 1952, shortly after the death of the King, when she was unsure of what her role was to be, Winston Churchill convinced her that the people would still need her and he has been proved right with every year that has passed since then. As one writer put it, 'Somehow her personality has kept alive some of the old-fashioned respect, admiration, even adoration, which is no longer automatically given to Majesties and Royal Highnesses.'[4]

For her part, the Queen Mother has never lost the interest in her job which was first noticed when she was Duchess of York. The annual round of engagements, one very much like another, has never become a matter of routine for her, according to her friends, because she never tires of meeting new people, talking to them and getting a glimpse into their lives. She particularly likes to meet children. At an agricultural show in 1977 a six-year-old boy was presented to the Queen Mother and, after speaking to her politely for several moments, suddenly came out with, 'Ma'am, I've also met your daughter. Do you know she's the Queen?' The Queen Mother gave the boy one of her famous smiles. 'Yes,' she said. 'Isn't it exciting?'

There is another reason why she enjoys her official duties: they give her a chance to express herself, often with a certain amount of humour. In 1977 she was invited to officiate at the opening of a new headquarters for the Pharmaceutical Society of Great Britain, and when she was told that champagne was to be served she asked that it should be changed to her favourite blend of tea, Earl Grey. It is not that she does not enjoy alcohol (she likes a gin and tonic with ice and a twist of lemon), but she felt that in Britain's straitened economic circumstances tea would do just as well as bubbly – as long as the cup was warmed before it was poured.

Nineteen seventy-seven was, of course, the year in which the Royal Family and the entire country was *en fête* to celebrate the silver jubilee of the accession of Queen Elizabeth II. Royalty went everywhere, and the Queen Mother was in the thick of the action. The event was not without its critics, however: badges proclaiming 'Stuff the jubilee' were in evidence and the students of the Queen Mother's 'own' university, London, chose that year to ban her from their annual union ball, saying that at a time when education was desperately short of money they saw no point in having college buildings 'tarted up' so that the Queen Mother could spend half an hour inspecting them. The militants were no match for their royal chancellor, though. The Queen Mother wrote to the students' union saying that she could see their point of view but was keen to meet members of the staff whom she had visited for the past two decades, so perhaps she had better make it an informal visit – which she did.

But whatever the attitudes of people for or against the jubilee, it was above all a family occasion as far as the Queen Mother was concerned. On 15 August 1977 she welcomed twenty-four members of the family – including the Queen and the Duke of Edinburgh, Prince Andrew and Prince Edward, Princess Anne and her husband, Captain Mark Phillips, and Princess Margaret and her children – to a get-together at the Castle of Mey. There was a splendid lunch followed by games on the secluded beach, then tea and later drinks aboard the *Britannia*, which had anchored in Thurso Bay. At half past seven the Queen Mother returned to her castle and the Royal Yacht sailed away amid a blaze of flares and rockets. It was the twenty-seventh birthday of Princess Anne, but the party was also the Royal Family's private celebration of the jubilee. Three months later there was something else for the Queen Mother to celebrate, the birth of her first great-grandchild, Princess Anne's son Peter Mark Andrew. The baby was the first so close to the throne to be born in hospital, and it was fitting that the place of his birth should be St Mary's,

Paddington, of which the Duchess of York had become president in 1930, shortly before the birth of Princess Margaret.

It might have been thought that after all the excitements of jubilee year, not to mention the hard work, the Queen Mother would at last have made some attempt to reduce her royal commitments. But every effort to persuade her to do so has been met with the disarming assurance that she could not possibly cut out such-and-such because that was one of her favourite engagements. In fact, far from lightening her load in 1978 the Queen Mother was accepting new responsibilities.

One peculiar honour accorded to her was her appointment as Lord Warden of the Cinque Ports. The post dates from the Middle Ages and the lord warden is governor of Dover Castle and has maritime jurisdiction as admiral of the ports, which are Lydd, Faversham, Deal, Folkestone, Tenterden, Margate, Ramsgate (the five original defenders of the South Coast, the 'cinque ports'), Winchelsea and Rye, the last two being latecomers to the group since they were only added to it shortly after the Norman Conquest. The lord warden is also chairman of the Dover Harbour Board and has the right to appoint the judge and marshal of the cinque ports admiralty court, the registrar of the ports and the salvage commissioners. The Queen Mother, who is the first woman ever to hold the post of lord warden, is now entitled to a salute of nineteen guns from ships which pass her while she is at sea, and to any flotsam and jetsam which is washed up on the south-east coast between Shore Beacon, in Essex, and Redcliff in Sussex. But she will also find that she has to pay for the disposal of any whales which happen to become stranded along that stretch of coastline.

The year 1978 also marked the 150th anniversary of the founding of King's College, London University, and to honour the occasion the Queen Mother, already chancellor of the university, was made a fellow of King's. But there was a slightly melancholy note to the year, too. In September the Queen Mother paid a farewell visit to the aircraft carrier HMS *Ark Royal*, the biggest ship remaining in the Royal Navy, which was taken out of service three months later. The Queen Mother, as Queen, launched the great ship in 1950, visited her often, and always received a telegram of congratulations on her birthday from the crew of the *Ark Royal*. As she toured the ship for the last time, the Queen Mother must have reflected that a tangible reminder of her former life with Bertie was being taken away, a footnote in the history of her reign as queen consort.

Epilogue: 'A Regular Royal Queen'

Considering that she never wanted it in the first place, the Queen Mother has been remarkably successful at her job over the past four decades. One way to judge the measure of her success is to note how none of the criticism of the Royal Family which has become so fashionable in recent years has ever attached itself to her. Even that fearless left-wing weekly the *New Statesman* could not bring itself to deride or denigrate the Queen Mother in its famous 'Anti-Jubilee Number' in 1977 – indeed the only time she was mentioned, it was in terms of something approaching praise. While others are upbraided or denounced as anachronisms who cost Britain too much money in these lean times, the Queen Mother, the dear old Queen Mum, is seen as 'the superstar of the British Crown', 'the best loved lady in the land', and, somewhat less respectfully but with equal affection, as 'a proud-bosomed imperial grannie', a 'Gainsborough lady with a hint of a Pearly Queen' and 'Elizabeth Regina who has picked up a sniff or two from Ena Sharples'.[1]

Why should this be? Part of the answer may perhaps be found in the words of a tribute to her published on her seventy-fifth birthday: 'The Queen Mother has displayed the virtues of ordi-

233

nary life in an extraordinary life . . . She made the British
monarchy much more easy and natural, much more good
natured and less severe than it was in the previous generation . . .'[2] And yet it could hardly be argued that the generations of royalty succeeding the Queen Mother's generation have
returned to the severity and formality of earlier times. Quite the
opposite is the case (there are even some die-hards who think
the Royal Family is far too informal these days). So there must be
something else about the Queen Mother that has made her the
revered figure she undoubtedly is.

That she has great courage is obvious, otherwise she would
never have been able to cope with the aftermath of the Abdication and with a husband who at the beginning felt that he could
not cope. That she remains calm under the stress of situations
dangerous or embarrassing she has proved a number of times.
Once during the war an army deserter half-crazed with grief at
the death of his whole family sprang out from behind the curtains in the Queen's bedroom at Windsor and seized her round
the ankles – she gazed down at him and said softly: 'Tell me
about it.' Years later it was a half-crazed lift that tested her
mettle. On a visit to the University of London in 1956 she was
descending from the first floor but the lift stopped only momen-
tarily at the ground floor and went on to the basement, whence it
returned once more to ground level. The doors opened and the
polite academics sharing the lift with the Queen Mother stood
back to let her step out, but just as she was about to do so the
doors closed again and the lift headed for the basement. This
time the Queen Mother was ready for it: as soon as the doors
began to open she stepped out smartly and, unruffled, set off up
the stairs, joining in the merriment of the watching undergraduates.

That the Queen Mother has the common touch is also clear.
She knows exactly what ordinary people like, and very often
likes it just as much as they do. During the war her favourite
radio programme was *ITMA (It's That Man Again)*, the zany
comedy show starring Tommy Handley. When Elizabeth and
Bertie sat down to listen to it at 8.30 on a Thursday evening they

were doing the same thing as most of their subjects. And in the days when television was emerging as the single most important organ of mass culture, the Queen Mother let it be known that she followed the serial which in 1957 was as popular as *Coronation Street* is now: 'We often look in at *The Grove Family*,' she told one of the stars of the show.

'She somehow always manages to put you at your ease,' says a Fleet Street newspaper editor, a leader of a breed not noted for its dewy-eyed sentimentality. 'You go in feeling nervous and uncomfortable, but before you know where you are you're chatting away to her as if you'd known her all your life.' He is supported by Bernard Delfont, producer of the Royal Variety Performance: 'She always says just the right thing to everyone.' And members of her staff agree. They say the Queen Mother treats them not like servants but more as gentlefolk who have fallen upon hard times – sometimes at the Castle of Mey, for example, she will sit with members of her staff watching television, just as she would with members of her own family.

She is full of energy, like most small people – she is only five foot two – and she has a tremendous capacity for work. In the growing materialism of the modern world, run as it is mainly by economists, the Queen Mother is seen to give value for money. Few people would seriously carp at the £175,000 she receives at present from the Civil List, because most would agree that she is worth every penny. The provost of London University, Lord Annan, once said to her, 'Whatever the institution, it seems that it only has to ask and you respond.'

But above all she is the very model of a queen, dignified, poised, elegant, regal. W. S. Gilbert's words might almost have been written for her:

> No half-and-half affair, I mean,
> But a right-down regular Royal Queen![3]

Her life has been privileged but certainly not easy. Looking back over it, the Queen Mother must sometimes wonder how it all happened and marvel at the strange chain of events which has brought her to the position of being one of the best-loved women in the world. And perhaps she sometimes reflects on the doubts that made her hesitate for two years before agreeing to marry the Duke of York. Had she possessed the ability to foresee the future when Bertie proposed to her for the second time in 1923, would her answer have been different? Almost certainly not, for she has never been one to retreat from a challenge or to shirk a job which she felt she had to do.

As she once told her daughters when they were young, 'Your work is the rent you pay for the room you occupy on earth.' All things considered, few people have paid a higher rent in this century than Her Majesty Queen Elizabeth the Queen Mother.

Elizabeth Mure = Robert II, King of Scotland = Euphemia, dau. o
1316-1390   Hugh, Earl of Ros
                 d. 1387

David, Earl of =
Strathearn

Robert III = Anna Bella   Sir John Lyon = Jean   Sir Patrick Graham, = Elizab
1337-1406   Drummond   slain 1382   k. 1412

James I = Joan Beaufort   Sir John Lyon, Knight = Elizabeth
1394-1437

James II = Mary of Guelders   Patrick Lyon, Lord Glamis = Isabel Oglivy
1430-60

James III = Margaret of   John Lyon, Lord Glamis = Elizabeth Scrymgeou
1451-88   Denmark   d. 1497

James IV = Margaret   John Lyon, Lord Glamis = Elizabeth, dau. of
1473-1513   Tudor   d. 1500   Andrew, Lord Gray

James V = Marie de   John Lyon, Lord Glamis = Janet Douglas
1512-1542 Guise   d. 1528

Henry Stuart = Mary   John Lyon, Lord Glamis = Janet Keith
Lord Darnley   1542-87   d. 1559

James VI & I = Anne of   John Lyon, Lord Glamis = Elizabeth, dau. of
King of England   Denmark   k. 1578   William, Lord
1566-1625   Abernethy

Frederick = Elizabeth   Patrick Lyon, Earl of Kinghorne = Anne Murray
El. Palatine   1575-1615
d. 1632

Ernest Augustus = Sophia   John Lyon, Earl of Kinghorne = Lady Elizabeth
El. of Hanover   1596-1646   Maule
d. 1698

George I = Sophia Dorothea   Partick Lyon, Earl of Strathmore = Lady Helen
1660-1727 of Brunswick-Celle   1643-1695   Middleton

George II = Caroline of   John Lyon, Earl of Strathmore = Lady Elizabeth
1683-1760   Brandenburg-Anspach   1663-1712   Stanhope

Frederick, = Augusta of   Thomas Lyon, Earl of Strathmore = Jean Nicholson
Prince of Wales Saxe-Gotha   1704-1753
1707-1751

George III = Charlotte of   John Lyon, Earl of Strathmore = Mary Eleanor
1738-1820   Mecklenburg-Strelitz   1737-1776   Bowes

Edward, = Victoria of Saxe -   Thomas Lyon-Bowes, Earl of Strathmore = Mary Carpenter
Duke of Kent Coburg-Saalfield   1773-1846
1767-1820

Victoria = Albert of Saxe -   Thomas Lyon-Bowes, Lord Glamis = Charlotte
1819-1901   Coburg-Gotha   1801-1834   Grinstead

Edward VII = Alexandra of   Claude Lyon-Bowes, Earl of Strathmore = Frances Dora
1841-1910   Denmark   1824-1904

George V = Mary of Teck   Claude Bowes-Lyon, Earl of Strathmore = Nina Cecilia
1865-1936   1855-1944   Cavendish-Bentinck

George VI = H.M. Queen Elizabeth   Patrick Bowes-Lyon,   John Herbert = Hon. Fenella Hepburn
            the Queen Mother   Earl of Strathmore   Bowes-Lyon   Stuart - Forbes-Trefusis
                                     = Lady Dorothy
                                     Godolphin Osborne

The Bowes-Lyon Family

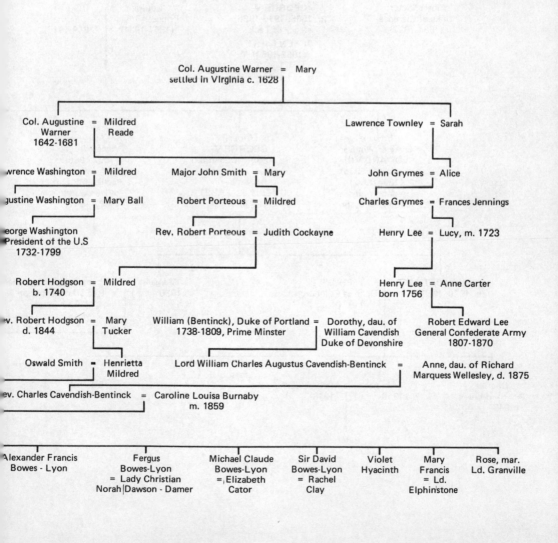

Col. Augustine Warner = Mary
settled in Virginia c. 1628

Col. Augustine = Mildred
Warner   Reade
1642-1681

Lawrence Townley = Sarah

wrence Washington = Mildred   Major John Smith = Mary   John Grymes = Alice

gustine Washington = Mary Ball   Robert Porteous = Mildred   Charles Grymes = Frances Jennings

eorge Washington   Rev. Robert Porteous = Judith Cockayne   Henry Lee = Lucy, m. 1723
President of the U.S
1732-1799

Robert Hodgson = Mildred   Henry Lee = Anne Carter
b. 1740   born 1756

ev. Robert Hodgson = Mary   William (Bentinck), Duke of Portland = Dorothy, dau. of   Robert Edward Lee
d. 1844   Tucker   1738-1809, Prime Minster   William Cavendish   General Confederate Army
        Duke of Devonshire   1807-1870

Oswald Smith = Henrietta   Lord William Charles Augustus Cavendish-Bentinck =   Anne, dau. of Richard
        Mildred   Marquess Wellesley, d. 1875

ev. Charles Cavendish-Bentinck = Caroline Louisa Burnaby
        m. 1859

Alexander Francis   Fergus   Michael Claude   Sir David   Violet   Mary   Rose, mar.
Bowes - Lyon   Bowes-Lyon   Bowes-Lyon   Bowes-Lyon   Hyacinth   Francis   Ld. Granville
        = Lady Christian   =,Elizabeth   = Rachel   = Ld.
        Norah|Dawson - Damer   Cator   Clay   Elphinstone

The Royal Family since Queen Victoria

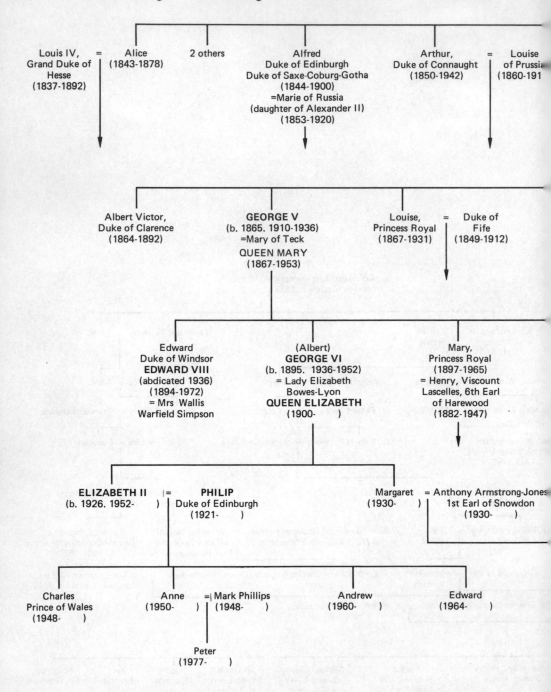

Louis IV, Grand Duke of Hesse (1837-1892) = Alice (1843-1878)

2 others

Alfred Duke of Edinburgh Duke of Saxe-Coburg-Gotha (1844-1900) =Marie of Russia (daughter of Alexander II) (1853-1920)

Arthur, Duke of Connaught (1850-1942) = Louise of Prussia (1860-191

Albert Victor, Duke of Clarence (1864-1892)

GEORGE V (b. 1865. 1910-1936) =Mary of Teck QUEEN MARY (1867-1953)

Louise, Princess Royal (1867-1931) = Duke of Fife (1849-1912)

Edward Duke of Windsor **EDWARD VIII** (abdicated 1936) (1894-1972) = Mrs Wallis Warfield Simpson

(Albert) **GEORGE VI** (b. 1895. 1936-1952) = Lady Elizabeth Bowes-Lyon **QUEEN ELIZABETH** (1900-)

Mary, Princess Royal (1897-1965) = Henry, Viscount Lascelles, 6th Earl of Harewood (1882-1947)

ELIZABETH II (b. 1926. 1952-) = **PHILIP** Duke of Edinburgh (1921-)

Margaret (1930-) = Anthony Armstrong-Jones 1st Earl of Snowdon (1930-)

Charles Prince of Wales (1948-)

Anne (1950-) =| Mark Phillips (1948-)

Andrew (1960-)

Edward (1964-)

Peter (1977-)

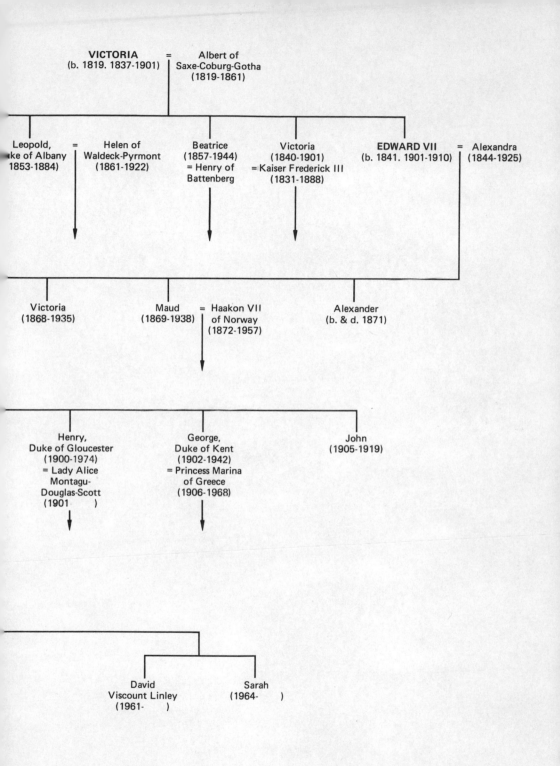

VICTORIA   =   Albert of
(b. 1819. 1837-1901) | Saxe-Coburg-Gotha
                       (1819-1861)

Leopold,   =   Helen of   Beatrice   Victoria   EDWARD VII   =   Alexandra
ke of Albany   Waldeck-Pyrmont (1857-1944)   (1840-1901)   (b. 1841. 1901-1910) (1844-1925)
1853-1884)   (1861-1922)   = Henry of   =Kaiser Frederick III
                                   Battenberg   (1831-1888)

Victoria   Maud   = Haakon VII   Alexander
(1868-1935)   (1869-1938)   of Norway   (b. & d. 1871)
                                         (1872-1957)

Henry,   George,   John
Duke of Gloucester   Duke of Kent   (1905-1919)
(1900-1974)   (1902-1942)
= Lady Alice   = Princess Marina
Montagu-   of Greece
Douglas-Scott   (1906-1968)
(1901   )

David   Sarah
Viscount Linley   (1964-   )
(1961-   )

Appendix I: The House of Windsor

The Royal House of Windsor came into being on 17 July 1917 by proclamation of King George V:

Whereas We, having taken into consideration the Name and Title of Our Royal House and Family, have determined that henceforth Our House and Family shall be styled and known as the House and Family of Windsor:

And whereas We have further determined for Ourselves and for and on behalf of Our descendants and all the other descendants of Our Grandmother Queen Victoria of blessed and glorious memory to relinquish and discontinue the use of all German Titles and Dignities:

And whereas We have declared these Our determinations in Our Privy Council:

Now therefore, We, out of Our Royal Will and Authority, do hereby declare and announce that from the date of this Our Royal Proclamation Our House and Family shall be styled and known as the House and Family of Windsor and that all the descendants in the male line of Our said Grandmother Queen Victoria who are subjects of these Realms, other than female descendants who marry or may have married, shall bear the Name of Windsor:

And do hereby further declare and announce that We for Ourselves and for and on behalf of Our descendants and all other the descendants of Our said Grandmother Queen Victoria who are subjects of these Realms, relinquish and enjoin the discontinuance of the use of the Degrees, Styles, Dignities, Titles and Honours of Dukes and Duchesses of Saxony and Princes and Princesses of Saxe-Coburg and Gotha, and all other German

243

Degrees, Styles, Dignities, Titles, Honours and Appellations to Us or to them heretofore belonging or appertaining.

Given at Our Court at Buckingham Palace this Seventeenth day of July, in the year of our Lord One thousand nine hundred and seventeen, and in the Eighth year of Our Reign.

God Save The King

A deep repugnance for all things German had swept through Britain with the outbreak of the First World War and the name of the royal house, Saxe-Coburg and Gotha, was a source of acute embarrassment, as was the close relationship between George V and Kaiser Wilhelm – they were first cousins. Of course, Queen Victoria had been a member of the house of Hanover, but then the Hanoverians had reigned in England since 1714 and had become thoroughly Anglicized. It was Victoria's marriage to Prince Albert of Saxe-Coburg which led to trouble. In 1917 the Prime Minister, Lloyd George, began to receive anonymous letters suggesting that there was not much chance of Germany being defeated while a 'Teutonic' King sat upon the throne of England, and George V was persuaded that his family's links with Germany had to be publicly severed. But if the name Saxe-Coburg was to go, there was the problem of what should replace it. Various suggestions were made: York, Lancaster, Plantagenet, Tudor-Stewart, Fitzroy. Finally Lord Stamfordham, the King's secretary, put forward the name of Windsor, which had been part of the titles of the great Edward III, founder of the Order of the Garter, and the martyred Henry VI.

A further difficulty arose in 1952 with the accession of Queen Elizabeth II. Her husband's family name, which he had assumed on his naturalization, was Mountbatten and that was the surname the Queen's children bore – thus when Prince Charles came to the throne he would be the first monarch of the house of Mountbatten. This, however, was not acceptable to the people of Britain, if the Press reports of the day are to be believed, and considerable pressure was exerted on the Queen to retain the name of Windsor: this she did officially on 9 April 1952. Eight years later, however, the Queen announced that it had long been her desire to 'associate the name of her husband with her own and his descendants' though 'without changing the name of the royal house established by her grandfather'. Thus on 8 February 1960 she informed the Privy Council that

while I and my children shall continue to be styled and known as the House and Family of Windsor, my descendants, other than descendants enjoying the style, title or attributes of Royal Highness and the titular dignity of Prince or Princess, and female descendants who marry and their descendants shall bear the name of Mountbatten-Windsor

Appendix I

This announcement caused a certain amount of confusion, for princes and princesses do not normally use or require a surname, and in any case the Queen had stated that she and her children would remain simply Windsors. The question was, who would actually use the new surname? It was thirteen years before the matter was cleared up. When Princess Anne was married to Captain Mark Phillips on 14 November 1973 her name was entered in the register at Westminster Abbey as Anne Elizabeth Alice Louise Mountbatten-Windsor. Presumably, therefore, this will be the style adopted by the Prince of Wales when he marries and the name Mountbatten-Windsor will become the style of the royal house.

Appendix II: The Civil List

Payments to members of the Royal Family under the terms of the Civil List have been mentioned several times in the course of this book, and a word of explanation is necessary.

The Civil List is the account which contains all the expenses applicable to the support of the Sovereign's household and the maintenance of 'the honour and dignity of the Crown'. The system used to be that Parliament voted an annuity to the Sovereign at the beginning of each reign, but in these days of inflation the sum tends to be reviewed regularly. The Civil List Acts passed by Parliament when they are considered necessary also allot various amounts to other members of the Royal Family.

The history of the Civil List goes back to the reign of William and Mary, which began in 1689. Before that time there was no distinction between the expenses of government and those of the Sovereign. The monarch's income from the hereditary revenues of the Crown, and certain taxes voted to him for life at the start of his reign, was supposed to maintain him, the civil government and public defence in peacetime: thus the Sovereign could swell his own coffers by skimping on public expenditure and, since he controlled vast revenues, he could act in large measure independently of Parliament. After 1689, however, the expenses relating to government were separated from the costs of maintaining the Crown. The revenues of the monarch were fixed by Parliament at £1,200,000 a year and of this sum £700,000 was allotted to the support of the Royal Household, the personal expenses of the

Sovereign, and payment of the Civil Service – hence the term 'civil list'. The annuity remained roughly the same during the reigns of Queen Anne, George I and George II, though in each case large debts against the Civil List were accumulated and met by Parliament.

A significant change in the system took place during the reign of George III. Instead of relying on revenues to defray the expenses, the King surrendered to the nation his life interest in hereditary income and received a fixed payment from the Civil List. The annuity was eventually determined at £800,000. The King, however, misused the funds allowed to him by spending them on bribes of various kinds for his supporters in Parliament and, in 1769 for example, incurred a Civil List debt of half a million pounds. By 1779, under the threat of national bankruptcy arising from the American War of Independence, loud criticism of the King's abuses of the Civil List began to be heard. Finally in 1782 an Act reforming the List was passed by Parliament. Limits were placed on the Sovereign's use of the List and its provisions were divided into distinct categories:

1 Pensions and allowances for the Royal Family.
2 Payment of senior members of the judiciary.
3 Salaries of ministers resident at foreign courts.
4 Payment for work carried out on behalf of the King or goods supplied to him.
5 Provision of servants for the Royal Household.
6 Pensions provided by way of royal bounty in cases of special merit or distress.
7 Salaries to the holders of certain offices.
8 Salaries and pensions for the Treasurer or Commissioners of the Treasury and for the Chancellor of the Exchequer.

The reform of 1782 stopped the abuses of the List, but it did not prevent the accumulation of debts, which cost Parliament £3,398,061 during the reign of George III. The List itself reached more than a million pounds in 1816 because provision had to be made not only for the King but also for the Prince Regent. By the time William IV came to the throne in 1830 the Civil List was ripe for further change and in return for the surrender by the King of more revenues, the List was relieved of all charges related to civil government – the £510,000 granted to William was meant to cover the King's expenses, salaries of certain offices and pensions, nothing more. In 1837 Queen Victoria's annuity was fixed at only £385,000, but the allowance for the royal pensions list was made separately.

King Edward VII obtained an annuity of £470,000 in 1901, and it is interesting to note that in 1952, when Queen Elizabeth II came to the throne, the Civil List allowance was only £5,000 more than Edward's. By 1972, however, the effects of inflation had made themselves felt and the Civil List annuity of the Queen rose to £980,000. Three years later it was £1,400,000 and in 1978 it became nearly two million pounds. The full List for 1978, including allocations for the Queen Mother and the other members of the Royal Family who benefit from it, was as follows:

The Queen, £1,950,000; the Queen Mother, £175,000; the Duke of Edinburgh, £93,500; Princess Margaret, £59,000; Princess Anne, £60,000; Prince Andrew, £17,262; Princess Alice, Duchess of Gloucester, £30,000; the Duke of Gloucester, £39,000; the Duke of Kent, £60,000; Princess Alexandra, £60,000; Princess Alice, Duchess of Athlone, £6,500. To cover the payments to the last four members of the Royal Family on the List, the Queen paid £165,500 into the Consolidated Fund, from which the Civil List allowances are taken. The allocations made to the various royals reflect the extent of the engagements and functions which they undertake. Supplementary payments may be made at the discretion of the Royal Trustees, who are the Prime Minister, the Chancellor of the Exchequer and the Keeper of the Privy Purse. No Civil List allowance is made to the Prince of Wales, who is Duke of Cornwall and receives the net revenue of the Duchy, half of which he gives to the nation.

Appendix III: The Wartime Broadcasts

The importance and the success of three major broadcasts by the Queen during the Second World War have been stressed in this book. These are the broadcasts in full.

1. TO THE WOMEN OF THE EMPIRE, 11 NOVEMBER 1939

The last time that I broadcast a message was at Halifax, Nova Scotia, when I said a few words of farewell to all the women and children who had welcomed the King and myself so kindly during our visits to Canada and the United States of America. The world was then at peace; and for seven happy weeks we had moved in an atmosphere of such good will and human kindliness that the very idea of strife and bloodshed seemed impossible. The recollection of it still warms my heart and gives me courage. I speak today in circumstances sadly different. For twenty years we have kept this Day of Remembrance as one consecrated to the memory of past and never-to-be-forgotten sacrifice, and now the peace which that sacrifice made possible has been broken, and once again we have been forced into war.

I know that you would wish me to voice in the name of the women of the British Empire our deep and abiding sympathy with those on whom the first cruel and shattering blows have fallen – the women of Poland. Nor do we forget the gallant womanhood of France, who are called on to share with us again the hardships and sorrows of war.

War has at all times called for the fortitude of women. Even in other days, when it was an affair of the fighting forces only, wives and

249

mothers at home suffered constant anxiety for their dear ones and too often the misery of bereavement. Their lot was all the harder because they felt that they could do so little beyond heartening, through their own courage and devotion, the men at the front. Now this is all changed, for we no less than men have real and vital work to do. To us also is given the proud privilege of serving our country in her hour of need.

The call has come, and from my heart I thank you, the women of our great Empire, for the way that you have answered it. The tasks that you have undertaken, whether at home or in distant lands, cover every field of National Service, and I would like to pay my tribute to all of you who are giving such splendid and unselfish help in this time of trouble. At the same time I do not forget the humbler part which so many of you have to play in these trying times. I know that it is not so difficult to do the big things. The novelty, the excitement of new and interesting duties have an exhilaration of their own. But these tasks are not for every woman. It is the thousand and one worries and irritations in carrying on wartime life in ordinary homes which are often so hard to bear.

Many of you have had to see your family life broken up – your husband going off to his allotted task, your children evacuated to places of greater safety. The King and I know what it means to be parted from our children, and we can sympathize with those of you who have bravely consented to this separation for the sake of your little ones. Equally do we appreciate the hospitality shown by those of you who have opened your homes to strangers and to children sent from places of special danger. All this, I know, has meant sacrifice, and I would say to those who are feeling the strain: Be assured that in carrying on your home duties and meeting all these worries cheerfully you are giving real service to the country. You are taking your part in keeping the home front, which will have dangers of its own, stable and strong. It is, after all, for our homes and for their security that we are fighting, and we must see to it that, despite all the difficulty of these days, our homes do not lose those very qualities which make them the background as well as the joy of our lives.

Women of all lands yearn for the day when it will be possible to set about building a new and better world, where peace and good will shall abide. That day must come. Meantime, to all of you, in every corner of the Empire, who are doing such fine work in all our services, or who are carrying on at home amidst the trials of these days, I would give a message of hope and encouragement. We all have a part to play and I know you will not fail in yours, remembering always that the greater your courage and devotion, the sooner shall we see again in our midst the happy, ordered life for which we long. Only when we have won through to an enduring peace shall we be free to work unhindered for the greater happiness and well-being of all mankind. We put our trust in God, who is our Refuge and Strength in all times of trouble. I pray with all my heart that He may bless and guide and keep you always.

2. TO THE PEOPLE OF THE UNITED STATES, 10 AUGUST 1941

It is just over two years since I spoke to the American people, and my purpose then was to thank countless friends for much kindness. It is to those same friends and of even greater kindness that I want to speak today. We, like yourselves, love peace and have not devoted the years behind us to the planning of death and destruction. As yet, save in the valour of our people, we have not matched our enemies, and it is only now that we are beginning to marshal around us in their full strength the devotion and resources of our great British family of nations, which will in the end, please God, assuredly prevail. Through these waiting months a heavy burden is being borne by our people. As I go among them I marvel at their unshakable constancy. In many cities their homes lie in ruins, as do many of those ancient buildings which you know and love hardly less than we do ourselves. Women and children have been killed, and even the sufferers in hospital have not been spared; yet hardship has only steeled our hearts and strengthened our resolution. Wherever I go I see bright eyes and smiling faces, for though our road is stony and hard, it is straight, and we know that we fight in a great cause.

It is not our way in dark days to turn for support to others, but even had we been minded so to do your instant help would have forestalled us. The warmth and sympathy of American generosity have touched beyond measure the hearts of all of us living and fighting in these islands. We can, and shall, never forget that in the hour of our greatest need you came forward with clothes for the homeless, food for the hungry, comfort for those who were sorely afflicted. Canteens, ambulances and medical supplies have come in an unceasing flow from the United States. I find it hard to tell you of our gratitude in adequate terms, though I ask you to believe that it is deep and sincere beyond expression. Unless you have seen, as I have seen, just how your gifts have been put to use, you cannot know, perhaps, the solace which you have brought to the men and women of Britain, who are suffering and toiling in the cause of freedom.

Here in Britain our women are working in factory and field, turning the lathe and gathering the harvest, for we must have food as well as munitions. Their courage is magnificent. I have seen them in many different activities. They are serving in their thousands with the Navy, Army, and Air Force; driving heavy lorries, cooking, ciphering, typing, and every one of them working cheerfully and bravely under all conditions. Many are on the land, our precious soil, driving the plough and making a grand job of it. Others are air raid wardens or ambulance drivers, thousands of undaunted women who quietly and calmly face the terrors of the night bombings, bringing strength and courage to the people they protect and help. I must give a special word to the nurses, those wonderful women whose devotion, whose heroism will never be forgotten. In the black horror of a bombed hospital they never falter, and though often wounded think always of their patients and never of themselves. And I need not remind you, who set as much store by your home life as we do, how great are the difficulties which our housewives have to face nowadays, and how gallantly they are tackling them. I could continue the list almost indefinitely, so manifold is the service which our women in Britain are giving. But I want to tell you that whatever the nature of their daily or nightly tasks, they are cheered by the evidence of your thought for them. We like to picture you knitting on your porches, serving in your committee rooms, and helping in a hundred ways to bring relief to our civilian garrison here.

Though I speak for us all in Britain, in thanking all of you in America, I feel I would like to send a special message of thanks to American women. It gives us strength to know that you have not been content to pass us by on the other side; to us, in the time of our tribulation, you have surely shown that compassion which has been for two thousand years the mark of the Good Neighbour. Believe me – and I am speaking for millions of us who know the bitter, but also proud sorrow of war – we are grateful. We shall not forget your sacrifice. The sympathy which inspires it springs not only from our common speech and the traditions which we share with you, but even more from our common ideals. To you, tyranny is as hateful as it is to us; to you, the things for which we will fight to the death are no less sacred; and – to my mind, at any rate – your generosity is born of your conviction that we fight to save a cause that is yours no less than ours; of your resolve that, however great the cost and however long the struggle, justice and freedom, human dignity and kindness, shall not perish from the earth. I look to the day when we shall go forward hand in hand to build a better, a kinder and a happier world for our children. May God bless you all.

3. TO THE WOMEN OF THE EMPIRE, 11 APRIL 1943

I would like, first of all, to try to tell you just why I am speaking to you tonight – to you, my fellow-countrywomen all over the world. It is not because any special occasion calls for it; it is not because I have any special message to give you. It is because there is something that,deep in my heart, I know ought to be told to you; and probably I am the best person to do it.

Most of us, at one time or another in our lives, have read some fine book that has given us courage and strength and fresh hope; and when we laid it down we have wished that, though we are strangers to him, we could meet the author and tell him how much we admire his work, and how grateful we are for it. Something of the same kind makes me feel that I would like to meet *you* this Sunday night. For you, though you may not realize it, have done work as great as any book that ever was written; you too, in these years of tragedy and glory, of crushing sorrow and splendid achievement, have earned the gratitude and admiration of all mankind; and I am sure that every man who is doing his man's share in the grim task of winning this war would agree that it is high time that someone told you so.

Some of you may feel that I am exaggerating your own share in that task. 'What have I done' you may ask, 'compared to what my boy has to put up with, dodging submarines in the Atlantic or chasing Rommel across Africa?' In your different spheres, believe me, you have done all that he has done in different degrees, endured all that he has endured. For you, like him, have given all that is good in you, regardless of yourself, to the same cause for which he is fighting – *our* cause, the cause of right against wrong; and nobody, man or woman, can give more. There is no need, surely, for me to say in detail how you have done this. Perhaps constantly travelling, as the King and I do, through the length and breadth of these islands, I am fortunate in being able to see a clear picture of the astonishing work that women are doing everywhere, and of the quiet heroism with which, day in, day out, they are doing it. The picture, I know, is being reproduced in many similar aspects all over the Empire, from the largest self-governing Dominion to the smallest island owing allegiance to the Crown. We are indeed very proud of you.

How often, when I have talked with women engaged on every kind of job, sometimes a physically hard or dangerous one – how often when I admired their pluck have I heard them say, 'Oh, well, it's not much. I'm just doing my best to help us win the war.' Their courage is reinforced, too, by one of the strongest weapons in our national armoury – a sense of humour that nothing can daunt. With this weapon of amazing temper, that turns every way, our people keep guard over their sanity and their souls. I have seen that weapon in action many, many times in the last few years and know how much it can help in really bad times.

'Work' is a word that covers a very wide field. It is hard to define in a single phrase, but if you take it as meaning doing something useful that helps others, then you will see that *your* work, whatever it may be, is just as valuable, just as much 'war-work' as that which is done by the bravest soldier, sailor or airman who actually meets the enemy in battle. And have you not met that enemy too? You have endured his bombs; you have helped to put out the fires that he has kindled in your homes; you have tended those he has maimed, brought strength to those he has bereaved; you have tilled our land; you have, in uniform or out of it, given help to our fighting forces and made for them those munitions without which they would be powerless; in a hundred ways you have filled the places of the men who have gone away to fight; and, coping uncomplainingly with all the tedious difficulties of wartime, you, the housewives, many doing whole-time and many part-time jobs – you have kept their homes for them against the blessed day when they come back. Many there are whose homes have been shattered by the fire of the enemy. The dwellings can be rebuilt, but nothing can restore the family circle if a dear one has gone for ever from it. A firm faith in reunion beyond this world of space and time, and a fortitude born of the resolve to do one's duty and carry on to the end are true consolations. I pray they may not be denied to all who have suffered and mourn.

All of us women love family life, our homes and our children, and you may be sure that our men overseas are thinking just as wistfully of these homes as we are – some of the dear and familiar homes they left behind, others of the new homes they mean to make for the young wives of the future. These men – both at home and abroad – are counting on us at all times to be steadfast and faithful. I know that we shall not fail them, but, fortified by the great experience in this war of our strength in unity, go forward with them, undismayed, into the future.

I feel that in the thinking and planning which we are doing for the welfare of our country and Empire – yes, and concern for other countries, too – we women as homemakers have a great part to play, and, speaking as I do tonight from my own dearly loved home, I must say that I keenly look forward to a great rebuilding of family life as soon as the war ends. I would like to add, with my fullest conviction, that it is on the strength of our spiritual life that the right rebuilding of our national life depends. In these last tragic years many have found in religion the source and mainspring of the courage and selflessness that they needed. On the other hand, we cannot close our eyes to the fact that our precious Christian heritage is threatened by adverse influences. It does indeed seem to me that if the years to come are to see some real spiritual recovery, the women of our nation must be deeply concerned with religion, and our homes the very place where it should start; it is the creative and dynamic power of Christianity which can help us to carry the moral responsibilities which history is placing upon our shoulders. If our homes can be truly Christian, then the influence of that spirit will assuredly spread like leaven through all the aspects of our common life, industrial, social and political.

The King and I are grateful to think that we and our family are remembered in your prayers. We need them and try to live up to them. And we also pray that God will bless and guide our people in this country and our great family throughout the Empire, and will lead us forward, united and strong, into the paths of victory and peace.

Notes

PROLOGUE CROWN IN CRISIS

1 *The Times*.
2 The brothers were: Prince Albert, Duke of York; Prince Henry, Duke of Gloucester; Prince George, Duke of Kent; Prince John. The latter died in 1919 at the age of thirteen.
3 David Lloyd George, born in Manchester of Welsh parents in 1863 and went to live with his uncle near Criccieth at age two, when his father died. Became solicitor and entered politics in 1890 as Liberal MP for Caernavon Boroughs. Chancellor of the Exchequer 1908–15, when he introduced Old Age Pensions Act and National Insurance Act. Prime Minister 1916–22. Remained an MP until 1945, when he was created Earl Lloyd-George of Dwyfor. Died 1945.
4 *The Times*.
5 *The Heart Has Its Reasons*, by the Duchess of Windsor (*see* Bibliography).
6 Stanley Baldwin, 1867–1947. Ironmaster who became MP in 1906. President of the Board of Trade 1921, Prime Minister 1923. Lord President of the Council in Coalition 1931–5, Prime Minister again 1935–7. Created Earl Baldwin of Bewdley, 1937.
7 Later Baron Hardinge of Penshurst.
8 Sir (Robert) Anthony Eden, Ist Earl of Avon, 1897–1977. Conservative MP for Warwick and Leamington 1923–57. Foreign Secretary 1933–8 (resigned over Munich Agreement); returned to Foreign Office for duration of Second World War and again in 1951 after downfall of postwar Labour Government. Succeeded Churchill as Prime Minister in 1955 and resigned owing to ill health in 1957.
9 Walter Turner Monckton, 1891–1965. Called to the Bar in 1919, Attorney-

257

General to the Prince of Wales 1932. Director-General of the Ministry of Information during Second World War; Solicitor-General in Churchill's caretaker government of 1945. Elected Conservative MP for Bristol West in 1951: Minister of Labour 1951, Minister of Defence 1955, Paymaster General 1956, created Viscount Monckton of Brenchley 1957.

CHAPTER 1   THE GIRL WHO WOULD BE QUEEN

1 The children were: Violet Hyacinth, born 1882; Mary Frances, 1883; John, 1884; Patrick, 1886; Alexander, 1887; Fergus, 1889; Rose Constance, 1890; Michael, 1893; Elizabeth, 1900; David, 1902.

2 This anecdote was recounted by Lady Cynthia Asquith in her book *The Duchess of York* (*see* Bibliography).

3 Princess Victoria Alexandra Alice Mary was born on 25 April 1897. She died on 28 March 1965.

4 The name is pronounced 'Lewson-Gore'. He later became Earl Granville and between 1945 and 1952 was Governor of Northern Ireland.

5 Later the Earl of Harewood (died 1947).

6 Diamond Hardinge was the sister of Alexander Hardinge, who figured in the Abdication crisis (*see* Prologue). She died in 1927.

7 Lady Cynthia Asquith, op. cit.

CHAPTER 2   'A PRINCELY MARRIAGE'

1 Andrew Bonar Law, 1858–1923. Born New Brunswick, but became iron merchant in Glasgow. Entered Parliament as Unionist 1900, became party leader 1911. Colonial Secretary 1915, Chancellor of the Exchequer 1916, Lord Privy Seal 1919, and Leader of the House from 1916 until retirement in 1921. Brought back to be Prime Minister in October 1922.

2 Daughter of Prince Arthur (1883–1938). She married the Hon. Sir Alexander Ramsay. Died 12 January 1974.

3 *The English Constitution* (*see* Bibliography).

4 Winston Leonard Spencer Churchill, 1874–1965. Grandson of Duke of Marlborough. A. J. P. Taylor calls him simply 'the saviour of his country'. In 1923 Churchill was out of the House of Commons, having been defeated as prospective candidate for Dundee because of his support for Lloyd George. The following year he became Conservative MP for Woodford and represented the constituency for the rest of his parliamentary life.

5 The property is now owned by the National Trust and is open to the public.

6 Bertie had become well known for the Duke of York's Camps, where boys from public schools mixed on holiday with youngsters from working class homes. He was also President of the Industrial Welfare Society.

7 Yugoslavia was at this time known as the Triune Kingdom of the Serbs, Croats and Slovenes. The crown prince who was being baptized became King Peter II in 1934, with Prince Paul as regent. When the Germans invaded Yugoslavia in 1941 King Peter assumed sovereignty, only to be deposed in 1945 when the country became a republic.

Notes

8 Emperor Haile Selassie died in 1975 after being deposed in a military coup the previous year.

CHAPTER 3 HOME AND FAMILY

1 The custom had arisen during the reign of James II, when it had been suspected that a child had been smuggled into the queen's bedchamber in a warming pan. The 'warming pan plot' was alleged to have been a cover-up for the fact that Mary of Modena, James's second wife, had either been delivered of a dead baby or simulated the confinement.
2 The house is no longer there. Its site has been incorporated into a hotel complex.
3 Kava is a narcotic drink made from the root and stem of a type of pepper plant, *piper methysticum*.
4 The schism occurred in 1843 over the interference of government in the appointment of ministers and other church matters. Out of the rift had grown the Free Church of Scotland, supported by some four hundred ministers.
5 Baldwin could have carried on at the head of a minority government, but he no doubt realized that Labour would be unable to govern and perhaps saw this as a way of allowing MacDonald and his colleagues to 'hang themselves'.
6 The *Sunday Times*.

CHAPTER 4 THE THREE KINGS

1 Morganatic marriage is a German concept applied to a marriage where the partners are not of equal rank or status and the wife does not assume the rank of her husband, as would normally be the case. Thus Mrs Simpson could have married Edward VIII but in doing so would not have been queen, and any children of the marriage would not have been in the line of succession. Morganatic marriages have taken place in several European royal houses and have been recognized by the appropriate churches. The word 'morganatic' comes from the medieval Latin phrase *matrimonium ad morganaticam* and is thought to refer to the German custom of *Morgengabe*, a morning gift presented by the husband to the wife on their marriage. Such marriages are sometimes known as 'left-handed', since the bridegroom gives the bride his left hand rather than the right.
2 Dawson had been at a function with the Bishop on October 31, but the editor's biographer states that Dr Blunt refuted any suggestion that 'The King's Matter' might have been discussed.
3 After the Abdication many people sympathetic to the King felt that Dawson had been involved in a plot to remove Edward from the throne, but if the editor's diaries are to be believed this was not the case, though by no stretch of the imagination could Dawson be described as in any way sympathetic to his monarch's position.
4 Lord Brownlow died in 1978.

259

5 Earl Baldwin of Bewdley.
6 Arthur Neville Chamberlain, 1869–1940. Lord Mayor of Birmingham 1915–16, Chancellor of the Exchequer 1923–4 and 1931–7, Health Minister 1924–9, Prime Minister 1937–40.
7 That date was the birthday of King George V.
8 Jardine and his wife were later reported in America, where the clergyman apparently had some success running what he called the 'Windsor Cathedral'.
9 *Berlin Diary*, by William L. Shirer, Hamish Hamilton, 1941 and Sphere Books, 1970.
10 Philip Wilson Steer, 1860–1942. Developed an English style of Impressionism. Taught at the Slade and helped to found the New English Art Club. Awarded the Order of Merit 1931. Some of his work can be seen at the Tate Gallery.
11 Augustus John, 1878–1961. One of the best-known British painters of the twentieth century, noted for his portraits and studies of gipsy life. Awarded Order of Merit in 1942.
12 Lord Strathmore died on 7 November 1944, aged eighty-nine.

CHAPTER 5   THE PALACE AT WAR

1 General Herzog, the Prime Minister, wanted South Africa to remain out of the war, but his parliament did not support him and he was replaced by General Smuts, who issued the declaration of war on 6 September 1939.
2 Louis Francis Albert Victor Nicholas, 1st Earl Mountbatten of Burma, born 1900, a great-grandson of Queen Victoria. Entered Royal Navy 1913, commanded 5th destroyer flotilla 1939, chief of combined operations 1942, later Viceroy and Governor General of India with the task of steering the country towards independence. Appointed First Sea Lord 1955, Chief of Defence Staff 1959–65.
3 Churchill succeeded Chamberlain as Prime Minister on 9 May 1940, following a debate on the disastrous Norwegian campaign. During that debate, Leo Amery made his famous speech demanding the resignation of Chamberlain and his War Cabinet in the words Oliver Cromwell had used to the Rump Parliament: 'Depart, I say, and let us have done with you. In the name of God, go!'
4 Named after the Minister of Food, Lord Woolton.

CHAPTER 6   JOY AND GRIEF

1 Clement Richard Attlee, 1883–1967. Entered Parliament for Labour 1919 after being Mayor of Stepney, Under-Secretary of State for War 1924, Postmaster-General 1931. Became deputy leader of Labour Party 1931 and leader in 1935. Deputy Prime Minister in war cabinet, Prime Minister 1945–51. Created Earl Attlee 1955.
2 The 'prefabs', provided at a cost of £61 million, were meant to last for ten years, but some saw service for double that time.
3 Sir Richard Stafford Cripps, 1889–1952. One of his tenets, which no doubt

Notes

prompted Churchill's comment, was that politics was an ideal sphere for the practice of Christianity.

4 The idea was to produce 800,000 tons of groundnuts annually in Tanganyika to make up a serious deficit in fats and oils in Britain. It ended in collapse in 1949, having cost the government millions of pounds.

5 Philip's mother, Princess Alice of Battenberg, (1885–1969), a great-granddaughter of Queen Victoria, married Prince Andrew of Greece.

6 The name Battenberg was changed to Mountbatten at the height of anti-German hysteria in Britain in 1917.

7 He became a Prince of the United Kingdom in 1957.

8 Sir John W. Wheeler-Bennett, *King George VI* (Macmillan, 1958).

9 Dr Geoffrey, Baron Fisher of Lambeth, 1887–1972. Headmaster of Repton School 1914–32. Bishop of Chester 1932, of London 1939, Archbishop of Canterbury 1945–61.

10 *The Times*.

11 The figure was 84 per cent.

12 On 18 September 1949 the pound was devalued from $4.03 to $2.80.

13 *See* Note 4, Chapter 1.

14 Ireland had become a sovereign republic in 1949.

15 Dorothy Laird, *Queen Elizabeth the Queen Mother* (Hodder and Stoughton, 1966).

16 *The Times*.

17 *The Times*.

CHAPTER 7   A NEW LIFE

1 Toc H is a well known organization for social service, founded originally in 1915 as a rest and recreation centre. It is an interdenominational Christian group.

2 Anne Edwards, writing in the *Daily Express*.

3 Cecil John Rhodes, 1853–1902.

4 After Egyptian nationalization of the Suez Canal, British and French troops occupied the Canal Zone while Israel invaded the region. After sharp condemnation by the United Nations, the forces were withdrawn and Eden's reputation suffered badly.

5 Lord Mildmay was drowned in 1950.

CHAPTER 8   PUBLIC PROPERTY

1 Nyasaland was granted internal self-government in 1963 and became a republic in 1966 under the name of Malawi. Northern Rhodesia, now Zambia, became an independent member state of the Commonwealth in 1964. Southern Rhodesia made a unilateral declaration of independence on 11 November 1965.

2 Maurice Harold Macmillan, born 1894. First entered Parliament 1924. Minister of Housing 1951, of Defence 1954, Foreign Secretary and Chancellor of the Exchequer 1955, Prime Minister 1957–63.

3 Kenya became an independent state within the Commonwealth in December 1963 and was declared a republic a year later.

4 CND was thought to be associated with extreme left-wing groups.
5 Dr Schumacher died in 1977. *A Guide for the Perplexed* was published in Britain in the same year by Jonathan Cape.
6 Prince William of Gloucester was killed in an air crash on 28 August 1972.
7 Interviewed by Audrey Whiting. *William of Gloucester*, *Pioneer Prince*, edited by Giles St Aubyn, Frederick Muller, 1977.
8 Lord Snowdon married Lucy Lindsay-Hogg in 1978.

CHAPTER 9   BUSINESS AS USUAL

1 Mr Wilson was Prime Minister until 1970, when the Conservatives won the general election. He returned to power in 1974 and unexpectedly resigned in 1976, when he received a knighthood. He remains Labour MP for Huyton.
2 The confrontation between the Heath Government and the miners' union led to a general election in February 1974 which resulted in the defeat of the Conservatives and the emergence of Mrs Margaret Thatcher as party leader in place of Mr Heath.
3 Benjamin Britten died in 1976. He had been created Baron Britten of Aldeburgh earlier in the same year.
4 Hilary Bonner in *The Sun*, 1 August 1975.

EPILOGUE   'A REGULAR ROYAL QUEEN'

1 These are descriptions applied to the Queen Mother by various popular newspapers.
2 *The Times*.
3 From *The Gondoliers*.

Bibliography

AIRLIE, MABEL COUNTESS OF, *Thatched with Gold* (ed. Jennifer Ellis), 1962

ARTHUR, SIR GEORGE, *King George V*, 1934

ASQUITH, LADY CYNTHIA, *The Duchess of York*, 1928

ATTLEE, C. R., *As It Happened*, 1954

AVON, EARL OF, *The Memoirs of the Rt Hon. Sir Anthony Eden, KG, PC – Full Circle* (1960), *Facing the Dictators* (1962), *The Reckoning* (1965)

BAGEHOT, WALTER, *The English Constitution*, 1867

BALDWIN, A. W., *My Father – The True Story*, 1955

BATTISCOMBE, GEORGINA, *Queen Alexandra*, 1969

BEAVERBROOK, LORD, *The Abdication of King Edward VIII* (ed. A. J. P. Taylor), 1966

BOLITHO, HECTOR, *Edward VIII*, 1937; *George VI*, 1937; *A Century of British Monarchy*, 1951

BROAD, LEWIS, *The Abdication Twenty-Five Years After*, 1961

BRYANT, SIR ARTHUR, *King George V*, 1936; *A Thousand Years of British Monarchy*, 1975

BUCHAN, JOHN, *The King's Grace*, 1935

BUCHANAN, MERIEL, *Queen Victoria's Relations*, 1954

CAMPBELL, JUDITH, *Elizabeth and Philip*, 1972

CATHCART, HELEN, *Her Majesty*, 1962; *The Queen Mother*, 1965

CHANCE, MICHAEL, *Our Princesses and Their Dogs*, 1937

CHANNON, SIR HENRY, *Chips: The Diaries of Sir Henry Channon* (ed. Robert Rhodes James), 1967

COLE, G. D. H. and POSTGATE, RAYMOND, *The Common People*, 1961

CRAWFORD, MARION, *The Little Princesses*, 1950

DARBYSHIRE, TAYLOR, *King George VI*, 1937

DONALDSON, FRANCES, *Edward VIII*, 1976; *King George VI and Queen Elizabeth*, 1977

DUFF, DAVID, *Elizabeth of Glamis*, 1973

ELLIS, JENNIFER, *Elizabeth the Queen Mother*, 1953

FISHER, GRAHAM and HEATHER, *Elizabeth, Queen and Mother*, 1964

FLOWER, DESMOND and REEVES, JAMES (EDS.), *The War 1939–45*, 1960

GORE, JOHN, *King George V, A Personal Memoir*, 1941

GORMAN, MAJOR J. T., *George VI, King and Emperor*, 1937

HARDINGE, LADY, *Loyal to Three Kings*, 1967

HARTNELL, NORMAN, *Silver and Gold*, 1958

HATCH, ALDEN, *The Fabulous Mountbattens*, 1965

HILL, C. W., *Edwardian Scotland*, 1976

HOWARD, PHILIP, *The Royal Palaces*, 1970

HUTCHINSON, T. H., *Economics and Economic Policy in Britain 1946–66*, 1968

HYDE, H. MONTGOMERY, *Baldwin – The Unexpected Prime Minister*, 1975

INGLIS, BRIAN, *Abdication*, 1966

JAMES, ROBERT RHODES, *Churchill, A Study in Failure 1900–1939*, 1970

JENKINS, ALAN, *The Forties*, 1977

JENKINS, ROY, *Asquith*, 1964

JUDD, DENNIS, *George V*, 1973

LAIRD, DOROTHY, *Queen Elizabeth the Queen Mother*, 1966

LIVERSIDGE, DOUGLAS, *The Queen Mother*, 1977

LONGFORD, ELIZABETH, *Victoria R.I.*, 1964; *The Royal House of Windsor*, 1974

MACKENZIE, COMPTON, *The Windsor Tapestry*, 1938

MACMILLAN, HAROLD, *Tides of Fortune 1945–1955*, 1969: *Riding the Storm 1956–1959*, 1971; *Pointing the Way 1959–1961*, 1972; *At the End of the Day 1961–1963*, 1973

MEDLICOTT, W. N., *Contemporary England 1914–1964*, 1967

MIDDLEMASS, KEITH and BARNES, JOHN, *Stanley Baldwin*, 1969

MIDDLEMASS, KEITH, *Edward VII*, 1972

MORGAN, KENNETH O., *Lloyd George*, 1974

MORRAH, DERMOT, *Princess Elizabeth, Duchess of Edinburgh*, 1950; *The Work of the Queen*, 1958; *To Be a King*, 1968

NICOLSON, HAROLD, *King George V, His Life and Reign*, 1952; *Diaries and Letters 1930–1939* (ed. Nigel Nicolson), 1966; *Diaries and Letters 1945–1962* (ed. Nigel Nicolson), 1968

PATIENCE, SALLY, *The Queen Mother*, 1977

PETRIE, SIR CHARLES, *The Modern British Monarchy*, 1961

PONSONBY, SIR FREDERICK, *Recollections of Three Reigns*, 1951

POPE-HENNESSY, JAMES, *Queen Mary 1867–1953*, 1959

TALBOT, GODFREY, *Queen Elizabeth the Queen Mother*, 1978

TAYLOR, A. J. P., *English History 1914–45*, 1965; *Beaverbrook*, 1972

TOWNSEND, PETER, *The Last Emperor, The Decline and Fall of the British Empire*, 1975; *Time and Chance*, 1978

TSCHUMI, GABRIEL, *Royal Chef*, 1954

VANDERBILT, GLORIA and FURNESS, LADY, *Double Exposure*, 1959

WENTWORTH DAY, JAMES, *The Queen Mother's Family Story*, 1967

WHEELER-BENNETT, SIR JOHN W., *King George VI, His Life and Reign*, 1958

WILSON, HAROLD, *The Labour Government 1964–1970 – A Personal Record*, 1971

WINDSOR, DUCHESS OF, *The Heart Has Its Reasons*, 1956

WINDSOR, H.R.H. THE DUKE OF, *A King's Story*, 1951; *A Family Album*, 1960

WRENCH, JOHN EVELYN, *Geoffrey Dawson and Our Times*, 1955

Index

Index

'Common Man' era, 157

Commonwealth replaces Empire, 158, 200

Communism: fears of, 171; United States crusade against, 187

Communist Party of Great Britain, 59

Complacency in 1930s, 119

Concorde, Queen Mother first 'royal' to fly in, 214

Connaught, Duke of, 85

Conservative Governments, 60, 79, 100, 126, 173, 177, 191, 192, 206, 225

Consumer society, 177

Corgi dogs, 104

Cornwall, King and Queen in, 125

Coronation: of George VI, 116–18; of Elizabeth II, 179

Coryndon, Sir Robert, 76, 77

Costermongers' Carnival, 95–6

Council of State, 96

Court Circular, 61q, 62

Covent Garden Royal Opera House and Queen Mother, 225

Coventry, 'Queen's Messengers' and, 148

Crathie Church, 190

Cranwell flying school, Prince Albert at, 52, 53

Crawford, Marion, 104

Crete in World War II, 150

Cripps, Sir Stafford, 159

Crown Estate Commissioners, 85

Cultural life, Queen Consort and, 127

Cumberland, Duke of, 102

Cumberland, 51

Curzon, Lord, 73

Curzon House, 81

Czechoslovakia, 129, 130

Dail, 172, 261n

Daily Colonist (British Columbia), 146q

Daily Express, 26, 126, 164, 261n

Daily Mail, 27, 83, 109, 219

Daily Mirror, 58–9q, 111, 193

Daily News (New York), 210

Daily Telegraph, 110

Dainty, Billy, 226

Dalkeith, Earl of, 181

Dambusters, 152

Darlington: the Yorks in, 81; Queen Mother in, 206

Dartmouth Naval College, 50–1, 136

Davidson, Randall, Archbishop of Canterbury, 66

Dawson, Geoffrey, 27, 28, 30, 110, 114, 259n

Dawson of Penn, Lord, 96

Deal, 231

Dean Water, 36

Deeside, Queen Mother at, 10

Delfont, Bernard, 235

Democracy and the monarchy, 222–3

Denmark invaded, 142

Depression, post-World War I, 59; thirties, 101–2

Derby stakes, Queen Mother and, 10

Devaluation of pound, 171, 261n

Divorce, 192–3, 195, 220

Dr Barnardo homes, 69

Doctor of Civil Laws degree, Oxford, conferred on Queen Consort, 102

Doctor of Law degree, Cambridge, conferred on Queen Consort, 167

Doctor of Laws degree, Columbia University, conferred on Queen Mother, 186

Doctor of Laws degree, Edinburgh, conferred on Queen Consort, 122

Launceston, Tasmania, Queen
   Mother in (1958), 203
Le Cateau, Battle of, 40
Lease-lend, 159
Leeds, Queen Mother in, 186
Leveson-Gower, Rose (née
   Bowes-Lyon), 47, 100, 258n
Leveson-Gower, William, 47,
   258n
Ley, Dr Robert, 121
Liberal Party, 60, 79, 100
Licensing hours, 59
Lichfield, Patrick Earl of, 216, 217
Lillibet (Princess Elizabeth), 97
Lindsay-Hogg, Lucy, 217
Lingfield races, 196
Linley, Viscount, birth, 216
Llewellyn, Roddy, 217, 218
Lloyd George, David, 18, 60, 119fn,
   257n
Locarno Pact, 79
Logue, Lionel, speech therapist, 87,
   89, 91, 125
London City Mission, 10
London, freedom of the City
   conferred on Queen Mother, 186
London, King and Queen's
   triumphal tour, 118
London and North Eastern
   Railway, 81
London School of Medicine for
   Women, 108
London University, 190, 229, 231,
   235
Loos, Battle of, 43
Lord Chancellor as Councillor of
   State, 96
Lord Warden of the Cinque Ports,
   Queen Mother appointed, 231
Lydd, 231
Lyon, Sir John, 35

MacDonald, Ramsay, 79, 101, 102

McGill University (Canada), Queen
   Mother at, 211
Macmillan, Harold, 201–2, 205–6,
   261n
Makwar Dam, the Yorks at, 78
Malaya occupied by Japanese, 150
Maldive Islands, independence, 200
Maloja, liner, the Yorks on, 78
Malta, 129fn, 171
Manchester, Duchess of York in,
   106
Manchester Guardian, 57q
Mann, Arthur, 110
Margaret Rose, Princess: birth, 23,
   99; problems as younger child, 100;
   upbringing, 103; and George V,
   107; at parents' coronation, 117; in
   World War II, 141; Elizabeth's
   influence on, 162; and Peter
   Townsend, 180–4, 189–95; and
   Royal Marriages Act, 62, 183, 191;
   renounces Townsend, 194q;
   marries, 208; MPs' criticisms,
   208–9; and Queen Mother, 215–16;
   and monarchy democratized, 222.
   See also Snowdon
Margate, 231
Marina, Princess, 136, 161
Marlborough House, 25, 30, 202
Marlowe, Thomas, 83
Marta, Princess, of Sweden, 98
Mary, Princess, 46, 54, 62, 66, 74, 78,
   85, 107, 258n
Mary, Queen, 25, 68, 99–100;
   mother of Prince Albert, 15; letter
   to Edward VIII on abdication, 17q;
   character, 17; public image, 19; and
   Abdication, 30; and Edward VIII,
   31; meets Elizabeth of Glamis, 48;
   on Elizabeth, 61q; wedding
   present to Elizabeth, 63; and
   Elizabeth's wedding, 64;
   modernizes White Lodge, 69; and

Index